Grierson Raids

and Hatch's Sixty-four Days March

Richard W. Surby

APPLEWOOD BOOKS
Bedford, Massachusetts

Grierson Raids
was originally published in
1865

9781429016605

Thank you for purchasing an Applewood book. Applewood reprints America's lively classics—books from the past that are still of interest to modern readers. This facsimile was printed using many new technologies together to bring our tradition-bound mission to you. Applewood's facsimile edition of this work may include library stamps, scribbles, and margin notes as they exist in the original book. These interesting historical artifacts celebrate the place the book was read or the person who read the book. In addition to these artifacts, the work may have additional errors that were either in the original, in the digital scans, or introduced as we prepared the book for printing. If you believe the work has such errors, please let us know by writing to us at the address below.

For a free copy of our current print catalog featuring our bestselling books, write to:

APPLEWOOD BOOKS
P.O. Box 365
Bedford, MA 01730

For more complete listings, visit us on the web at:
awb.com

Prepared for publishing by HP

GRIERSON RAIDS,

AND

HATCH'S SIXTY-FOUR DAYS MARCH,

WITH

BIOGRAPHICAL SKETCHES,

ALSO

THE LIFE AND ADVENTURES

OF

CHICKASAW, THE SCOUT.

BY R. W. SURBY.

CHICAGO:
ROUNDS AND JAMES, STEAM BOOK AND JOB PRINTERS.
1865.

Entered according to Act of Congress, in the year 1865, by
RICHARD W. SURBY,
In the Clerk's Office of the District Court of the United States, for the Northern District of Illinois.

To the officers and men, who have so kindly assisted me in getting out this work, and those who accompanied the various expeditions, this work is most respectfully dedicated by the

AUTHOR.

C. B. GRIFFIN, General Agent for the United States. Address Box 2779, Chicago, Ill.

TESTIMONIALS.

HEAD-QUARTERS DEP'T 7TH ILLINOIS CAVALRY,
MEMPHIS, TENN., Nov. 1, 1864.

To whom it may concern: This is to certify that Sergeant R. W. SURBY has been a member of my regiment for the three past years. I have been intimately acquainted with him during that time, and know him to be a man of undoubted loyalty, strict morality, integrity, and temperate habits. Since October, 1862, he has acted as Quartermaster-Sergeant for the regiment, the duties of which office he has discharged with promptness and ability—often doing all the business in the absence of the Quartermaster. I therefore unhesitatingly recommend him to any one or any position he may seek for employment.

Respectfully,
GEO. W. TRAFTON,
Lt.-Col. 7th Illinois Cav.

MEMPHIS, TENN., January 10, 1865.

To whom it may concern: The bearer, L. H. NARON, has acted for me as guide and scout, and has rendered valuable services to the government in that capacity. He was formerly a resident of Chickasaw County, Miss., from whence he was driven by the enemy early in the war. He has proven his loyalty and devotion to the cause of our country by his acts, and the sacrifices of property which he has made. I earnestly recommend him to the favorable notice of all commanding officers of the United States forces.

B. H. GRIERSON,
Brig.-Gen'l.

BURNETT HOUSE, CINCINNATI, OHIO, Feb. 8, 1865.

My Dear Sir: L. H. NARON, of Chickasaw, Mississippi, acting in the capacity of a scout, behaved while with my command as became an honest, brave, loyal and reliable citizen of the United States; and for his good services and noble devotion merits the high respect and good wishes of all Union men. God bless him and his family.

W. S. ROSECRANS,
Maj.-Gen'l.

HEAD-QUARTERS DEPARTMENT OF THE MISSOURI,
ST. LOUIS, MO., June 24, 1865.

R. W. SURBY, Esq., Arcola, Ill.—*Dear Sir:* I have your letter of the 23d inst. L. H. NARON, ("Chickasaw") was in my employ as Chief of Scouts, and secret service corps, for more than a year. Daring, bold and shrewd, he rendered me most valuable services, by keeping me informed of the movements of the enemy in Tennessee, Alabama, Mississippi and Georgia, and by operating against the enemy's outposts —killing and capturing their spies, scouts and couriers, destroying their bridges, telegraph lines, &c., and annoying them generally. He, together with my other scouts and spies serving with him, performed many exploits of singular daring.

Very Respectfully,
Your Ob't Serv't,
G. M. DODGE,
Maj.-Gen'l.

MEMPHIS, TENN., Dec., 14, 1864.

I have carefully perused the manuscript of the work upon the expedition from "La Grange, Tenn., to Baton Rouge, La.," in April, 1863, of which MR. RICHARD W. SURBY is the author, and I pronounce it correct in every particular.

Very Respectfully,
B. H. GRIERSON,
Brig.-Gen'l.

PREFACE.

DEAR READER:—After waiting a sufficient length of time for some competent writers to place before the Public the particulars of these world-renowned Raids, and as yet nothing but imperfect reports have appeared in print, I therefore take the responsibility of offering to you the contents of my journal, together with items furnished by others. It was written under most embarrassing circumstances; just imagine yourself trying to write in an army tent, with six jolly comrades seated and standing around, talking and laughing on various subjects, (for soldiers like ladies gossip over the incidents of the day before retiring,) and you will need no other apology. Having performed a conspicuous part on the Raid, I will try and furnish you with some items of a startling and amusing character, but nevertheless true.

AUTHOR.

BREVT. MAJ. GENL. B. H. GRIERSON.

Biographical Sketches.

BRIG.-GEN. BEN. H. GRIERSON.

BRIG.-GEN. BENJAMIN H. GRIERSON was born in Pittsburg, Penn., July 8th, 1826, of Scotch and Irish parentage; he removed at an early age to Youngstown, Mahoning Co., Ohio, where he resided for eighteen years. While a boy he evinced a remarkable talent for music, and at the age of thirteen was the leader of a fine band. He afterwards devoted himself for many years to music as a profession, composing and arranging for bands, orchestras, the piano and guitar, playing with ease on all.

In October, 1849, he removed to Jacksonville, Ill., where he resided at the commencement of the war. Early in May, 1861, he entered the volunteer service as aid to General Prentiss, then commanding at Cairo. In October, 1861, he was commissioned Major of the third battalion Sixth Illinois Cavalry, but remained on detached service with General

Prentiss until the first of December, when he joined his regiment at Shawneetown, Ill. His energy and perseverance in drilling his battalion soon gained for him the good will of both officers and men of the Regiment. In February, 1862, Major Grierson was stationed with his battalion at Smithland, Ky., and in March rejoined the regiment at Paducah, Ky. Upon the resignation of Colonel Cavanaugh, March 28th, 1862, Major Grierson being the choice of the regiment was promoted to the vacancy. In June the regiment moved to Columbus, Ky., and soon after to Memphis, Tenn.; from this point Colonel Grierson with his command made frequent dashes into Northern Mississippi and West Tennessee, often attacking superior numbers and always with remarkable success.

At Hemand, Cold Water Station, Olive Branch, and near Cockrum's Cross-roads, Mississippi; Germantown, Colliersville, Wolf River, and near the Looschatchie, Tenn., he had brisk fights inflicting serious injury on the rebels, with slight loss to his command. His rapid, intelligent and decisive movements soon taught the rebels to fear Grierson's Cavalry.

On the twenty-sixth of November, 1862, he left Memphis with his regiment in advance of General Sherman's army corps, and from the middle of January, 1863, to the 17th of April Colonel Grierson's brigade was stationed at La Grange, Tenn., to guard the Memphis and Charleston railroad; from this point he surprised Colonel Richardston near Covington, Tenn., capturing his entire camp equipage, a large amount of ammunition, a quantity of arms, wagons, mules and horses; killing and wounding about thirty and capturing forty prisoners, (including Colonel Richardson himself who was wounded) without the loss of a man.

On the seventeenth of April, 1863, Colonel Grierson left

La Grange, on his great raid through Mississippi, arriving at Baton Rouge, La., on the second day of May. He co-operated with General Banks before and during the siege of Port Hudson, having various engagements with the enemy. On one occasion, at Clinton, La., June third, he fought successfully against a force more than double his own. On the third day of June, 1863, Colonel Grierson was, for gallant and distinguished service, appointed by the President of the United States, Brigadier-General of Volunteers.

On the eighteenth day of July, General Grierson embarked with his command at Port Hudson for Vicksburg, upon his arrival at that place the meeting between Major-Gen. Grant and himself was most cordial, and his course of action met General Grant's hearty approval. From Vicksburg General Grierson was ordered to Memphis to report to Major-Gen. Hurlburt, by whom he was immediately placed in command of the Cavalry of the Sixteenth Army Corps.

On the fourteenth of September, the officers of the sixth and seventh Illinois Cavalry, who accompanied General Grierson on his expedition, presented him a valuable sabre, as a token of their respect and esteem. In person, General Grierson is tall, with dark complexion, hazel eyes, black hair and beard, and prominent nose. Though not robust in appearance, he has an iron constitution, and is capable of enduring great hardships and fatigue; modest and unassuming in his manner, he is loved by his officers and men, and has the confidence and respect of his commanding officers.

---

* See account of fifty days travel of the Sixth Illinois Cavalry.

EDWARD PRINCE
COL. 7TH. RGT. ILL. VOL. CAV.

COLONEL EDWARD PRINCE.

COL. EDWARD PRINCE was born in East Bloomfield, Ontario Co., N.Y., Dec. 8th, 1832; his parents removed to Payson, Adams Co., Ill., in the fall of 1835. Edward entered college in 1847, at Jacksonville, and graduated in 1852; after receiving his degree he read law in the office of Williams & Lawrence, in Quincy, Ill., and for several years practised his profession in that city.

When the South rebelled, he entered with zeal into the service of his country. Having a taste for military life he studied the cavalry tactics, and became so familiar with the drill, that upon offering his services to Gov. Yates in the summer of 1861, he was appointed Cavalry Drill Master, with the rank of Lt.-Col. in the Seventh Ill. Volunteer Cavalry. He has always shown great genius in developing the systems and intricate manœuvres of troops, and in inventing and improving many things which have been of great value in the field and at home.

While in front of Port Hudson, his active mind conceived a plan by which the enemies works could be brought under our observation. He applied to General Banks for permission to carry out his plan, it was granted, and he immediately commenced building (what we called caviliers) high mounds of earth overlooking and commanding the enemies' parapets, Colonel Prince set his troopers to transporting from all the the sugar houses the hogsheads, (which could be found in quantities in that section of country,) these he filled with cotton and moved within a short distance of the Fort, and soon five hundred men were able to take a position in line behind this novel breastwork; the arc of the semi-circle was then thrown within fifty yards of the rebel works, and by mining sufficient dirt was thrown out from inside to make a complete protection against all kinds of missiles; the hogsheads were mounted one upon another until they commanded the enemies' position and demonstrated the plan of Col. Prince.

During the early part of the siege, Colonel Prince ascertained from negroes along Thompson's Creek that the rebels had two steamers nicely moored under their river batteries, and but slightly guarded, (on account of the supposed impossibility of getting at them,) Colonel Prince obtained permission to undertake the capture of these boats; he succeded where others failed, and moved them from under their batteries to the protection of the Stars and Stripes, showing great tact, energy and perseverance.

He was promoted Colonel of the Seventh Ill., in the fall of 1862. This regiment was organized at Camp Butler, near Springfield, in August, 1861, and mustered into the United States' service in October.

It would be too lengthy to enter into a detailed account of all the raids, skirmishes and battles in which this regiment has taken an active part. I will only state through what States they passed, and the number of miles traveled—

Missouri, Kentucky, Tennessee, Mississippi, Alabama and a portion of Louisiana have all been visited by this regiment, and in every place left behind it a token of their presence, in railroads destroyed, government property burned, and prisoners taken, of which they count four thousand; they have traveled by water over one thousand miles, by railroad about five hundred, and by land not less than twelve thousand; have never done garrison duty, but always been in active service, and ever distinguished themselves, while their loss has been less than many other regiments in the same brigade.

Colonel Prince was mustered out on expiration of his term of service by order of General Washburn about the middle of October, 1864.

LT. SAMUEL L. WOODWARD.

LT. SAMUEL L. WOODWARD, acting assistant Adjutant General on the staff of Colonel Grierson, was born in Burlington Co., New Jersey, on the 28th day of October, 1840. When he was eight years old his parents removed to Philadelphia, where he was educated. At the age of sixteen he embraced mercantile business. In 1860, he removed with his parents to Paducah, Ky., where he resided at the commencement of the war.

In consequence of his strong Union sentiments and of those of his father and family they were subjected to a series of persecutions. On three different occasions was he waited upon by rebel sympathisers and allowed so many hours to leave the State, twice was himself and father mobbed in the streets, their lives threatened as well as the destruction of their property; all of which they withstood for sometime, but finally they became so severe that young Woodward was compelled to leave his home. He went to Illinois where he engaged in business until February 1st, 1862, when he enlisted in the Sixth Illinois Cavalry as a private soldier. On the first of March he was detailed from his regiment as clerk in the office of Brig.-Gen. W. T. Sherman, in that capacity he served for eight months. Was in the battle of Shiloh and the numerous engagements during the advance on Corinth, Miss.; after the fall of this place General Sherman's command moved towards Memphis, Tenn., to which point he accompanied the General.

In November, 1862, upon the recommendation of General Sherman, and Colonel Grierson, of the Sixth Illinois Cavalry, he was promoted to second lieutenant in his company. In December, 1862, Colonel Grierson being assigned the command of a brigade, Lieutenant Woodward was detailed as Acting Assistant Adjutant General on his staff, and served with distinction in all the expeditions and engagements in which his command was employed. While acting in this capacity, in March, 1863, he was promoted to First Lieutenant in his company. He accompanied Colonel Grierson on his Raid, in April, 1863, and in all the numerous expeditions and engagements in Lousiana, and during the siege of Port Hudson. Upon the promotion of Colonel Grierson to the rank of Brigadier General, he was highly recommended to the President, by both Generals Banks and Grierson, for promotion to Assistant Adjutant General with the rank of Captain. He received the appointment and has since served in that capacity with honor to himself, and the command to which he was attached.

GRIERSON RAIDS.

It was in the spring of eighteen hundred and sixty-three, that considerable emotion could be perceived in and about the camps of the sixth and seventh Illinois cavalry regiments, also the second Iowa, all of which were stationed at La Grange, Tennessee, on the line of the Memphis and Charleston railroad, fifty miles southeast of Memphis, at one time a very pretty, enterprising town, situated on a high ridge of land, commanding a fine view of the surrounding country; but this place, like many others of importance, has felt the effects of a civil war, and now presents a truly sad picture. It was upon this day that I shall commence my narrative.

"What's up?" is the question asked by a score or more of voices.

"A big scout, I reckon," is the general reply. A certain member is seen to emerge from headquarters, when the inquisitive ones gather around him.

"Come, John, tell us all about it; where are we going, and how long will we be gone?"

John's retreat being cut off, he replies as follows: "Now, boys, I'll tell you, but you must not say a word to any one, for it must be kept secret."

"Oh! no; we'll not tell; you know us."

"Well, boys, we are going on a big scout to Columbus, Mississippi, and play smash with the railroads."

"All right; we'll keep mum, and when we get to Columbus we'll make it pay." The sequel will show how correct John was in his opinion.

General W. S. Smith was at that time commander of the post, a gentleman and a soldier. The men had been complaining for more active service, or as they expressed it, "spoiling for a fight." General Smith finally announced to them, through their officers, that they should in a few days have a chance to try their fighting qualities, which report was received with loud cheers; and a few days after this an order was issued to the commander of the first cavalry brigade to be ready for a march or scout, requiring all effective men, with five days rations in haversacks, with the understanding they were to last ten, and double rations of salt.

On the morning of the seventeenth of April, eighteen hundred and sixty-three, at an early hour, the following regiments left camp: the second Iowa cavalry, numbering between six and seven hundred men, rank and file, commanded by Colonel Edward Hatch, the seventh Illinois cavalry, numbering five hundred and forty-two, rank and file, commanded by Colonel Edward Prince, the sixth Illinois cavalry, with about five hundred men, commanded by Lieut.-Col. Loomis, and accompanied by Company K, first Illinois battery, numbering six pieces light artillery, under the command of Captain J. B. Smith, the whole commanded by Colonel B. H.

Grierson. Before proceeding further, I will state that Colonel Grierson planned this expedition some three months previous to this time, and it was submitted to General Hurlbut and remained null until again referred to by Colonel Grierson, when it was forwarded to General Grant, then near Vicksburg, who readily approved it, and sent suitable instructions how Colonel Grierson was to proceed.

The morning upon which the command moved out was a beautiful one, with a gentle breeze from the south. The fruit trees were all in full bloom, the gardens were fragrant with the perfume of spring flowers, the birds sang gaily, all of which infused a feeling of admiration and gladness into the hearts of all true lovers of nature. The men seemed to feel highly elated, and, as they marched in column of twos, some were singing, others laughing, while many were speculating as to our destination.

The following poetry I thought would express the feelings of the men at the time of our departure.

SONG OF THE FIRST BRIGADE.

The morning star is paling,
 The camp-fires flicker low,
Our steeds are madly neighing,
 For the bugle bids us go;
So put the foot in stirrup,
 And shake the bridle free,
For to-day the fearless first
 Are bound for Mississippi.

CHORUS.—With Grierson for our leader,
 We'll chase the dastard foe,
'Till our horses bathe their fetlocks
 In the Gulf of Mexico.

GRIERSON RAIDS.

Our men are from the prairies,
  That roll broad, proud and free;
From the loyal State of Illinois
  And brave old Iowa;
And their hearts are open as their plains,
  Their thoughts as proudly brave;
With Hatch for their commander,
  They'll resist the rebel wave.

    CHORUS.—Then quick into the saddle,
        And shake the bridle free,
        To-day with gallant Grierson
        We'll leave old Tennessee.

'Tis joy to be a trooper,
  To fight for this free land,
'Tis joy to follow Grierson,
  With his gallant, trusty band;
'Tis joy to see our Prince
  Plunge like a meteor bright
Into the thickest of the fray,
  And deal his deathly might.

    CHORUS.—Oh! who would not be a trooper,
        And follow Grierson's eye,
        To battle for their country,
        And, if needs be, to die.

By the many streams of water,
  And the deep, murmuring shore,
On our soft, green peaceful prairies,
  Our homes, we may see no more;
But in those homes our gentle wives,
  And mothers, with silvery hairs,
Are loving us with tender hearts,
  And shielding us with prayers.

    CHORUS.—So trusting in our country's God,
        We draw our stout good bladé,
        For those we love at home,
        And those who need our aid.

It is under such circumstances, with nothing to mar the feelings, that time passes swiftly away. The order of march for this day was to be as follows: Sixth Illinois cavalry in advance. Through some mistake the sixth took the wrong road near La Grange, was thrown to the west, and did not join the command until near camp, which was on the plantation of Dr. Ellis, four miles northwest of Ripley, Mississippi, distance from La Grange thirty miles. Just before going into camp five or six rebels were discovered crossing a field, and immediately a party was sent in pursuit, who captured three of them. Our advance met a young man who looked rather seedy; he was driving an ox team, and, unfortunately for him, wore a very good looking hat, which one of the boys took a fancy to and relieved him of, leaving the poor fellow looking rather sad. Colonel Prince, on coming up, noticed the man and inquired of him what was the matter; he stated his loss, when the Colonel pulled out his pocket-book and gave him a two-dollar greenback, which seemed to please him very much.

SECOND DAY.

Next morning, the eighteenth. At seven o'clock the command moved out, the seventh Illinois in advance. At eight o'clock we passed through Ripley, in Tippah County, making a halt of one hour, then moved south towards New Albany. The day was delightful, and nothing occurred to interrupt the quiet prevailing, until we had marched four miles, when our ears were startled by the report of fire-arms. A party of eight rebels had fired on our advance, then retreated rapidly. A few shots were sent after them, no harm done to either side, and all became quiet again. Colonel Prince then detached the first battalion, under the command of Captain Graham, who took the direct route to New Albany, while the main column passed through Arizabee, crossing the Tallahatchie River two miles east of New Albany, arriving there at five o'clock, P. M.

Captain Graham arrived at the bridge near the latter place in time to prevent a rebel picket demolishing it. He had been there an hour when the main column arrived, and crossed in safety. Previous to leaving Ripley Colonel Hatch had been detached to move with his regiment eastward and southward, to cross the Tallahatchie about five miles above New Albany, with a view of rejoining the brigade some five or six miles below the latter place, (which Colonel Hatch accomplished with success). The seventh Illinois captured this day four prisoners, two of Bartue's and two of Wetherall's men. The command camped for the night at Mr. Sloan's plantation, five miles below New Albany, a small place composed of a few dry-goods stores, whose stock needed replenishing; also some fine residences; altogether a pleasantly situated country town.

THIRD DAY.

The morning of the nineteenth day was anything but agreeable, a heavy rain having fallen all night and continued the next morning until noon. At an early hour Colonel Prince, by order of Colonel Grierson, sent two companies of the seventh Illinois, under command of Captain Trafton, back to the Tallahatchie, who drove a force of the enemy out of New Albany and rejoined the command at ten o'clock the same morning. Two companies of the same command being sent to the right to look after Captain Wetherall's (Confederate) company, which was camped in that vicinity, they had taken the hint and retired during the night. They however captured from Major Chalmers' command four prisoners, and destroyed some camp and garrison equipage. Two companies were also sent to the left to find some horses, said to be hid in the woods. They returned to the column in a few hours, having had very poor success. The command left camp at ten o'clock in the morning. The road being slippery and muddy somewhat retarded our progress and damped our feelings. At a late dinner hour we stopped to feed, and while so doing some of the fortune-seeking ones were searching a house close by, in which they found concealed one keg of powder, several revolvers, and a few old United States muskets, which unfortunately resulted in the burning of the house and most of its contents. The officers made every effort to find the guilty party, but it occurred mysteriously, no one knew anything about it.

The sixth Illinois, occupying the advance, entered Pontotac, county-seat of Pontotac County, at four o'clock, killing a rebel who persistently fired on the advance; (his name was Beers.) A small party of rebels were in town, when hearing of our advance skedaddled, leaving a wagon-load of ammunition and camp equipage which we destroyed. Captain Graham, of the seventh Illinois, with three companies, found and destroyed between four and five hundred bushels of salt, (government property.) Pontotac is, or rather was before the war, a brisk business place, boasting a population of about three thousand inhabitants, a fine brick court-house, and beautiful residences, denoting wealth. After remaining about an hour we proceeded eight miles south, and encamped on the plantation of Mr. Wetherall, (brother of Captain Wetherall,) and Mr. Daggett. The whole command camped in sight of each other, having marched in the last two days sixty miles.

FOURTH DAY.

Next morning, the twentieth, at three o'clock, boots and saddles was sounded. Lieutenant Wilt and sixty men with a number of lead horses belonging to the seventh Illinois, together with about the same number of the sixth Illinois and second Iowa, and one piece of artillery, all under the command of Major Love of the latter regiment, were sent back to Le Grange; the rest of the command, with the second Iowa in advance, continued south passing through a good section of country somewhat rolling. The day being cloudy and damp, there was little interest displayed in viewing the country, and it was not until I had discovered that we had left the main road, and was making a new one through a wheat field of some extent; it was about six inches in height and of a beautiful green, which was a change from the mud; the question arose, what does this mean, and various were the conjectures.

The prevailing opinion was, that the enemy was near at hand, and we were on a flanking expedition, however, our fears were soon dispelled, the column had been conducted through the fields in order to avoid passing through the town of Houstan, leaving it on our right; a very pretty little place in Chickasaw County. Either the citizens had held out some inducements, or our commanders through a pure motive avoided marching the troops through, that pillaging might be avoided; there may have been some other motive, that of disguising our forces as much as possible—however, Houstan this time was favored by a side view of our column, while house tops and church steeples presented a picturesque appearance to us, we proceeded on to Clear Springs and camped for the night, having marched forty miles.

FIFTH DAY.

Left camp on the morning of the twenty-first at daylight, the seventh Illinois in advance; Colonel Hatch with the second Iowa and one piece of artillery turned eastward from Clear Springs with orders to proceed toward Columbus, Mississippi, and destroy as much as possible of the Mobile and Ohio railroad, and make his way to Le Grange again. Some fears were felt for his success, as forces were concentrating in our rear, expecting to intercept us on our return, it was of the utmost importance that a feint should be made in the direction of Columbus in order to draw the enemies' forces that way and conceal the real movement which was then making all speed south. Colonel Hatch was just the officer to be entrusted with this perilous task, he accomplished the object but had some hard fighting, reaching our lines in safety. The sixth and seventh were now alone and various were the opinions expressed by the men as to our destination. The proceedings of the past few days showed that something was to be done; they felt equal to any task and, notwithstanding the heavy rain that was falling, they were cheerful and enlivened the march with songs and jokes.

The citizens were somewhat surprised to see so many "Yanks" so far down in "Dixie," and many were the questions asked,

"Where are you'ens all going to?"

Rebel courriers were ahead, and for several days our arrival was expected by them; they having had warning had concealed all of their valuable horses, mules, and negroes. Now the question will arise, how did we manage to subsist? Why, we just helped ourselves, or rather, when we stopped at a plantation to feed, a detail of men for guards was immediately made and stationed at the smoke-house, kitchen and dwelling house, with instructions not to allow anything to pass without permission of a commissioned officer, also a suitable person was appointed to issue out to the different companies a proper quantity of hams, shoulders, meal, and so forth, for one or two meals as the case required; this duty devolved upon William Pollard, commissary sargent of the sixth Illinois, he being the only representative of that department along, and fully competent to the task. Respecting the horses, it was seldom that there was any scarcity of corn and fodder, if there was not enough at one plantation, for the command, part went to the next, always keeping within supporting distance of each other.

Belonging to the non-commissioned staff I was a priveleged character, and undoubtedly took many liberties not allowed me, consequently I had a good opportunity of observing many things, and learning some of the designs of our commanders. Possessed of a venturesome disposition I naturally wanted to be in the front, and it occurred to me I could do so; I immediately suggested my ideas to Lieut. Col. Blackburn (formerly my captain,) that of having some scouts in the advance dressed in citizens clothes, they could by proper management gain much valuable information, although not without running some danger. Colonel Blackburn immediately had an interview with Colonel Grierson stating the object of the organization; Colonel Grierson approved the plan provided the right men could be found, Colonel Blackburn said he knew just the men, and without further consideration, he had full permission to organize and control the scouts; it was not long before I was ordered to report to him, and was somewhat surprised when he requested me to act as scout, and take command of a squad of men. This suited me, and without any hesitation I accepted the position with thanks, fully resolved not to abuse the confidence reposed in me. I received orders to take six or eight men, proceed at once on the advance and procure citizens dress, saddles, shot guns, and everything necessary for our disguise. It did not take long to do this, and by noon reported myself and men ready for duty; we excited some little curiosity and sold the sixth Illinois boys completely, they thought we were prisoners and bored us with a thousand questions; after this we went by the name of "The Butternut Guerillas;" our old uniforms and carbines were placed in the hands of friends.

My instructions from Colonel Blackburn were to keep in the advance, from a quarter of a mile to two as the case required, to obtain all information respecting different roads, their destination, distance, and condition, also that of the streams, bridges, and the whereabouts of the enemy, their force, and was to exercise my own judgment in all cases where it required immediate action, to report to him or Colonel Prince from time to time. Another advantage was, that we would more easily find forage, and save trouble and delay by sending out squads for that purpose.

The advance guard each day being advised and cautioned about us, did not find or take us prisoners, and our signs were soon understood by both parties. We passed through Starkville, Ochtibleher County, and camped eight miles south of that place. Between Starkville and camp the scouts captured a Lieutenant belonging to Vicksburg, who was seated in a fine buggy with a beautiful span of iron gray horses attached; the horses Colonel Grierson assigned to the battery. Also a mounted rebel was secured and taken along.

SIXTH DAY.

Morning of the twenty-second left camp at an early hour,—weather favorable. Before leaving camp Captain Graham of the seventh, commanding a battalion, was sent to burn a Confederate shoe and saddle manufactory near Starkville; he succeeded in destroying several thousand pairs of boots and shoes besides a large quantity of leather and hats, capturing a quarter-master from Port Hudson, who was getting supplies for his regiment (the twelfth Tennessee,) previous to leaving camp, the field officers had a consultation and were convinced that it was of the utmost importance to intercept and destroy the railroad and telegraph between Okalona and Macon, as near Macon as possible. This work Colonel Prince offered Captain Forbes, Company B, seventh Illinois, whose company numbered thirty-five men and officers; Captain Forbes accepted at once, though he knew he would be obliged to repulse all attacks and travel at least fifty miles more than the command, would run great risk in being captured, as it was not known what force was at Macon, nor what force was following us; he was instructed, that if a force should be at Macon, to endeavor to cross the Ranox Bar and move toward Decatur, in Newton County, by the shortest route.

The Captain proceeded on his perilous journey, and many feared that they would never see him again. The country through which we were passing was not of a prepossessing appearance—it was low and swampy. The scouts were quite successful during the day in finding several droves of horses and mules, with negroes concealed in the woods, to avoid being captured by our forces. The manner in which we obtained our information was quite easy in our assumed characters, when conversing with the hunters we passed ourselves off as confederates, belonging to commands in Tennessee; that we were ordered to keep in advance of the Yankies, watch their movements and when opportunity presented, to report to the nearest post; this story invariably was credited among them, and in a little while by ingratiating ourselves into their favor, we obtained their confidence, and was told where they had concealed their fine animals; I would then leave a man to inform the Colonel when the column came up, and a squad of men would often bring in twenty-five horses and mules, with as many negroes, who would of their own accord accompany us.

I was very much amused one day; had taken three of my men with me and proceeded two miles from the main road expecting to find a Confederate captain at home, but he had left quite suddenly; found some good mules, upon which I mounted some negroes who were standing round with mouths wide open showing teeth like circular saws, at the sight of a Yankee, having never seen one before. On my return I passed a very fine residence—my attention was suddenly attracted by a motion made at one of the windows, I gave the order to halt; no sooner done than the front door flew open and three lovely looking females dressed in white appeared at the opening, their faces beaming with smiles, and in a voice soft and sweet invited us to dismount and come in. It was raining, we were all wet to the skin, and spattered with mud, contrasting strongly with the elegant appearance of everything around; I therefore begged to be excused as my time was limited, and we were watching the advanced movements of the Yankies; no sooner said than out they bounded, regardless of the rain, and coming to the gate (were joined by an elderly lady who they addressed as mother, insisted upon our remaining over night. Various were the questions asked about the "Yanks" all of which we could answer satisfactorily; they informed us their father and brothers were in the Confederate Army.

One of the boys complained of being hungry; no sooner said than one of the ladies ran into the house, and soon returned with two black servants following, loaded down with eatables; we had to accept half a ham, that would make a hungry man laugh; biscuits, sweet cakes, fried sausage, and peach pie, all in abundance were pressed upon us, while one of the young ladies plucked some roses and presenting one to each bade us adieu, with many blessings and much success in our "holy cause;" on my way back I met a company of the sixth Illinois, and cautioned them to still deceive the "ladies," and I presume it was some time ere they learned how bad they had been sold.

Another instance occurred where I visited a plantation, accompanied by two of my scouts. We found two young men at home, both belonging to the Confederate army. They were somewhat surprised to hear the Yankees were coming that way; all was excitement, the negroes were called up, and received orders to get all the horses and mules, and saddle two of them. We were invited into the house. Having told them that we would accompany them some distance, the demijohn was brought out, glasses placed upon the table, and a cordial invitation given to help ourselves to some "old rye," which invitation a soldier never refuses. The blacks soon announced all ready, and we started out, the young men armed with shotguns, eight negroes following with fourteen mules and six fine horses. It was about one and a half miles to the road, upon which the column was advancing, and in the direction that we were going; when about half way I had a curiosity to examine their guns, which they seemed proud to exhibit; making a motion to one of my men he followed suit, thus we had them disarmed, and in a good humored way informed them they were our prisoners; they laughed, thinking it a good joke, saying they were old soldiers, and not easily scared. We soon came in sight of the column, when our Confederate friends "smelt a rat," and with downcast countenances became uncommunicative. Shortly after this we passed through Whitefield, a small place of little importance.

After leaving this place the country began to look decidedly swampy, we were crossing the Big Black or Okaxuler River, which was much swollen by the recent rains. In many places we had to swim our horses and mules. Many troopers lost their animals and equipments, barely escaping with their lives. It was a tedious task piloting our way through this bottom, which extended in breadth nearly six miles, and was covered with water to the depth of three feet. You will ask how did we get our artillery over; this was accomplished by taking the ammunition out of the caissons, and packing it over our own horses, thereby keeping it dry. Unfortunately one of the gun carriages broke down, causing some delay, but through the ingenuity of Capt. Smith, commanding the guns, it was mounted next day on buggy wheels.

The sixth Illinois cavalry succeeded in crossing and reached camp about two o'clock; the seventh did not arrive until three the next morning. After leaving this dismal swamp, the country became more rolling, the roads were in better condition, vegetation more forward, and the citizens were impressed with the idea that we belonged to the rebel General Van Dorn's command, and complimented us on our fine appearance, and said we were right good looking men. No couriers had preceded us on this road, and we enjoyed ourselves very much at the expense of the deluded citizens.

While passing a schoolhouse the teacher gave her pupils recess; the way they flocked to the roadside was not slow, hurrahing for Beaureguard, Van Dorn, and the Southern Confederacy. One little urchin imagined she recognized in one of the men an old acquaintance, and very impatiently inquired how John was, and if her uncle was along.

Before reaching Louisville the scouts captured a mailcoach containing the Port Hudson mail, together with some Confederate money, which was handed to Colonel Grierson. The letters were mostly in French, which was translated into English by Sergeant-Major Le Sure of the seventh; they contained some valuable information. Louisville is a neat little town of pretty location, in Winston County. After leaving it ten miles in our rear, we camped for the night, having traveled this day fifty miles. On this evening Captain Lynch of Company E, of the sixth Illinois, and one of his men, Corporal W. H. H. Bullard, disguised themselves in citizens' dress, and started on a reconnoitering expedition towards Macon, with what success will appear hereafter.

SEVENTH DAY.

We left camp at an early hour and were now drawing near Pearl River Valley. A glance at the map will show the importance of this river on the Talla Hoga, and knowing it to be quite high from recent rains, and a possibility of news of our approach reaching them from other routes, it became necssary to secure the bridge. I was instructed to proceed rapidly and cautiously forward, and if possible, to secure it with my squad. When within two miles of the bridge,

I met an old citizen mounted upon a mule. We passed the time of day and entered into conversation; he informed me that a picket was stationed at the bridge, composed of citizens, numbering five in all, his son being one of the party; all were armed with shot-guns. They had torn up several planks from the centre of the bridge, and had placed combustibles on it ready to ignite on our approach.

I then wrote down the old man's name, and the whereabouts of his residence, which was on the opposite side of the river. He began to mistrust that all was not right, and says, "gentlemen you are not what you seem to be, you certainly are Yankees, for we got news in Philadelphia last night that 'you'ens' all were coming this way." I had now fully resolved upon scaring the old man into an unconditional surrender of the bridge. So, looking him in the face, I told him it now lay in his power to save his buildings from the torch, his own life, and probably that of his son, by saving the bridge. We started, and when within one half mile of our object we descended into a low bottom land, considerably flooded with water, making progress slowly. Unless the enemy had a picket, or videt, thrown out we could approach to within three hundred yards without being discovered. I now told the old man, who was trembling with fear, that he was to visit his friends, and tell them, that if they would surrender, they should not be harmed, but would be paroled as soon as we reached town, but if they did any damage to the bridge, his property would suffer for it.

The old man said he was confident of saving the bridge, but would not promise the surrender of his friends; that we cared nothing about—the bridge was the important point. I impatiently followed the figure of the old man with my eye; when within a dozen yards of the bridge, he halted, and commenced telling his errand; but ere he had hardly half through, I could perceive some signs of uneasiness on the side of his listeners, they all at once jumped upon their horses and away they went. We then advanced to the bridge, replaced the planks, found two shot guns, that they had left in their flight, and leaving one man to wait for the column and turn the old man over to the Colonel, I proceeded with the rest to Philadelphia.

This incident is mentioned as one of the many in which the *Power above* seemed shielding us from harm, as the destruction of the bridge would have been fatal to the expedition. In my case others might have acted differently; my object was to save life if possible, the bridge at all hazards. We now proceeded toward Philadelphia, occasionally firing a shot at some mounted citizen who were armed but took care to keep at a respectful distance. The nearer we approached the larger the force became in our advance, yet, they showed no disposition to come within range, until within about three hundred yards of town, when they were discovered drawn up in line across the road, upon which we were approaching. I immediately sent a man back, requesting the commanding officer of the advance guard to send me ten men. I waited long enough to see they were coming, and turning to my men ordered them to charge, and as we neared them amid a cloud of dust, we commenced to discharge our revolvers at them, which had the desired effect of stampeding them; they fired but a few shots, and in a few minutes we had full possession of the town; resulting in the capture of six prisoners, nine horses with equipments. One of the prisoners being the county judge—a very worthy man. At first they evinced much uneasiness and thought their time was near to depart from this world. Colonel Grierson soon quieted their fears by telling them that he did not come among them to insult them, or destroy private property, that he was in quest of Confederate soldiers and government property. We left the Philadelphians in better humor and with a more favorable opinion of our intentions, and the conduct of our army.

The last I saw of them they were standing in line with arms extended perpendicular, and Colonel Prince was swearing them not to give any information for a certain length of time. Just as we were leaving Philadelphia, up came Captain Lynch and his corporal in disguise, having just arrived from their expedition to Macon, the particulars of which I obtained from Captain Lynch.

On his departure from Louisville he pushed through to Macon, traveling all night, arriving within half a mile of the place at eight o'clock next morning; traveling seventy-five miles, meeting with no trouble until haulted by the picket in sight of the town; they demanded his business. The Captain told them that he had been sent out from Enterprise to ascertain the whereabouts of the Yankees. "Why," says the guard, "you need not go any further, they are now within two miles of here. General Loring sent out a squad of cavalry to reconnoitre; they have all returned but one who is either killed or taken prisoner." The Captain then inquired what force they had to defend the place, and was told that re-enforcements had arrived from Mobile—two regiments of cavalry, one of infantry, and two pieces of artillery. The Captain made an excuse to withdraw by stating that he had left two men at a plantation about a mile from there; he would return for them and be back in a few hours. The guards thought it all right and allowed him to depart.

The Captain made good time, forfeiting his word to return. After traveling all night and next day until about one hour of sunset, they reached the command, just as they were leaving Philadelphia. After proceeding seven miles south of the latter place the command haulted to feed and rest for a few hours on the plantation of Esquire Payn. While so doing, at a council of the officers Lieut. Col. Blackburn offered a proposition, which was to take two hundred men and proceed to Newton Station, on the Southern railroad, to intercept the trains and destroy the track; his plan was favored by Colonel Grierson, and at ten o'clock Colonel Blackburn started with the first battalion of seventh Illinois. I was ordered by him to take two of my men and accompany him. The night was a beautiful starlight one, the roads in good condition, and meeting with no enemy, nothing occurred to interrupt the stillness that reigned until midnight, when the column was startled by the report of fire-arms, in the advance, which occurred in the following manner: In coming to a point where the road forked, I was at a loss which one to take, and to decide the question, sent George Stedman back to a house to inquire, in the meantime I had advanced on the road leading to the right a short distance, and haulted, with my horse standing crosswise the road, leaving a narrow neck of timber between me and the other road. Scout number two had preceded me a short distance, and was waiting by the shade of the timber. In a few minutes Stedman came trotting back, and as he neared me I asked him if this was the right road; he did not seem to comprehend what I said but came up within a few feet of me and peering into my face a moment, without saying a word, wheeled his horse and galloped off. His actions puzzled me a little at first, and was giving no further thought to it, supposing he had gone back to the column with his information, when the first thing I heard was the report of firearms; though somewhat startled at first I did not move my position until the third shot had been fired, which impressed me with the idea that some one was firing at me, by hearing and seeing the fire-sparks fly from a stone the ball hit just beneath my horse's head, the next whizzed a few feet over me. I began to think it was time for me to get out of that, so I turned left about and retreated a few yards into the timber. Soon, whiz, whiz, came another shot, tearing through the timber; I immediately decided on a retreat, and went pell-mell through the scrub-oaks and briars for about two hundred yards, then coming to a halt, I heard another shot, then all was quiet again.

I now took time to think, and was of the opinion that we were ambushed from the point of timber between the two roads, and that the enemy had let us pass, and were firing into the advance of our column; still I could not account for the shots fired at me. I concluded to flank around and get to the column if possible. At that moment up came scout number two. We struck out and circled about a mile, striking the middle of the column, and soon learned that I was the sole object of all the firing. It appears that Stedman, when he rode up, did not recognize me, but hastily retreated to the fork of the road, and commenced firing at me with his revolver, causing the advance to hurry forward, who in turn began to fire with their carbines. Loss sustained, one hat. George was cautioned against firing upon his comrades again. It reminds me of the saying, "better born lucky than rich."

When within four miles of Decatur I was ordered by Colonel Blackburn to take one of my men and proceed to the town and try and ascertain if there was any force stationed at Newton Station, their position; if any artillery, and any information I could obtain. We started, feeling secure of our disguise, and no couriers ahead to tell of our coming. About three o'clock in the morning we entered the quiet town of

Decatur, in Newton County. No one was astir, the sleeping occupant little dreaming that two "Yanks" were treading on their sacred soil. After going up and down, surveying all the streets, and satisfying ourselves that no one was astir, we halted in front of an old fashioned country inn, with its pigeon-hole windows standing half way up the slanting roof. Dismounting and leaving my horse in care of my comrade, I stepped boldly up on the verandah, approached the door, knocked loudly; no answer. Repeated the summons; still no answer. Tried another door, with the same result. Began to think the hotel was evacuated. Made a forward movement, which proved the right one. After knocking at the door, a gruff voice on the inside inquired "who's there?" I answered in a loud voice, "a Confederate soldier, on important business, in quest of information." In a moment the door opened, and an invitation to come in was extended, which I at once accepted, stepping into what appeared to be a sitting room and bed chamber in one.

I begged to be excused for disturbing them at so unseasonable an hour. No excuses were necessary. The old gentleman, who proved to be the proprietor of the establishment, scraped out a few coals in the fire place, which threw a lurid light across the room, drew forth a chair, and told me to be seated. At the same time he sprang into bed again, from beneath whose covering I could see a pair of sparkling, roguish black eyes, tresses black as the raven's wing, a mischievous mouth, belonging to a young and charming woman. Can it be possible, thinks I, that she is married to this old man. It must be so, for it is quite fashionable in the South, old husbands and young wives. My hospitable friend, in a mild tone, at once demanded my business. I told him in a few words. Before answering me he was careful to ask me to whose command I belonged, where I came from, and why I was sent through there. I answered him by stating that I belonged to Van Dorn's command, a portion of which was stationed at Columbus, Miss., and I was sent with a portion of them across the country to obtain all the information I could respecting a Yankee raid, which was then being made somewhere in the interior of the State, and supposed to be meditating an attack on the Southern railroad. I wished to know how far it was to any of our forces, at what points stationed, their strength, &c., as it was of the utmost importance that I should communicate to them.

This story seemed to satisfy the old gentleman. He then told me that the nearest force was at Newton Station, that our hospital was there, and about one hundred sick and wounded soldiers occupied it, and he was under the impression that two corps of infantry were stationed there. He also said that a considerable force of cavalry had passed a few days previous within five miles of Decatur, going east. He had heard the day before many conflicting reports about the Yankees, but had no idea that they would ever reach this far. Had he known that the "blue coats" were then within rifle shot, that dreaded disease, the "cholera," would not have caused more consternation in town. My partner called me. A sweet voice invited me to call if I came that way again. I promised, and, bidding good-bye, left them to slumber.

I met the column just entering the town, reported to Colonel Blackburn, and again assumed my place in front. It was not long after leaving this town that streaks of daylight began to appear in the east, and a glorious sun arose to crown the day.

EIGHTH DAY.

The eighth day found us passing through a timbered country somewhat rolling, and displaying but little cultivation. Decatur is a small place in Newton County. It being night, I could see but little of the town. When within five miles of Newton Station Colonel Blackburn ordered me to proceed lively with my two men to the station, reconnoitre, and report what force was stationed there, what time the train would arrive, and so forth.

This suited us. On we went, meeting with no obstacles, approached to within half a mile of town, found an elevated position, from whence I could obtain a pretty good view of the place; could not see any camp; saw several persons walking and standing around a large building, which I took to be the hospital. I felt pretty well satisfied that there was no force stationed there, or we would have seen their pickets ere we approached so close to town.

I told the men we would proceed and see a little more before reporting. We started leisurely along and stopped at a house just at the edge of town; found a white man, called for a drink of water, and asked him how long before the train would be in. He said it was due in about three quarters of an hour. I ascertained that no force was stationed here. Was obtaining other information, when my ears were startled by the whistle of a locomotive. It seemed a long way off. I then inquired what train that was. The man said it was the freight train coming from the east, due at nine o'clock, A. M.

I now allowed there was no time to lose in order to capture the train. The column must be here. I at once sent back one man to tell the Colonel to hasten with all speed or lose the train. I then, with my scout, made for the depot to secure the telegraph, but found, upon reaching there, no office. By this time the convalescents began to pour out of the hospital, (which building stood within one hundred yards of the depot) to see who and what we were. I knew the column would be here in a few minutes, and, with revolver in hand, approached it and told them to remain inside, not to come out on peril of their lives.

In a moment the column came charging down the street, which was immediately picketed to prevent any one leaving town. The horses were led back behind the buildings, and one man sent to each switch, to lay concealed until the train passed, then to spring forward and alter it. Every "blue coat" was ordered to lay behind the buildings until the train was secured. On she came, puffing and blowing with the weight of twenty-five cars, loaded with railroad ties, bridge timber and plank. In a few minutes this train was in our possession and switched on a side track. Another train would be due in a few minutes from the West. Men were placed near the switches. The command was ordered to hide themselves from view, and everything was perfected just as the whistle sounded. On she came rounding the curve, her passengers unconscious of the surprise that awaited them. The engineer decreased her speed. She was now nearly opposite the depot. Springing upon the steps of the locomotive, and presenting my revolver at the engineer, told him if he reversed that engine I would put a ball through him. He was at my mercy, and obeyed orders. It would have done any one good to have seen the men rush from their hiding places amid the shouts and cheers which rent the air of "the train is ours." It contained twelve freight cars and one passenger car, four loaded with ammunition and arms, six with commissary and quartermasters' stores, and two with dry goods and household property belonging to families moving from Vicksburg. Several passengers were aboard, and as soon as they learned what was up, commenced throwing out of the windows on the opposite side from us their valuables, which fell into the water, it being low and swampy on that side of the track. A few revolvers, some papers and a considerable amount of money was unceremoniously thrown out. Some of the men, who never let anything pass unobserved, accidentally picked up a few articles. One old watch, which was floating on the water, contained about eight thousand dollars in Confederate "greenbacks."

This train being switched off on the side track with the other, the private property thrown out, fires were kindled in each car. The whole soon became one continuous flame. By eleven o'clock the heat had reached the shells, which began to explode, and must have sounded at a distance like a sharp artillery duel. Such was the impression it had on Colonel Grierson and the rest of the command, who were eight miles in our rear, following us up. As soon as they heard the reports of the bursting shells, they allowed that Colonel Blackburn was attacked, and the order was given, "trot, gallop, march," and on they came, expecting battle, but instead, found the men had charged on a barrel of whisky, which they were confiscating. I did not see a man that had more or less than a canteen full.

As soon as Colonel Grierson came up, two battalions, under command of Major Starr, of the sixth Illinois, was sent to destroy the bridges and tressel-work for six miles on the east side of the station, while one battalion of the seventh, under command of Captain Hening, destroyed them the same distance on the west, also effectually destroying the telegraph lines for some distance. A building was found containing a large quantity of United States rifles and clothing which was burned. Seventy-five prisoners were captured and paroled, (which duty devolved upon Adjutant George Root, 7th Illinois). One depot, two locomotives and all the cars, everything was destroyed. Colonel Blackburn was highly complimented for his success.

Everything being completed, rally was sounded, men fell into line, and at two o'clock, P.M., the command moved forward. Passing the railroad we proceeded south, which pleased the men very much. In justice to them I will mention that while at the railroad station they allowed the patients of the hospital to supply themselves with sugar, coffee and clothing before destroying it. It was now useless to disguise our character further; the news of "Yanks" was too far ahead. Couriers were going in all directions, spreading various reports respecting our strength. Some had estimated it as high as fifteen hundred, and some as many thousand; that we burned all the towns, insulted the females, and shot and hung all defenceless old citizens.

It was very annoying to listen to the stories repeated by many that we captured during the day; and many was the load of bacon, flour and household goods and valuables that we captured, which the poor deluded owners were trying to run off from the "Yanks," deserting their mansions, leaving all to the mercy of the invaders.

Great credit is due the commanders of this expedition for their efforts to prevent the destruction of private property, and the men for abstaining from destruction, which they could have done quite easily. It now required more energy and perseverance on the part of the scouts; the rumors ahead were contradictory, and the designs upon us, hard to tell; the roads must be found, so that there should be no delay to the column, at the same time, through our assumed character, find all the horses we could, and get them, or give information to the command where they could be found. The roads being good, we made good time, passing through Garlandville, where we found the citizens organized, armed and ready to receive us; they fired on the advance, wounding one man and killing one horse; we charged them, capturing nearly the entire party.

They were all aged men and very much alarmed, supposing that we would murder them and their families, burn their homes, and commit other unheard of outrages. We disarmed them and quieted their fears by releasing them, assuring them that we had come among them not to make war upon defenceless women and children but upon the armed rebels; they appeared elated at what they deemed their good fortune, and one old man ventured to remark that hereafter his prayers should be for the Union Army.

The column stopped to feed on the plantation of Mr. Bender, twelve miles from Newton Station. After two hours' rest we started again, feeling somewhat old and tired. We would occasionally see citizens dodging about, watching but avoiding us; we would sometimes give chase, but they escaped in the by-paths.

We continued our journey this night, through timber land. I was so sleepy that, after trying all in my power to keep awake, and finding I could not, I dropped back to the column, and was aroused several times; but it was no use, sleep I must have, and sleep I got, for when I awoke I found that my horse was nibbling the grass, and I was on the eve of taking a somersault over his head. I was alone, and, reader, I was awake at once; not a sound could I hear. The night was intensely dark and dreary, and the shade from the timber made it dismal enough. It was only a moment before I acted. I could not see anything of the road, so I dismounted and commenced feeling for it; I found it several yards to my left. To get on the right course was the next thing; this I did by feeling for the toe and heel of the horse-shoe prints. Mounting my trusty steed I put him on the track, with a slack bridle and smart canter, trusting to his instinct to keep the road. After traveling about two miles I was rewarded by overtaking the rear-guard to the column. I assure you I felt relieved.

My horse was seen to turn out from the column, but supposing I had left the column purposely, to fix something about my saddle, which is nothing unusual on a march, besides the men were so sleepy and tired that nothing but a shot fired would arouse them. I found that I was no sooner out of one danger—that of being captured—than I was into another. When within one mile of camp, and as the column was passing a plantation, my attention was attracted to a barn-yard, where were apparently some fine horses. A wide lane extended between the barn-yard and house. I proceeded up the lane a short distance, hitched my horse to the fence and sprang over into the yard, and joined in the chase after a fine cream colored horse. While thus engaged an officer belonging to the sixth

Illinois rode up the lane, and seeing my horse with citizen's saddle and shot gun attached to it, concluded that some Guerillas were around, and was calling for some of his men, who did not appear to be there; he continued to ride back and forth. My chase after the steed proving unsuccessful, I was returning to my horse, when I discovered the officer, as described; my first impulse on seeing him, which was a very indistinct view, was that he was a Rebel, and without further investigation I drew my revolver, jumped on the fence presenting it at him, demanded his surrender, or I would fire; he had his revolver in his hand, but dare not raise it for fear of my putting my threat into execution, which I certainly should have done, had he made any show of resistance. Just at this stage of the game, when I was going to order my prisoner to drop his arms, I was startled by the report of firearms just in my rear, at the same time I felt a stinging sensation on my left side. I was hit, and like a flash the thought occurred to me, that I was fired on by one of my own men; and still keeping my men in view, I shouted, I am one of the seventh, what are you firing at me for; this explained all; the person who fired was William Pollard, commissary sergeant of the sixth; the moment I spoke he knew my voice. "Why," says he, "sergeant —that is Captain Skinner, of the sixth; but, my God, you are hit." "Yes," I replied, "I am; but it is nothing serious." It turned out that the sergeant knew the Captain, but my back being turned toward him, and my clothes being decidedly "butternut," he came to the same conclusion respecting my character that I had that of the Captain.

They allowed it was a good joke, but I could not view it in that light, but in my heart I thanked God that it was no worse. Upon examining my side I found that the ball had ruffled the skin for about three inches just over my hip (for a few days it burned and smarted considerable.) We repaired to camp, which was a short distance from there. It was eleven o'clock, and for the first time in forty hours did we take off our saddles from our weary horses.

NINTH DAY.

On the morning of the twenty-fifth, we left camp at eight o'clock; the sky obscured by clouds indicating rain. Our progress was impeded by the bad roads; the country was thinly settled, and we had to swim our horses across the streams. Being considerably in advance, I stopped at a plantation, the appearance of which did not denote much wealth; a double log-house, and a few out-buildings. On approaching the stoop I was met by five females, who betrayed in their countenances, much uneasiness and fear—the cause was soon explained.

I at once inquired if there was any men about, and with one voice they all replied, "No sir," "our husbands are all in the Army of Vicksburg."

"And so, ladies, you are all married?"

"Yes, sir; is there anything strange about that."

"Oh no," I replied, laughing, "only it is strange to see so many married ladies at one house." To this they replied, that they had met to sympathize with each other. I then asked them for a drink of milk; they said that they had none, but would bring some water, which we accepted with thanks; one of the number, an old lady, wanted to know how soon this cruel war was going to end.

I concluded to utter a few Union sentiments, to see with what effect they would be received. I answered her by saying, that I thought it would stop just as soon as the old Stars and Stripes floated triumphantly over all the South. Looking at me with some surprise pictured in her countenance, she said, "I always did like that old flag, and I think this ere war all wrong, and if it had'nt been for these big larned folks, we'd all be living in peace. There's my husband, he'd no lawing nor law-suits in court, but minded his own business, and had nothing to do making this war; but they had to come and conscript him, and take him off to Vicksburg, and I don't expect to see him agen— after being together for thirty-six years to be parted this way—" the tears trickled down her cheeks as she continued, "I suppose you are conscripting; well, you'll find no men around here; you'd better conscript all the women too; we have no one left to care for us; we don't own any blacks." By this time I began to think there were still some sparks left burning for the old Union—that they were not all extinguished by the adulterated fluids of secession, and finally I asked the old lady what she thought about the "Yanks."

"Well," says she, "we've hearn a heap about them that wasn't good, and I've hearn tell a heap about them that was right smart in their favor. I've never seen but one, that is Mr. P——, who lives four miles from here; he came all the way from Ohio, and is a good man."

"Now, madam," says I "what would you think if I should tell you that we were Yankees?"

Picking me up before I had scarcely finished the sentence, she replied, "Now, young man, just stop that thar kind of talk; I aint going to be fooled in that thar way; you aint no Yankees, and you can't make me believe it, and I aint going to tell you a word about where the men are." By this time I looked up the road and saw the column advancing. I beckoned the old lady to me, and pointing to them told her they were all Yankees, "and, my good woman, we are Yankees, too."

The old lady's eyes opened to their widest extent, and turning around she raised her hands in a praying attitude, said "good Lord deliver us! what will we'uns all do;" and calling the "gals," as she termed them, showed them the column. At first they felt very much alarmed; we soon quieted their fears, and assured them that they were perfectly safe.

We were called into the house, and in a few minutes pies, bread, butter and milk in abundance was placed upon the table, and we were invited to help ourselves. While so doing the old lady was pulling an old chest from under the bed, and soon displayed to us a good sized flag, representing that good old flag for which we were fighting, and to protect its beautiful folds, so that it may continue to wave

"O'er the land of the free,
And the home of the brave."

This was sufficient to satisfy me that the old lady was all right on the Union question; at the same time one of the other ladies expressed a wish that "John and William only knew what we were, how soon they would come out of the woods." I left the old lady wishing that God, in his mercy, would spare her husband, and that peace would soon be permanently restored to our afflicted country; then she need no longer keep concealed the "banner of liberty," which, though

Thousands of true and brave,
Their heroic lives may end;
O'er thousands that flag shall wave,
Thousands its folds defend.

And as I journeyed on I thought how many of our readers, were they to take a trip through the interior of Mississippi, would be most bitterly disappointed; where they expected to find educated minds, elegant mansions, beautiful fields, quiet retirement luxuriating in wealth, they would find a double log cabin or frame house, with plain furniture (very scant), a feint show of comfort, a little garden spot, profuse with flowers of various hues (not very tastefully arranged), fields that show a lack of proper cultivation. Altogether, there is no show of wealth. And as for the high-toned intellect, with few exceptions, it is not to be found. Many words they express have the negro accent, and their knowledge of the geography of our country, its population, and resources, is very deficient. No free schools to educate their children, and not sufficient wealth to send them from home, they continue in ignorance—so I thought as a pretty girl of some eighteen summers remarked one day as we were passing, "why, ma, they all look like we'uns do." Their minds prejudiced, they will continue to be the tools and dupes of the educated classes, who are building up their hopes on establishing a monarchical government; but when the time arrives that these prominent leaders are brought before the bar of justice, and their evil designs frustrated, and our country cleansed of those evils, then will knowledge flow like lava into the minds of those who now think there is no soil equal to that which raises cotton.

We passed through Pineville—a small place—and at noon stopped at a plantation and fed. The proprietor was absent—about a mile from the house, with his slaves, cultivating corn. I was ordered by Colonel Blackburn to go and request him to come to the house. I found him, as I expected, with a large leather-bound whip. He was seated on a stump, from which he commanded a view of the negroes, about twenty-five, male and female. I approached him, and passed the time of day; he did not seem at all surprised to see me, and at once asked me what success I had hunting, and how Pemberton was getting along at Vicksburg. I answered that I thought the latter place was safe against the whole Northern army; but as for hunting, I was not on that kind of business; that there was a large force of us up at his house, and I was sent to request him to come up. He at once called an old negro, giving him his whip, and instructing him what to do. We started, he on foot, I mounted. While on the way he asked me whose command I belonged to, and where we were going. I told him we belonged to "Williams'" command, late from Tennessee, but now from Jackson, Miss., and were in quest of commissary stores, and picking up deserters and conscripts. As we came in sight of his barn-yard he was perfectly astonished to see so many troops; but what worried him the most was that they had all helped themselves to his corn and fodder, without asking his permission—besides he had none to spare; not but what the Confederate vouchers were good enough, and he was willing to loan his share, that he had fed several squads, but he did not have more than he wanted for his own use. As we passed through among the men he remarked how well they were dressed, how healthy they looked, and what fine arms we had. I told him we were the best equipped cavalry in the Confederate service, and had been in several battles. I entered the house with him, and not letting him have an opportunity to talk with his wife, ushered him into the room occupied by Colonel Grierson and other officers. I at once introduced the Colonel to him as "Colonel Williams, from Jackson, Mississippi, formerly from Tennessee, at the same time intrusting to the Colonel that our friend could give information of deserters, conscripts and provisions, which hint was sufficient for those present. I then withdrew, to lay down and rest my weary limbs upon the verandah. Considerable information was obtained from this planter. While here some of the men found a negro imprisoned in a log-hut, with manacles fastened about both ankles, and a chain attached to it, fastened to a ring in the floor. Colonel Blackburn had the irons cut off, and it was a sickening sight to look at those ankles; the flesh was worn off to the bone and almost in a state of mortification; the rings that went around the ankle were one inch in thickness, the whole weighing about twenty-five pounds. The poor fellow felt quite grateful, and never once complained about his scars. He accompanied us through to Baton Rouge. His only offence for all this treatment was trying to run away from bondage.

Just as the shades of night began to set in we halted and camped on the plantation of Dr. D——. Information had been obtained that a force of "rebs" were making their way from Mobile to intercept us. It was necessary that we should know something about their movements and force. About nine o'clock, after holding a consultation, Colonel Grierson requested Colonel Blackburn to select one of the scouts and report with him. In a few minutes Colonel Balckburn appeared with scout Samuel Nelson, of the Seventh Illinois. He was then instructed to proceed due north to Forest Station, thirty miles from where we were camped, and cut the telegraph line between Jackson and Meridian, on the Southern railroad, and if successful, bring a piece of the wire, as proof of its accomplishment; and if he had time to fire the bridge before daylight to do so, if not return to the command. After being supplied with a quantity of Confederate money, Samuel started on his perilous journey. After proceeding sixteen miles he met a force of Rebel cavalry, about eighteen hundred strong. He was halted and asked who he was and what he was doing here. He replied that he had been "pressed in" by the "Yanks" and compelled to guide them; that they kept him two days, releasing him the day before on a parole; that he was then on his way to a friend, residing at Forest Grove. He was then asked what force the Yankees had and where he left them. He replied that he had left them the day before at noon near Garlandville; that their force was about eighteen hundred men, well armed, enough, he thought, to whip them. He was then asked the nearest route to Garlandville, and which course the Yankees went from there. Sam directed them so as to lead them away from the proper trail, telling them the Yankees had left before he did and gone in the directoin of the Mobile railroad. Apparently satisfied with the information they started, allowing Samuel to pursue his journey. After he thought they had gone far enough he turned about, retraced his steps about one mile, then taking a right-hand road, and pressing in a negro as guide, reached camp about five o'clock the next morning. This valuable information was at once conveyed to Colonel Grierson, who decided on evacuating immediately. Boots and saddles was sounded, and the command moved out at once. It was a fortunate thing that this scout was sent out, as there would have been a force upon us by daylight that would have annoyed us to some extent. As it afterwards proved, they were thrown two days in our rear. The telegraph project was abandoned.

TENTH DAY.

Left camp at five o'clock—the sixth Illinois in advance. Three soldiers had to be left behind this morning, they being too feeble to travel further. About eight o'clock we passed through Raleigh, Smith County, a small place having rather a deserted appearance. On entering the place I discovered a man hastily mounting his horse and riding away at full speed, which looked rather suspicious; he was requested to halt, but paying no attention, kept increasing his speed. I told two of my men to give him chase; they being well mounted soon came up within pistol shot of him, when a few shots fired convinced him that there was danger in his rear, he concluded to halt, and very reluctantly returned to town, where he was delivered over to Colonel Grierson, together with five thousand Confederate "greenbacks," and a bundle of papers; he proved to be the county sheriff, and possessed some valuable information.

During the day we traveled through considerable pine timber plantations, few and far between. We experienced some scarcity of forage. It was just about dusk when I stopped at a plantation to dry my clothes, it having rained all the afternoon; had a very lively conversation with the proprietor who proved to be another sheriff (but minus the five thousand,) one that had no little conceit of his own abilities; he imagined we were hunting up deserters, and did not trouble himself to ask our business particularly, not half so much as we did to try the quality of his home made whisky, which he very generously supplied.

Imagine his astonishment when I ordered his negro servant to bring his masters horse to the door without delay, at the same time allowing the sheriff permission to procure a change of clothing, which he crammed into his saddle bags with an oath, exclaiming that it was d——d strange that he should be ordered round in his own house in this style, that he was not subject to conscription, and he be d——d if somebody should not have to pay for this trouble. He did not seem well posted in military matters. By this time up came the column, and Mr. Sheriff was introduced to Colonel Grierson, under the impression that he was in the presence of some noted general in the Confederate army. He was ready to tell all he knew, and more too. We were now nearing Stony River and near Westville, in Simpson County, when the column was overtaken by two messengers from Captain Forbes, who was then about thirty miles in our rear, requesting us not to burn any more bridges, as he was endeavoring to overtake us. This was joyful news to us. One of the messengers, whose name is Wood, was one of the scouts, and had rendered much valuable assistance on the expedition that was now trying to reach us, of which I will speak hereafter. About nine o'clock the Sixth Illinois camped on the plantation of Major ———; the Seventh, going a mile further, crossed Stony River bridge and camped at Mr. Smith's plantation. The rebel Major was quietly seated in his house, when Colonel Grierson halted before it. Coming out he wished to know whose command this was. No one seemed to pay any attention to him, but riding in through his gate into his garden, dismounting and hitching their horses to the beautiful shade trees. This was more than he bargained for, and he foamed and tore around, swearing that it was an insult upon his dignity, and he'd be d———d if he would not report the commanding officer to General Pemberton; he would not stand such abuse and insult on his own premises; his garden was ruined, and they were feeding up all of his corn and fodder. The Major learned his mistake before morning, respecting our character, and had nothing more to say about his garden. Distance marched this day forty-two miles. Though tired and sleepy, there were those who did not rest or sleep longer than to feed their horses and prepare supper. As the citizens were arming themselves, and the news was flying in every direction, it was a matter of life or death that Pearl River should be crossed and the New Orleans and Southern railroad reached, without any delay. So thought Colonel Prince; and acting on the impulse he had an interview with Colonel Grierson, and obtained permission to move directly forward, and with two hundred picked men of his regiment to secure the ferry across Pearl River before the enemy should destroy it. The following companies were detached: I, C, E and L. The distance to the river was thirteen miles, and from thence to Hazelhurst Station twelve miles. The remainder of the two regiments were to come forward as soon as they were sufficiently rested. The Colonel left with the four companies at two o'clock on the morning of the twenty-seventh. Some of the scouts accompanied him, they being permitted to sup.

ELEVENTH DAY.

At daylight the remainder of the command moved out, and it was discovered that Mr. Sheriff number two had effected his escape during the night, and availed himself of a fine horse belonging to one of Colonel Grierson's orderlies. Taking the advance I reached Pearl River, and found that Col. Prince had succeeded in crossing about one hundred of his men. He had reached the bank of 'the river before daylight, and, contrary to the information he had received, the flatboat was upon the opposite side. Not daring to arouse any of the citizens, the Colonel called for a volunteer, who, with a powerful horse, undertook to swim the river; but the rapidity of the swollen stream carried him far below the landing, where there was quicksand, and he barely escaped to the shore with his life; his name was Henry Dower, company I, Seventh Illinois. A few minutes later a man from the house came down toward the river, and, with North Carolina accent, wanted to know if we wished to cross, to which the Colonel replied, in a very fair imitation of the same tongue, that a few of us would like to get across, and it was harder to wake his negro ferrymen than to catch the d——d conscripts. The proprietor apologized, and woke up his ferrymen, who brought the boat across, from which time it remained in federal possession. For all the proprietor knew it was in the possession of the first regiment Alabama cavalry, from Mobile. The Colonel says the breakfast he gave the first Alabama will long be highly appreciated. The importance of this dispatch in this instance was proved half an hour later, by the capture of a courier, who was flying to the ferry with the news that the "Yanks" were coming, and that the ferry must be destroyed immediately. By the time that Colonel Prince had crossed his two hundred men the rest of the command came up, having left a guard at Stony River bridge to await the arrival of Captain Forbes. It was known that a rebel transport was some seven miles up the river, that carried two pieces, six-pounders. Colonel Grierson sent a detachment of men two or three miles above the ferry, where they could lay behind the river bank, secure from artillery, and engage the transport if she attempted to come down; but she did not make her appearance, probably apprehending capture. Leaving the rest of the command crossing—a slow, tedious task, as only twenty-four horses could go at a time—Colonel Prince with his two hundred men proceeded toward Hazelhurst.

The scouts were ordered ahead, and had not advanced more than four miles before we began to pick up citizens, who were collecting together and arming themselves to repel the invader. One small man, with sandy whiskers and foxy eyes, trying to look as savage as a meat-axe, had secured in an old belt around his waist two large old flint-lock dragoon pistols, and slung over his shoulder a large leather pouch and powder-horn, and on his left shoulder, with his hand resting on the stock, and old United States musket, flint-lock. As I came up to him he brought his gun to a carry arms, and between a grin and a laugh exclaimed: "They is coming, Capting, and I am ready; I've jist bid the old woman good-bye, and told her that she need not expect me back until I had killed four Yankees, and they were exterminated from out our Southern *sile;* I'm good for three of them, anyhow; I've been through the Mexican war, and know how to use them ere weapons." I gave the men the wink, which they understood, and approaching the "exterminator" began to compliment him on the appearance of his arms, and requested to look at them. Without any hesitation he passed over his musket to me; the other men in the meantime had his pistols. I informed him he was a prisoner, and would soon have a chance to see the General. Leaving him with one of the scouts, to be turned over to the Colonel, I proceeded some two miles further, when I saw some ten or twelve men together, some of them mounted, while others were standing and sitting on some pieces of timber. We boldly advanced, and when within speaking distance I discovered there was a small building, and further that it was a gunsmith's shop, on rather a small scale. A few questions were asked by the crowd respecting the "Yanks," which were answered by letting them know that they were supposed to be advancing toward Pearl River. They had flocked here with their old shot-guns, muskets, rifles and pistols, some of which looked as if they were made in the year one. Taking them all prisoners, which somewhat surprised them, we proceeded into the shop and threw out twenty-five guns, of all descriptions; taking them one at a time and striking the stock on the ground, breaking them off at the breech, then taking the barrel and putting one end under some weighty substance and giving it a jerk or two, it was no longer fit for anything but to shoot around corners. These prisoners were turned over to the column.

When within four miles of Hazelhurst, Colonel Prince handed me a written dispatch and ordered me to send two of my men with it to the station, to be handed to the telegraph operator. I at once hastened forward and sent Stedman and Kelly. The dispatch was addressed to General Pemberton, at Jackson, Miss., stating that the Yankees had advanced to Pearl River, but finding that the ferry was destroyed, and that they could not cross, had left, taking a northeast course. The scouts had no difficulty in reaching the station, found the telegraph office, the operator and six or eight Confederate officers and soldiers standing and seated around, not having the least idea that any Yankees were on the south side of Pearl River. The dispatch was examined and various questions asked by the parties, all of which were satisfactorily answered. The dispatch being sent the men complained of being hungry, and said they would cross over to the hotel, and mounting their horses they were half way over when up rode, in great haste, Mr. Sheriff number two, who had escaped the night before. He at once recognized the scouts as two of the party who had helped to drink his whiskey; the men knew him, too, and began to feel for their revolvers, while the sheriff, with naked sword in one hand and horse-pistol in the other—which proved to be empty— began to assume rather a dangerous character; at the same time shouting for help, and ordering everybody to stop them d——d Yankees. The men thought it would not pay to resist, so they prudently commenced a retreat. Several persons tried to stop their horses, but the sharp crack of a revolver impressed them with the idea that it would not be a safe business, and gave them a wide berth. They met me within one mile of town. After stating their adventures I immediately sent one man back to report to the Colonel, also to tell the advance guard to come on double quick, while with the remainder of my men we charged back into town, the rain at the time pouring down in torrents. The first place to visit was the depot. Not a soul was there except two old men; the rest had all absconded, the operator tearing up his instrument and taking it with him. He had not countermanded the dispatch, as was ascertained. When the two scouts retreated the

Confederates thought that the Yankees were then in sight, and without waiting to secure their private property skedaddled, the honest sheriff with them. Upon inquiry we learned that a train was soon due from the north. The usual precaution was taken to secure it; but after waiting half an hour beyond the time for its arrival the command became careless, and no further attention was given it, supposing that news had reached the next station of our approach. This was a sad mistake, for when every one was scattered around town, thinking of anything else, the train came around the corner, from which point the engineer had a good view of a score of "blue coats." He "smelt a rat," and reversing his engine retreated safely with seventeen commissioned officers and eight millions in Confederate money, which was *en route* to pay off troops in Louisiana and Texas. A large lot of empty and loaded freight cars was burned, considerable commissary stores, four car-loads of ammunition, the telegraph cut in several places, the track torn up and some tressel-work destroyed.

The depot was spared on account of its being so near private buildings; they would undoubtedly have caught fire. This was a humane act, and was highly appreciated by the citizens. Though every precaution was taken by the officers to prevent the destruction of private property, the flames were soon seen to burst forth from a drug-store on the east side of the depot, resulting in the burning of three other buildings, two of which were empty stores and the third a private residence; none of the buildings were of very large dimensions. Every exertion was made to extinguish the fire and prevent its spreading.

Hazelhurst is in Copiah County, and is not a very large place; the buildings are somewhat scattered. But little taste or neatness is displayed, though we found some very clever people there, and some who still entertained a strong feeling for the old Union, and were bitterly opposed to secessionism. Two or three barrels of eggs and a quantity of sugar, flour and hams was found in the depot, which was taken to the hotel and cooked for all hands as long as it lasted.

The explosion of boxes of ammunition and bursting of some shells not only alarmed the citizens to some extent, but had a startling effect on Colonel Grierson and the column with him, which was about half way between the station and ferry. The order was given at once to "trot," then "gallop, march!" and they came charging into town, expecting to find Colonel Prince hotly engaged with the enemy. It was only the explosion of the ammunition and shells, that we had purposely fired, and they were sold again, as at Newton Station.

Captain Forbes, who was sent to Macon, rejoined the command just as the rear guard was crossing Pearl River. After the whole command reached Hazelhurst they rested four or five hours, giving me a good opportunity to listen to Captain Forbes relating his adventures, which I give as near as possible. On his way to Macon he was preceded by two of his scouts, Isaac E. Robinson and Wm. Buffington, both members of his own company. When within three miles of Macon they concluded to camp. Before reaching this place the scouts had captured twelve Confederate soldiers, picking them up one, two and three at a time. While selecting the camp-ground Robinson was ordered to advance toward Macon about a mile, to see what he could learn about the force at that place. When he had gone about that distance, and dismounted, he heard the tramp of horses, and in a few minutes there approached him a squad of six Confederate soldiers. When within fifty yards he halted them, and demanded, "Who comes there?" The answer came, "Friends." The scout then said, "Advance one and give the countersign," whereupon one of them advanced, a captain, and the following conversation took place:

"You appear to be a picket here?"

"Yes, sir; have you not heard the 'Yanks' are coming?"

"Yes; I have learned that they are about six miles from here. I was not aware of any pickets stationed here."

"Oh, yes; I was sent here, and told to watch these cross-roads," (which were between him and the camp.)

"How many men are there of you?"

"Only about sixteen of us."

"What are your instructions about passing, &c?"

"The orders from General Loring (commanding forces then at Macon) are not to pass any soldiers, except commanding officers, and citizens."

"Well, my friend, I am a commanding officer, and

have permission to take a squad of men and scout around the country."

"I will call the sergeant of the guard." He shouted at the top of his voice two or three times "sergeant of the guard," but no answer. By this time the soldiers began to be suspicious that all was not right, and two of them dropped back, soon followed by two more, leaving but one, who turned round and wanted to know "what in h—l they meant by leaving in that manner." They did not seem to pay any attention to him, but were soon on a gallop.

"Why, Captain, you must have queer men, to leave in that way; I would not give much for such men to look after 'Yanks.'"

"I'll know what this means," he replied, and calling the fifth man, who still remained at his post, ordered him to remain there, and he would bring back the rascals, and away he went.

Robinson thought this was his opportunity, and he would improve it. The Confederate sat on his horse, with his double-barreled gun elevated, cocked and ready for instant use. Robinson had on a long grey coat, beneath which his carbine hung, attached to a string; he slid his hand down beneath his coat, seizing his carbine and cocking it silently, unbuttoned his coat, and in an instant had it presented at the rebel's heart— ordering him to drop his gun, ride forward and dismount, which he did. Robinson draws his revolver, drops his carbine, breaks the shot-gun, mounts his horse; ordering the reb to follow suit, hurries him back to

Captain Forbes, who made the fellow believe that he would hang him if he did not tell all that he knew about the forces in Macon. The man had not been long in the service, was young and easily frightened, and informed the Captain that there was about four hundred troops, mostly conscripts, stationed there, but there had arrived that day nine hundred troops from Mobile. This was the same man captured by Federal forces as reported by Captain Lynch on his return from scout previously mentioned. Captain Forbes concluded not to visit Macon, and early next morning started back. After marching eight miles the scouts picked up a soldier belonging to the Second Mississippi Artillery. He happened to be one of those individuals that had been opposed to the war, but rather than be conscripted had volunteered. This man proved of considerable service to the Captain, he having a good knowledge of the country; just the man the Captain wanted, and he used him to good advantage. Striking towards the railroad, with the intention of cutting the telegraph and burning a bridge between Macon and Enterprise, to prevent a force being sent from the former to the latter place; but on nearing the railroad he learned that the bridge was strongly guarded; he concluded to avoid it, and destroying the telegraph proceeded towards Newton Station, at which place he was informed that Colonel Grierson had gone to Enterprise. The Captain had a tedious time reaching this point, having to go through swamps, swim streams, travel through timber without any roads, for hours at a time, in order to avoid forces that were patroling the country in quest of us. From Newton Station he went the nearest route to Enterprise, and when within one mile of the town learned that a force of three thousand rebel troops were just getting off the cars. He promptly raised a white flag and rode forward, demanding the surrender of the town in the name of Colonel Grierson! To this demand the rebel commander, Colonel Goodwin, asked an hour to consider upon it, and inquired of the Captain where he would be found at the end of that time. Captain Forbes replied that he would fall back to the reserve. It is not known whether Enterprise surrendered or not, although an article was read in the Jackson-Granada-Memphis-Appeal, of April 26th, that fifteen hundred "Yanks" had demanded the surrender of the place. The Captain made good use of the hour in getting to the reserve. He followed our trail for four days, making forced marches of sixty miles a day, swimming streams, over which we had burned the bridges, to prevent the enemy following us. At one time they were taken in a windfall purposely by a guide, with the intention of having them captured, but their scheme was discovered in time to avoid it. Previous to this, and near Philadelphia, one of the scouts was shot dead from an ambush, (William Buffington,) also a member of the company wounded, (C. E. Martin,) both good and brave soldiers.

When near Raleigh, Robinson learned that a company of guerrillas were in that place. The Captain ordered a charge, and so complete was the surprise (they thinking that all the "Yanks" had passed) that not one of them escaped. They were taking dinner, and ere they knew it, they were surrounded; they numbered twenty-nine men. Their arms were destroyed, men turned loose, the horses and captain of the company taken along. After leaving this place, Lieut. McCausland suggested to Captain Forbes that if he would let him he would send three men, well mounted, to overtake Colonel Grierson. His request was granted, and I have previously mentioned how successful they were. Captain Forbes and men deserve great praise for their bravery and perseverance. He was highly complimented by Colonel Grierson for his success.

At seven o'clock the command left Hazelhurst, the Sixth Illinois in advance. Taking a northwest course it proceeded towards Galiton. It now became necessary to use every precaution. We had passed withtn twenty-five miles of the capital of the State—cut the railroad and telegraph communications on the New Orleans and Great Northern Railroad. The enemy's scouts had been sent out, and were watching our movements; couriers were flying in every direction, spreading the news, forces were concentrating and sent to intercept us, hem us in and annihilate us, as they boasted, and felt confident of accomplishing. They certainly had every advantage on their side;—a perfect knowledge of the country—every road, public or private—every stream of water, small or large—the fordable places and bridges—forces above and below us on the railroad, in our front at Port Gibson, Grand Gulf and Port

Hudson—following in our rear—retreat was impossible, even if such an idea had occurred to us, we having destroyed our only hope in that quarter—bridges and ferries. Colonel Grierson was not one of the retreating kind; his motto was "onward." In wood craft I do not think I ever saw his equal. He reminded me of an old deer hunter; he understood the runways and the shortest way to get to them; besides he had good supporters in the following persons: Colonel Prince and Lieut.-Col. Blackburn, of the Seventh Illinois; Lieut.-Col. Loomis and Adj't. S. L. Woodward, of the Sixth Illinois. It was seldom that any citizen was found to act as guide, except when dodging across through the woods from one road to another. With one of Colton's maps—a small pocket companion—with the states and counties on it, he made his way through the enemy's country. The road selected, it was then the duty of the scouts to keep its communication open, thereby causing no delay to the column.

Colonel Grierson was, just at this time, executing one of his flank movements, which had so many times thrown the enemy off our track, leaving them far in our rear. It was about nine o'clock when we entered the small town of Galiton, driving out a few guerrillas. We had not proceeded many miles further when a train of wagons was discovered ahead, drawn by oxen. The scouts were withdrawn; the Sixth Illinois dashed ahead, and after a few shots fired, captured a thirty-two pound Parrott gun, fourteen hundred pounds of powder, two wagons, and some provisions, *en route* for Grand Gulf.

The gun was spiked, wagon and powder destroyed. After proceeding a few miles further, we went into camp at Hargrove's. Distance traveled, thirty-seven miles.

It was very amusing, sometimes, to witness the astonishment depicted on the countenances of the negroes when they learned that we were Yankees. So many falsehoods had been told them by their masters and mistresses that we were a different people—ugly, deformed, and very wicked, that the poor slaves had conjured up in their minds a fearful picture; they being naturally superstitious and ignorant, are easily worked upon. I had stopped one day to feed at a large plantation, and was somewhat surprised at not seeing any negroes about; however the mystery was soon solved, by finding an old negro in one of the cabins, whose aged locks of wool had turned "gray." I asked him where all the negroes were. "I tell you, massa, dey am in de woods; you see I'se an old nigger, but I knows better, massa; I tell dem not to run to de wood to hide, de Lord knows I did; yes, massa, dey am in de woods over dar,"—pointing with his hand. I asked him why they had run away; we would not harm them. "Well, I tells you, massa; de white folks tell we black ones dat you all's will kill us; so dey hear dat the "Yank's" be coming, and dey runs; now, massa, Ise like to ax one question." "Well, Uncle, go ahead." "I wish you tells dis old nigger when am all de black folks to be free." Smilingly I replied, "just as soon as Uncle Abraham sounds his trumpet, so that it will be heard throughout the whole land, then he will fold you all in his bosom, and you will become a free and happy people." I left the old darkey repeating to himself, "De Lord send him this way soon!" Upon reaching the yard I found that some of the men had flanked around into the woods, looking for horses, and discovered the negroes hid behind stumps and logs. They thought their time had come, and exhibited much fear, which was soon quieted by the kind manner in which our men approached them. They became quite docile, and had a great curiosity to see the "horns" they had heard stuck out of our heads.

TWELFTH DAY.

After a good night's rest we left camp at seven o'clock. We had changed our course, and were going due south—the roads in good condition. Nothing occurred to interrupt us except now and then a chase, and frequently capturing one or two guerrillas, who were in our advance. Thus we continued until about ten o'clock, when the column was halted, and after a council of half an hour among the officers, the following companies of the Seventh Illinois were detached: A, H, F and M under command of Captain Trafton, (acting major) whose instructions were to proceed to Bahala, on the New Orleans and Great Northern Railroad, below Hazelhurst, to destroy the track and otherwise injure the enemy.

Colonel Blackburn ordered me to take one man and accompany this expedition. Away we went, taking a left-hand road, while the rest of the command moved forward on the road to Union Church, the Sixth Illinois in advance, which I will leave to resume their journey while I take my place in the advance with Stedman. Not meeting with anything until within one mile of Bahala, when on gaining the top of a hill (country thickly timbered), I was somewhat startled, at first, to discover two army tents not more than seventy-five yards distant. I immediately halted, cautioned my command to be silent; taking a hasty survey, could not see a living being. We then retreated and reported to Captain Trafton; the column was halted, we concluded there was either no person with the tents, or they knew of our approach and were ready to ambush us. The captain at once decided to advance, by deploying one company as skirmishers, and throwing one company on the right and left flank, the fourth bringing up the center, moving up cautiously, each moment expecting to hear the sharp crack of the rifle. The skirmishers are within a few yards of the tents, still no signs of life; the tents are surrounded, they are captured, they are ours; contents—one darkey asleep; loss—none. It appears that a squad of cavalry had been camped here, and were engaged in burning coal for the Confederate Government, and had been withdrawn the day previous, being ordered to Osako. The negro had been left to take care of the tents, which were destroyed, together with a large quantity of coal. I was then ordered to proceed forward and reconnoitre the town. I did so by flanking around through the timber. Could see no signs of any force there—all appeared to be quiet. Reported back to the command, which went in on a charge, capturing a Major Weader, belonging on General Gardner's staff, and was chief commissary of subsistence, and very much of a gentleman. After destroying depot, water-tank, tressle-work, and steam-engine for pumping water and sawing wood, we rested a short time and then began retracing our steps, taking the Major along. After traveling about seven miles we stopped at a plantation and fed, then continued our journey. On coming into the main road upon which we were to follow up Colonel Grierson, it was eight o'clock, and we had thirty miles to travel before reaching the command. After proceeding about a mile I stopped at a plantation, and what was my surprise to learn that a force of the enemy had passed about five hours before, and were following up Colonel Grierson, but were in ignorance of any Federal force sent to Bahala. They were under the impression that all the Yankee forces had passed. This was most fortunate for us, and in another respect we were favored —the night was very dark. I immediately reported to Captain Trafton. The men were all ordered to observe silence, arrangements were perfected so that the column should halt whenever the scouts requested it, and all seemed to depend on them for a safe re-union with the command. Only Stedman and myself were acting as scouts. Half a mile further I saw a candle-light, apparently out of doors. I advanced boldly, and when near enough discovered an old man standing out upon the front stoop of the house, holding the light in one hand and shading his eyes with the other. He appeared to be conversing with a man that was mounted on a horse, and inside of the garden lot. As I drew up to the gate, not more than fifty yards from the house, I cried out "Hello, step this way;" this seemed to come unexpectedly, and in a moment the mounted man disappeared in the darkness. The old gentleman wanted to know who was there. "A friend," I replied; "please step this way a moment, I want to ask you some questions." He toddeled out to the gate, and as soon as he could see asked if I was not a soldier. I answered that I was, and wished to know how long since our troops passed.

"Do you mean Colonel Adams, sir?"

"Yes, and what force has he?"

"Well, I don't know as I can tell; I can't see but a short distance, but there appeared to be a good many pass, then some cannon."

"How long since?" I inquired.

"Well, about five hours, or it may be six."

"Who was that man that was talking with you when I came up?"

"Well, I really don't know; he is a soldier and a stranger to me, and was inquiring the way to Port Hudson."

"Well, good night, we must go, for we have got reinforcements for Colonel Adams. Tell that man, if you see him, not to be alarmed, the Yankees are all ahead, and we expect to overtake them to-morrow."

"I hope you will," said the old man, "they took two horses and a mule from me, and my neighbor down here lost three mules and one horse, besides four of his best working hands."

I turned and left him, thinking the horse and mule business was nothing new to me. I had no sooner returned to the head of the column and reported to Captain Trafton, then up came a single horseman. It at once occurred to me that this was the man talking with the old man at the house. I told the men to keep still, at the same time ordering him to halt, which he obeyed promptly, and in a loud voice said, "I am all right, I belong to the Confederate army; I heard you talk with the man at the house." Captain Trafton then told him to advance; coming up rapidly he displayed a double-barrelled gun laying across the pommel of his saddle. I asked him if he was not tired, at the same time requesting him to hand me his gun and I would have one of the men carry it for him; he handed it over and I passed it back. Just then Captain Trafton says to me, "This man may be a Yankee for all we know." "Oh, no, gentlemen, you are mistaken; I am a Lieutenant, and belong to Port Hudson, and can tell you all about it, and who commands there, then Captain you can tell if I ain't all right." He was rather young, had been on furlough, and was now on his way back to join his company. He said we would find six men stopping at the next plantation, patrols and pickets, belonging to Wirt Adams' Louisiana cavalry—just what we wanted to know. He was allowed to ride in the ranks, upon being persuaded to accompany us. The men all understood the game, and the Lieutenant proved very sociable, little dreaming that he was a prisoner. After traveling another mile I met a mounted soldier, with a small boy behind him, passed them back as prisoners and continued on until reaching a plantation —a barn on the left of the road, the house on the right; from the barn to the house was about three hundred yards. Approaching the barn we found three men feeding their horses, which they had unsaddled, their saddles laying on the ground; two shot-guns and one carbine standing against the fence next the road. They heard us coming up. I stopped at the gate; they appeared to be expecting us, and expressed no surprise —entered into conversation; questions were asked on both sides and satisfactorily answered. I then told Stedman—in an under tone—to go back and tell the captain to send a few men forward, and as Stedman started I spoke loud, telling him to tell the captain that all was right, that we would soon join Colonel Adams. In a few minutes the men came up, and without further parley we took them prisoners, which proceeding somewhat surprised them. They had stated that three of their number were at the house, and as some loud talking had been done, might they not have heard it? An idea occurred to me, which I at once put into execution. Telling four or five men to come with me, I galloped up to the house, and speaking in a loud voice said, "Come along, men; you know what the captain's orders are, that we must find and bring along every man that is straggling behind; every man is needed to whip those d———d Yankees." This had the desired effect. They were in the house—one a lieutenant—having a good time conversing with the ladies. Skulking was beneath their dignity, and as they heard what I said came boldly out. The men had dismounted, and slipping through the gate took the gentlemen by surprise. Their arms were secured and they put under guard. The Port Hudson lieutenant for the first time "smelt a rat," and exclaimed, "D—n me, if I ain't sold!"

A sad accident occurred at this place. Several shot-guns were found; I had destroyed all but one, a very fine double-barrelled shot-gun, which Sergeant G. M. Vaughn, company F, took a fancy to, requesting me not to break it, but give it to him, and he would carry it. I handed it to him, at the same time saying that he would soon get tired of it, which proved to be the case sooner than I anticipated. We were just going to start when we were startled by the report of fire-arms. The sergeant had concluded not to keep the gun, and dismounting went a few steps to a tree, and grasping the barrel in both hands near the muzzle raised it up, striking it against the tree. He had not taken the necessary precaution to remove the caps, and the result was he lodged the contents of one barrel of buck-shot in his thigh. He had to be left, and I never expected to see him again. The inmates of the house promised to show him every kindness. We resumed our journey, and while passing a cross-road five rebels came trotting into our column, thinking we were Confederates. They were taken quietly, without firing a shot. A short time after this occurred two patrols were met and secured.

It was now about midnight, when on consulting with the captain he thought it was advisable to know something more about the force between us and Colonel Grierson, as well as the locality of the country, and see that, if necessary, we could not flank around the enemy and join our command. We were then within sight of a large plantation. It was a dim starlight night, and the country through which we were traveling principally timbered, with tolerable good roads. The column halted, and taking two men we jumped over a fence, crossed an open space about two hundred yards and stopped in front of a neat log house. I then stationed one man on each side, to prevent any one from leaving it, and then stepping upon the verandah knocked loudly at the door. A voice from within inquired, "Who's there?" I answered, "A soldier; my captain has sent me here to find out something about the roads, and how long since Colonel Adams passed; we are trying to overtake Colonel Adams with reinforcements." By this time he told me to come in. The door not being locked I turned the knob and stepped into a small-sized room, containing one bed, a few chairs, a table, a looking-glass, and a fire-place in which were a few burning embers, giving sufficient light to see that the room was but scantily furnished. He requested me to light a candle and then be seated, which I soon accomplished, while he remained in bed. The following conversation then took place. He was a lawyer and a bachelor, living at his ease, owning considerable property, and did not appear to have seen more than thirty-five years, very good looking, with penetrating eyes, rather prepossessing countenance, and no doubt prided himself on his cuteness as a lawyer.

"Well, you say you are a soldier, and that your captain has sent you here to obtain information about Colonel Adams and the condition of the roads. Now, sir, before answering your questions, I will ask you a few. To whose command do you belong?"

"To Colonel Faulkner's First Mississippi Cavalry, stationed at Granada, and sent by railroad to Jackson, to assist in intercepting the Yankees at Pearl River, but we arrived too late; the Yankees had crossed, and we were ordered by a dispatch from General Pemberton to pursue the enemy, and, if possible, fall in with Colonel Adams and report to him."

"Is Colonel Faulkner in command of this force."

"No, sir; Major Williams is in command. We number about two hundred men, well armed and uniformed. Having been engaged in several battles with the enemy, most of the men have captured Yankee clothing sufficient to clothe themselves."

"You do not speak like a Southern man."

"That is easily accounted for; I came from Missouri formerly; belonged to Jeff. Thompson's command; when he disbanded I came to West Tennessee and joined this command. But I must not delay; can you send a negro along to guide us through to Union Church?"

"I have several blacks, but my horses and mules I sent away when I received news that the Yankees were coming this way, in order to save them. I would go myself as your guide if I had my riding horse here, for I am acquainted with Colonel Adams, and it will be a capital idea, this reinforcement; yes, I would like to go—the Colonel stopped here half an hour and rested his column."

"Do you know, sir, how much force Colonel Adams had?"

"About four hundred men, with six pieces of artillery. He left here about sundown, and intended to attack the Yankees at three o'clock in their rear, while a force from Port Hudson will meet them in front, on the Natchez road."

"I would like very much you would accompany us; I can mount you on a good horse."

"I will go;" and suiting his action to his word sprang out of bed and commencéd dressing, saying that he would be ready in five minutes, and that I would find a saddle, bridle and sheepskin on the door-steps."

"What may I call your name, sir?"

"My name is Mosby."

"Well, Mr. Mosby, I will step out and tell the Major, and have a horse brought up for you." So out I went, feeling very much relieved; told the Captain all about my conversation and my representations of the command, also the information I had obtained, thoroughly posting the captain. I then had the horse brought forward, and the two men withdrawn from the house, the captain in the meantime procuring a long grey coat and cap of the same color. All was now ready, and Mr. Mosby made his appearance at the fence, jumped over, and I introduced them. The captain occupying the advance the lawyer had no opportunity of seeing the column. I proceeded to the front, leaving the Captain and lawyer riding side by side, on intimate terms. We were now within twelve miles of Union Church, and it was of the utmost importance that Colonel Grierson should be informed, at all hazards, of the designs of the enemy. I had gone about two miles when I met two patrols; unarmed them, turning them out on one side of the road, in order that Mr. Mosby should not see them near enough to recognize their features or dress.

As we continued to move on, tired and hungry, I thought some one might try and reach Colonel Grierson before three o'clock; I dropped back so as to ride in company with Mr. Mosby, and inquired of him, where he thought Colonel Adams would stop to feed and prepare before making the attack, and if it was a possible thing for any person to get around his camp without being discovered, as my design was to reach as near the "Yanks" as possible and find out their position, which would be a great advantage to us. Mr. Mosby thought Colonel Adams would feed near the Fayette road on a plantation; that it was impossible to get around Colonel Adams' camp and return in time, owing to the rugged state of the country; "But," continued he, "I am well acquainted with Colonel Adams, and I will go with you, and can pass you through his lines, then you can have a good road to proceed on." I then inquired how far it was to where the Colonel would camp, Mr. Mosby replied about four miles. It was near one o'clock, P.M. I told Mr. Mosby I would consider his proposition, and if I concluded to go through Colonel Adams' camp I would return for him. I started ahead, accompanied by Stedman. We had now made up our minds to go ahead and see if we could obtain a view of the rebel camp, and if possible reach Colonel Grierson.

I bid some of my comrades good bye, telling them that I did not know whether ever I would see them again or not. We started alone; the road was shaded— the overhanging trees on either side, which, together with the darkness of the night, made it very lonely. I began to reflect; what, if we should be detected, our fate was certain death—we would be treated as spies. Then imagination pictured home with all its inducements, and I could see many sad countenances and bitter tears. I thought of all this; what if we should be successful in the attempt, might we not be the instrument of saving the lives of many brave comrades, (we said we would go, and go we must,) and I prayed in my heart that God would guide us safely through. We had advanced to within one half mile of the supposed camp ground, when I could distinctly hear somebody talking and laughing; we came to a halt, and when near enough I could see the figures of the men mounted upon horses; I allowed them to come within about twenty-five yards, when I cried halt, which sound came rather unexpected to them, and at first they did not know whither to turn and run or not, but raising their guns I could distinctly hear the sharp click of the hammers as they cocked their pieces. Our revolvers were grasped in our right hands ready for instant use, (a precaution we always used after night.) I immediately inquired "who comes there?" One of them answered, "friends," I then said, "advance one and give the countersign." They answered they had no countersign, at the same time one of them advanced, and as he came up, inquired who I was, and if I was alone. By this time I could see my man plain enough to feel satisfied that he was a Confederate soldier. I answered him that I was not alone, that the column would be here in a few minutes, that we had been traveling all day and that night to overtake Colonel Adams and reinforce him; "all right," says he, "we belong to old Wirt Adams' cavalry, and to-morrow we intend to give the 'Yanks' h——l." By this time the other two came up and many questions were asked as to the command we belonged to, all of which we answered satisfactorily. They informed me that the "Yanks" had a fight going into Union Church last evening, and that Colonel Adams had gone to Fayette there to be reinforced by troops from the river, and they intended to ambush the "Yanks" in the morning between Fayette and Union Church; that the "Yanks" intended to make Natches but would get slipped up; they farther stated that they had been left on the corner where the Fayette road turned off to notify forces coming up where they could join Colonel Adams. This was just what I wanted to know and I felt really good. I knew the column would soon be along, and telling my friends that I would go back and meet the advance, and tell them of their presence, so that no accident would occur. This looked plausable enough, and without any objections they permitted me to depart. I then procured two men from one of the company's, proceeded ahead, and without any trouble took my three friends in "out of the wet"—two of them were lieutenants, they had left their post and were going to a plantation about a mile from there to visit an old acquaintance. They were taken a few yards into the timber to prevent Mr. Mosby seeing them, fearing that he would know them. As soon as the head of the column had passed the prisoners were turned over to company M. I started forward and as I passed Mr. Mosby he inquired who those men were that we had taken; I told him they were "Yanks" and had been straggling from their command, probably to plunder, and had lost their way. He allowed it was a capital idea, and hoped we would shoot them, that they should not be permitted to live.

The coast was now clear, and we had only six miles to go before joining our command. I now told Mr. Mosby that Colonel Adams had gone to Fayette, and explained the reason. Mr. Mosby then wanted to know from the Major whether he intended joining Colonel

Adams or following up the "Yanks." The Major (which we will continue to call Captain Trafton,) replied, that on considering the matter he would follow the "Yanks" and send a courier through to Colonel Adams, notifying him of the force here and the intention, which was to attack the enemy in the rear, in conjunction with their attack in the front.

Mr. Mosby thought it was a capital idea and offered his services to carry this dispatch through to Colonel Adams—in fact insisted upon it. But the Major allowed that he could not part so easily with his excellent company, and turning to me, ordered me to send a courier through to Colonel Adams on the Fayette road which we were now leaving to our right; I absented myself a short time, then reported to the Major that his order was obeyed. I then trotted forward beside my friend Stedman and we congratulated each other on the success attending us, and it was not without a feeling of gratitude to the Most High for our safety thus far.

We now felt comparatively safe. It was but five miles to the command, and I gave myself up to thoughts of our numerous adventures, of the past few hours, and could hardly realise that we had had so many narrow escapes; I thought of the delay I had occasioned the column so many times, knowing how tired and sleepy the men were, how they must have cursed me, but they were ignorant of the proceeding in front, and as the prisoners continued to be sent back they began to realise the importance of the scouts, and their show of gratitude toward myself and comrade afterward has more than repaid me for the risk incurred. When within a few miles of Union Church I could see our picket fires, so riding briskly up, though not without being halted by the vidette. I advised the men of our having a guide who was under the impression that he was rendering the Confederate service a great benefit by guiding us. I requested them not to make any remark while the head of the column was passing, that would excite suspicion in the mind of Mosby. I dropped back to see what effect the presence of this picket post would have on him; at first, he was much surprised and remarked that he did not know that we had any force ahead. I told him that it was only one company, that had been sent down on the east side of the railroad, and were waiting here expecting us—that we still had a force at Union Church. This was satisfactory; he allowed it was a capital idea. We soon entered town, and with it came daylight—half-past four o'clock. We found the command scattered, and laying stretched out on the ground fast asleep—for the weather was quite warm and pleasant. We at once dismounted, the men feeding their horses, while Captain Trafton—no longer major—repaired to headquarters and communicated his information to Colonel Grierson. The prisoners were put under guard, except Mr. Mosby, who remained most of the time in my company, and not suspecting anything wrong. Colonel Grierson at once arose from his bed and sent for Colonel Prince, Lieut.-Col. Blackburn, Lieut.-Col. Loomis, and Adj't

S. L. Woodward; the latter he consulted on all such occasions.

After Captain Trafton left on his expedition to Bahala, the rest of the command kept on the direct road to Union Church, not meeting with any trouble until within two miles of the place, except eight or ten guerrillas, who were picked up by the scouts. Companies A, C, and D, the advance of the Sixth Illinois, met the enemy about one hundred and fifty strong, but without any delay drove them into and through town some three miles, wounding two and taking several prisoners. Our loss one—slightly wounded. Captain Trafton brought in twenty-one prisoners, having met with no loss, except the accident, and having traveled about thirty miles more than the rest of the command. While Colonel Grierson was consulting the map, Adj't Root was busily engaged writing paroles, and soon the prisoners were brought up to sign their names. This was what I wanted; now was the time to witness the surprise and discomfiture of our worthy friend, Mr. Mosby, the learned lawyer, the Yankee exterminator, "a capital idea." As the prisoners were brought around to the front of the house, and going through the ceremony of being paroled, my friend the lawyer's curiosity was excited; he thought he recognized among the prisoners a few familiar faces, and expressed a desire to cross the garden and see. "Most certainly," I replied, "there's no objection to any one conversing with the prisoners." He started, and I remained standing where I could see and watch his countenance.

On the verandah was a table, and seated around it the buisy clerks, while the prisoners crowded around, awaiting their turn to be called, apparently feeling in good spirits. On approaching the crowd one of them turned around and at once recognized, in the form and features of Mr. Mosby, an old acquaintance, and extending his hand exclaimed, "Why, friend Mosby, you here; I did not expect to see you a prisoner."

"Why, explain; what do you mean? are these not our troops?"

"Our troops? No! I wish they were; I'd feel a d——d sight better than I do now. No, sir; they are the genuine Yankees; but they will not do anything with you, being a citizen, and not a soldier; but I am surprised, lawyer Mosby, that you had not noticed the difference."

I could see his face change—color half a dozen times —and turning around he looked "daggers" at me. In a few minutes he returned, and looking me full in the face said, "This is a d——d Yankee trick." I was full of laughter, and laying my hand familiarly on his shoulder said, "Mr. Mosby, you are sold, but it is all fair in war times, and do you not think 'a capital idea?'" He twitched his mouth a little, and at last assuming a contented look said, "Sergeant, you have done well, but for God's sake do not ever mention this to any person." I promised, but it was too good to keep. From that time until he left the place he was very sociable. On inquiring how he was to get back home, he said he could not walk so far, and there would not be a horse or mule left. I told him that I thought I could raise him a horse of some kind, as several had to be left behind. I left him, and finding the Colonel, asked him if there would be any horses left behind, if so, I would like one for Mr. Mosby to return on. The Colonel told me to find one and mount him. I soon found one, and putting on a good saddle called Mr. Mosby, and handing him the reins told him to keep this horse in remembrance of the Yankees. He seemed much pleased, and when I left him he had a very favorable opinion of Yankee hospitality. Prisoners all paroled, exhausted horses turned loose, by six o'clock in the morning we left Union Church.

THIRTEENTH DAY.

The twenty-ninth found us directing our course towards the railroad—the Seventh Illinois in advance —passing through the woods for several miles without any signs of a road—another flank movement—leaving Colonel Adams with a considerable force on the Natchez road, expecting to ambush us. We afterwards learned hat he did not discover we had evacuated Union Church until two o'clock that day.

We were now directing our course towards Brookhaven, on the New Orleans and Great Northern railroad. Considerable dodging was done the first three or four hours' march of this day. I do not think we missed traveling toward any point of the compass. We were making tolerably fast time, occasionally "taking in" a prisoner. Finally we struck the main road leading to

Brookhaven, and met ox and mule teams drawing hogsheads of sugar, running it off from the station across the country to Port Gibson; of course it was destroyed, but not before the men replenished their haversacks. When within four miles of the station we surprised and took prisoners five guerrillas, without firing a shot. Upon searching a house near by we found eight shot-guns and rifles, and three revolvers. Destroying the former we advanced to within two miles of the station, when I was ordered to proceed and reconnoitre the town, and see what I could discover. About one mile from town I met a squad of eight soldiers walking; they had no arms and were on their way to join their command at Port Hudson. I sent one man back with them to the column. Coming within sight of the town I could see a considerable number of men collected here and there on the corners of the streets, but could not see any armed soldiers. I reported back to the column, which advanced, and as soon as in sight, and not more than four hundred yards from town, a single shot was heard to our left, in the timber. This place being entirely surrounded by woods, the column formed fours, and on a charge dashed into town through the streets, causing some confusion, excitement, and a considerable running among the citizens; they anticipated a visit from the "Yanks," but not so soon. The shot was a signal of our approach, but ere the echo of the report died away we were in and among them. While the Seventh was charging in this gallant style, the Sixth was making good time towards a camp of instruction, one and a half miles south of town, which they charged into, expecting to find a considerable force, principally conscripts; but they had left the evening previous—some eight hundred. This camp was capable of accommodating about fifteen thousand troops. Long rows of small frame buildings, a few tents, a quantity of arms, and a large supply of commissary stores were destroyed. It was truly a most delightful camping-ground, situated on a high hill, in a shady grove of live oaks.

Captain Lynch, of the Sixth Illinois, with companies E and F, was sent to destroy one mile of tressel-work. After accomplishing this work, the Sixth visited town, in time to see the flames devouring the depot and some dozen freight cars, fired by the Seventh; also a railroad bridge. The depot contained quite a quantity of commissary stores.

Two hundred and sixteen prisoners were captured and paroled here, principally sick and convalescent soldiers. They were quartered in a very fine building, used as a hospital; they seemed to court our society rather than avoid it, and evinced a strong desire to be paroled, which was a long, tedious task, they having to be written out, which duty devolved on Adjutants Root, and Woodward, both young men possessing a large share of patience and perseverance. Several citizens were hiding themselves in the woods, and as soon as they learned that we were not destroying private property came into town, and urgently requested that they be paroled, so as to avoid the conscription. In the meantime somebody was enjoying a good meal. Lieut.-Col. Blackburn had ordered at one of the hotels dinner for two hundred of his men, paying the proprietor in Confederate money. The landlord expressed a wish that the "Yanks" would come every day, if they all acted like "we'uns" did.

When the depot was burning there was great danger of a private building taking fire on the opposite side of the street, owing to the excessive heat thrown upon it; and had it not been for the exertions of some twenty soldiers, who brought pails of water and kept the roof wet, it would have burned and destroyed many more with it. The saving of the property was personally superintended by Colonel Grierson.

I must say that the citizens of this town were generally very clever, opening their doors and inviting us to partake of their hospitality; there was none of that bitterness and hatred displayed. They were mostly of an educated class, whose minds had not been prejudiced by the extravagant tales circulated through the South concerning us. A show of neatness and taste prevailed around these dwellings. Brookhaven has a very pretty location. It is in Lawrence County, and has a population of about fifteen hundred. It was near sundown when we took our departure, leaving the people enjoying a much better opinion of us than they had before. From this place we marched six miles and camped, and for the first time in thirty-eight hours did a portion of the command take the saddles off their horses, and obtain time to sleep.

FOURTEENTH DAY.

The command moved out just at sunrise, with every appearance of a lovely day—the Sixth Illinois in the advance. Without any interruption we proceeded to Boyachitta, a small station on the railroad, consisting of not more than a dozen houses. While the Sixth Illinois was destroying the depot and six or eight freight cars, Captain Hening, of the Seventh, with his company, was sent to destroy some tressel-work and a railroad bridge. Upon reaching them he found it to be a bigger job than he could complete in the short space of time allowed on such occasions, so the Captain sent back to the Lieut.-Col. of the Sixth Illinois to send fifty or one hundred men to assist in destroying the very large railroad bridge and two hundred and fifty feet of tressel-work—a very important item. Captain Lynch, of the Sixth Illinois, with company E, destroyed three hundred feet of tressel-work. From here we proceeded towards Summit, crossing the railroad to the east between the former and latter place, destroying railroad bridges and tressel-work as we went along. Two couriers were captured by the scouts. We arrived in Summit about noon; marched in quietly and leisurely.

The people seemed to expect us, and there were no signs of excitement or fear displayed, either in actions or features. They had received a favorable report of our conduct at Brookhaven, and Colonel Grierson was almost as much of a favorite with them as General Pemberton. We spent nearly half a day here, improving the time by destroying a large number of freight cars and a large quantity of sugar, salt, molasses and meal —government property—which was loaded into the cars and then run down the track, away from private property, and burned. The depot was spared from the flames because it would endanger dwellings.

Some of the men discovered that there were thirty or forty barrels of Louisiana rum hid in the swamp, about a mile from town—the meanest stuff in existence, warranted to kill further than any rifle in Uncle Sam's service. Some of the men began to feel quite uneasy, and the swamp became a place of much resort. The Colonel soon heard of it, and sent a commissioned officer, with a squad of men, to destroy it; they with great reluctance stove in the head of each barrel, and thus did waste the balm of a thousand flowers. In justice to the citizens, I will say they knew what good liquor was, and kept it, too. You will ask, where? buried in a pile of old chips. Now, who but a Yankee would think of looking in a pile of old rubbish, in a dirty door-yard? A four-gallon demijohn was pulled out from its hiding-place, filled to the brim with good "old rye," such as would make a temperance man forget his pledge. Upon entering a house one day I heard the latter part of a conversation between a mother and daughter. The latter was in a mild way trying to convince her mother that it was no use trying to hide anything from the Yankees; "Aunty hid her wine out in the cornfield, and some of the nasty scamps found it."

Some of the men had a curiosity to see the inside of a large hall; the door being fastened they did not wish to break the lock, but took the trouble to find the proprietor, who, on learning the object of their visit, was very reluctant to comply with their request. He was informed that if he did not produce the keys they would break it down. This was enough; he handed over the keys and the men entered the hall, finding several old United States muskets, and folded neatly underneath them was a silk battle-flag, with a motto inscribed on it—" God and our rights," "Fort Donelson," "Shiloh"—belonging to a Mississippi regiment—I have forgotten the number. The men of course confiscated it. At this place we found plenty of feed for our horses. The citizens were kind to us, and, like their neighbors at Brookhaven, showed many signs of loyalty toward the old Union. This place showed many signs of once having done considerable business; of a neat, lively appearance, a pretty location, situated in Pike County, and before the war could boast of a population of about three thousand.

Just as the sun was sinking to rest "boots and saddles" was sounded, and we left town amid smiles and the waving of many handkerchiefs, following a southwest course in the direction of Liberty. After traveling eight miles we camped for the night. After leaving Summit we passed through some fine country and over good roads. The climate was delightful. We were not more than one hundred miles from New Orleans. Were we going there? that was the question.

A rebel courier had been captured since leaving the railroad. The scouts had learned that there was a force at Osyko Station. There was now every indication that the enemy were exerting their utmost to intercept us. Large forces were reported in various directions—delay would prove fatal to us. Colonel Grierson concluded to abandon the railroad and take a straight line for Baton Rouge, Louisiana. We had completely destroyed forty miles of the road, and the command was becoming very weary for want of proper rest. So far as horses were concerned there was no scarcity; many troopers had to change four or five times, abandoning their worn out ones, and but few of the horses we started with were taken through; besides we were in poor trim for fighting, there being only forty rounds of ammunition to each man, and it was not the intention of Colonel Grierson to engage the enemy, but rather avoid him. I am satisfied of one thing—that had we been compelled to fight it would have been a desperate one. A better understanding and feeling never existed between two regiments than between these two so linked together. I will speak more of them hereafter.

FIFTEENTH DAY.

On the morning of the first of May, just as daylight began to appear, the command left camp, taking a southwest course—Seventh Illinois in advance—and as we wended our way through the woodlands, we little dreamed what a change would be produced in a few hours. The sun arose in all his glory—not one cloud visible in the sky to obscure its dazzling brightness.

A gentle breeze floated through the trees, causing a rustling among the green leaves of the oaks. Perched among the branches was the mocking bird, singing a variety of notes, the whole impressing the beholder with a sense of a Creator of all this beauty. The command felt inspired, and various were the conjectures as to what point on the Mississippi River we would make. We were sometimes pursuing by-roads, and it was on one of these, and within four miles of the Clinton and Osyko road, that we met a sutler driving his team, seated in a wagon. Following him was a man mounted on a fine horse, from whom I obtained some information respecting their forces. They were on their way to Osyko, not expecting to meet, but rather avoid us, under the impression that we were advancing on another road. Among the stock was some tobacco, to which the men helped themselves.

About ten o'clock we emerged into the Clinton and Osyko road. I at once discovered, by the newly-made tracks, that a column had passed, and could not have been long before. Sending a man back to Colonel Grierson, he soon came up and examined closely. It was the opinion of all the officers that a considerable force had passed, and were going in the same direction as ourselves. I was then ordered by Colonel Grierson to advance cautiously, to let nothing escape my observation on either side of the road, and if I saw any object that I could not satisfy myself about, to report at once to him, and not to get more than half a mile from the advance. After receiving these instructions

I started, followed by my scouts; had proceeded about two and a half miles when I discovered horses hitched in the edge of the timber, near the road-side on our left; I could see that they were saddled, but could not discover any person around. We were then about three hundred yards from them. I immediately sent one man back to report to Colonel Grierson, and taking two of them with me started on, using the necessary precaution of having our revolvers ready at hand. As we approached nearer I could see that there were but three horses and three men, two of them sitting upon a log talking, the third lying down. They were well armed, each man carrying a carbine and revolver. They did not seem to think strange of our approach. We rode up to them and I said, "Hello, boys, on picket?" "Yes; been on about an hour and feel devilish tired; been traveling night and day after the d——d "Yanks," and I'll bet my horse they will get away yet." "That is just our case," I replied; "but where is your command?" "Over in the rush bottom, resting"—pointing with his hand. "Whose command is it, and how many have you?" Just then two shots were heard in our rear, and sounded as though fired on the right of the road. At this they began to open their eyes and prick up their ears. There was no time for further questioning, so giving the men the sign, each one of us covered his man with his revolver, demanding their surrender, and to hand over their arms at once or we would blow them through, and ordering them to mount, double-quicked them back to the column, which was halted some four hundred yards in our rear. In order that the reader may more fully understand the situation of affairs, I will try and describe the surrounding country. On our left as we advanced was timber; on our right a large plantation, a two-story frame-house, painted white, standing back from the road some three hundred yards; between the house and main road the ground was covered with a dense growth of live-oaks and silver-poplars, completely hiding from the house the view of any passing column. Two roads wended their way through this little forest from the main road to the house, one above and the other below it, taking an oblique direction. It appears that when the column was stopped, the advance was just opposite the house, and while waiting for further developments from the scouts, several men under command of Lieutenant Gaston, company G, Seventh Illinois, proceeded to the house. As they rode up to the gate they were surprised at seeing four armed rebels standing around in the yard, their horses being tied outside the gate. The "rebs" were surprised as well, and both parties showed a disposition to fight. Our men demanded their surrender, which they had no notion of complying with. Both parties commenced firing upon each other, which resulted in our men taking two, putting the other two to flight, and an easy capture of the four horses. One of our men was struck in the breast by a buck-shot, striking one of his ribs and glancing off without inflicting a serious wound. This explained the firing while at the picket-post, and these four "rebs" belonged to that post, but had gone to the house to procure something to eat, not expecting the "Yanks" to come that way. They paid little or no attention to their duty.

I was again ordered to proceed cautiously, and upon reaching the place where we had taken in the picket I thought I could see two mounted men off to my right, in an oblique direction, and about one quarter of a mile off; an open field was between us, having a gradual descent towards them. On surveying the road with my eye I could see that after following it for a quarter of a mile it turned a right angle, and then at the distance of another quarter it entered the timber, at which point those two men appeared sitting on their horses, and not moving but looking very earnestly at us. That a force was down in the bottom, and that not very far off, was pretty well understood; but what that force was, and their number, we did not know, but, as the game says, we had to "go it blind." Leaving a man at this point with instructions to stop the column, which could advance this far without being seen by those who appeared to be watching us from below, and at the same time see all that was going on in the bottom, outside of the timber, I proceeded with Stedman. Fowler and Wood had taken the right-hand road, and advanced on it about one hundred yards, when one of the horsemen cried out in a loud voice, "What in h—l does all that firing mean?" I answered that reinforcements were coming up, and that his picket had fired on our advance, thinking that they were

"Yanks," but no one was hurt, and it was all right. At this one of them broke out in a roar of laughter, and said "Is that all?" and putting spurs to his horse started towards us at a gallop, leaving his comrade behind. I told Fowler to let him ride up between us, and I would manage him. Each one of us carried our revolvers in our hands ready for instant use. Up he came, looking much pleased, and said, "How are you, boys; how much force have you got?" We had now halted, and as he rode in between us I turned my horse in an oblique direction, changing my revolver into my left hand, cocked it, and pointing it at his breast, attracted his attention to it, and in a quiet way told him not to speak or make a motion, but hand over his arms to Fowler or I would blow him through; he at once complied, though not without some astonishment at our proceedings. I then directed my attention to "reb" number two, and discovered that he was coming slowly towards us. Stedman, who had dismounted for some reason, was leading his horse and advancing to meet him. He had returned his revolver to its holster, feeling confident that he had an easy prey. They met about one hundred yards from where I was then standing. Stedman was so anxious to secure his man that he forgot for a moment the character he was to play, which came near proving fatal to him. As they met Stedman let go his bridle-rein and grasped that of his opponent, at the same time laying his hand firmly on his revolver holster and ordered him to surrender. This proceeding somewhat confused the "reb's" ideas, and for a moment he did not know what to think, at the same time he looked up the hill and must have seen the column advancing. He was a large, athletic man, while Stedman was very small. With a quick movement he tried to release the hold Stedman had on his holster, at the same time saying. "Who and what in h—l are you?" It only took a moment to see something was wrong, and calling to Wood to come on I put spurs to my horse, and in a few moments was presenting a revolver at his head, threatening to blow his brains out if he did not surrender; he at once complied. I could not but admire his manly proportions, and face beaming with courage and bravery. I noticed the gold bars on his collar, which in the Southern army denotes captain. I ordered him to follow me, and told him not to be alarmed, that we were Illinois boys and he would be treated well. Smilingly he said, in a clear, firm voice, "I am not afraid, sir; I would not have been your prisoner had it not been that I was deceived in your dress." He proved to be a Captain Scott, and commanded the force then within rifle-shot. Just at this time Colonel Blackburn came galloping up, alone, and said to me, "Sergeant, bring along your scouts and follow me, and I'll see where those rebels are." I called one of my men and told him to take the Captain back to the column, which by this time had descended the hill, and were advancing within four hundred yards of us. I then started, followed by Kelly, Wilson and Wood. The Colonel being some distance ahead we had to increase our speed to a gallop to overtake him. It seemed to me that this was a rash movement on the part of Colonel Blackburn, but he had ordered me to follow him, and it was my duty to obey. As soon as we reached the spot where the two horsemen were first seen, we were at the end of a lane, and a few yards further all was timber. A considerable stream of water could be seen wending its way through the marshy and heavily timbered bottom. A little to the left, about seventy-five yards, is the crossing, a narrow plank bridge, some fifty feet in length, better known as Wall's Bridge, across the Trickafaw River, in Hunt County, and within one mile of Wall's post-office. Just before we reached the bridge we were saluted by a few shots fired from the opposite side of the stream, which did not check our speed, but rather increased it. Closely following Colonel Blackburn all dashed upon the bridge, but ere the last one of us had reached the opposite side we were greeted by a loud volley of carbines and musketry, coming from some eighty of Colonel Wirt Adams' cavalry, who lay in ambush not more than fifty yards distant. It seemed as though a flame of fire burst forth from every tree. The Colonel fell, along with his horse, both pierced by the fatal bullet. One of my comrades had his horse shot under him. A minnie ball struck me on my right thigh, passing through it into my saddle, just grazing my horse's back. Three shots were all I could get. I began to feel a faintness creeping over me, but still clinging to my revolver I turned my horse about and tried to retrace my steps amid the flying bullets. When the first few shots were fired it was heard by Colonel Grierson, who then occupied the advance, and was the advance guard of the column. On they came, most gallantly, led by Lieutenant Styles, who charged across the bridge, followed by only twelve men. No sooner over the bridge than they were checked by a well directed volley. They rally and charge, but it is useless—they were too few and exposed, while the enemy were protected by the surrounding timber. The little band have to retreat back across the bridge, leaving one man killed and two wounded, and seven dead horses. They had no support; the column was too far behind to lend assistance in time, but just as they re-crossed the bridge the column came up on the double-quick. Colonel Prince, by order of Colonel Grierson, ordered companies A and D of his regiment to dismount. They were sent to the right and left as skirmishers. One section of Captain Smith's battery was brought up, the woods were shelled, the enemy put to flight, and our men were pursuing them, and as they pass Colonel Blackburn, who laid mortally wounded, with one leg under his horse, cries out to them, "Onward! follow them, boys!" and cheers. The Sixth now take the advance—no halt is made—the Seventh look after the killed and wounded; they are all borne by friendly hands, and with tender care placed in the ambulances and carried forward one mile and left at the plantation of Mr. Newman. Their horses, equipments and arms are turned over to comrades and friends to take through with them. Many a kind farewell was given, and friends parted, some never to meet again on this side of the grave.

The following are the casualties sustained at this place, all belonging to the Seventh Illinois: Lieut.-Col. Blackburn, mortally wounded; Quartermaster-Sergeant of the regiment, R. W. Surby, flesh-wound; William Roy, Company G, seriously; R. W. Hughes, Company G, mortally; and Geo. Reinhold, Company G, killed. The following members were left to nurse and attend to the wants of the wounded: Serg't-Maj. A. Le Suer, Seventh Illinois; George W. Douglass, Company A, Seventh Illinois; and Dr. Yole—whose services were very valuable—of the Second Iowa Cavalry, who accompanied the expedition.

And now, as my thoughts at that time were with the command, thinking of their safety, with the reader's permission, I will still continue to be with them, until they again return to old Tennessee, and then, not forgetful of the sufferings of those who we were compelled to leave behind, will return and tell you of their fate.

The Sixth was pursuing the fast retreating foe, for they began to scatter in all directions. It was amusing to see some of them grasping their horses' manes, while their lower extremities were half suspended in the air; their saddle-girths have broken, and off tumbles saddle and blanket, leaving the rider bare-backed, with his legs pressed close to his horse's sides, his body thrown forward, resting upon his neck, and bare-headed. Occasionally a ball whizzes past him; he is fortunate enough if he escapes capture. The road is strewn with old saddles, blankets, coats, hats, and firearms. It was rarely we participated in such a chase; but it is not quite so fine when the joke is on the other side. While we are enjoying the prospect of such a chase I will go back to the scene of the last few hours and endeavor to show you how, in my opinion, the loss of our few brave hearts could have been avoided. You will remember of reading, a few pages back, of the manner in which I approached the picket-post, accompanied by two of my men, and how, just as I was on the eve of obtaining information respecting the forces in the bottom, and whose command, that a few shots were heard at the house on our right; it was those shots that frustrated our plans and left us in the dark. Had Lieutenant Gaston and squad not entered the house, thereby meeting the enemy, firing upon each other and giving the alarm, all would have no doubt ended well. With the information I should have obtained from the picket it would have been sufficient for Colonel Grierson to so perfected his plans as to have surprised the enemy and taken them prisoners, and that very probably without the loss of life, thereby still securing to the country a few good soldiers, a brave and efficient field-officer, and prevented the sorrow and anguish that was inflicted on the loved ones at home. Another sad mistake was that Lieut.-Colonel Blackburn, unfortunately with too much daring, proceeded across the bridge with no other support than a few scouts. He being a very large man, dressed in full uniform, and mounted upon a very fine horse, was a most conspicuous mark. There was no call for this movement. The scouts had performed their duty up to this time, and having every assurance that the enemy was near by they should have been withdrawn, at least long enough to have changed their costume; however, it is all past, and I often think that it was a miracle that any of us escaped the first volley; but the ways of Divine Providence are very mysterious, and I have every reason to be thankful that my fate was no worse.

We will now see how the advance is progressing. The command was now in Louisiana, Amit County being the last county passed through in Mississippi. We found the roads in good condition, and were making not less than six miles per hour. It was about two o'clock, P.M., the column was about six miles from Wall's Bridge, and the scouts, who were in the advance, discovered off to the right about forty rebels advancing on a side road leading into the main one. The scouts made a halt at this corner and fired several shots, which was replied to by the "rebs," who still kept advancing, seeming determined to gain the main road, but ere they could accomplish this the Sixth came in sight, and at the distance of six hundred yards brought one of their guns into position and threw a few shells among them, which had the desired effect, causing them to beat a hasty retreat. This was most opportune, for had they gained the main road nothing could have prevented them from reaching the Amit River and effectually destroying the extensive bridge over that stream, which would have resulted most seriously with us. About four P.M. the command passed through Greensborough, a small town in St. Helena County. It was here that Lieutenant Newall, company G, Sixth Illinois, overtook the command, having been sent early that morning with a few men to procure horses and provisions. He was not aware of the fight until he had passed over the battle-ground, which somewhat increased his speed until he overtook the column. He had a narrow escape from being captured.

As the scouts entered this place Samuel Nelson discovered a mounted "reb," who was armed with a shot-gun, and apparently standing picket on a cross-road. Samuel approached him, and saluting him inquired who he was and what he was doing there. He replied that he was the County Clerk, and was waiting for a courier to come up that he might learn the news. Samuel then asked him if he knew who he was talking too. The fellow replied that he did not remember of seeing him before, but thought he was a soldier and belonged to Port Hudson. Samuel says, "No, sir; you are mistaken —you are talking to a live Yankee, and here is some Yankee whisky." "Reb" looked somewhat surprised at first, but displayed good taste and judgment—took the proffered canteen, and raising it to his lips took a good drink. As soon as the column came up Samuel turned him over, but before they parted company he very politely asked Samuel for " another nip of that

Yankee whisky." Of course Samuel gave it to him, and he appeared to be very well satisfied with his new quarters.

On leaving town the column took a southwest course, and met with nothing of note until they had gone about four miles, when the scouts brought in two couriers, who were on their way to Osyko Station. The column was now proceeding on a good road, level as a floor, beautifully shaded on both sides by tall forest pines, interspersed with a small growth of other kinds of timber, now and then passing a small plantation, until within four miles of Amit River, when the country became more open, displaying considerable cultivation and some fine residences, with extensive plantations.

The night was a clear, starlight one, and moderately warm, the moon not making its appearance until about eleven o'clock, which added to the beauty of the surrounding country. Yet there was little interest displayed in the scenery, the men being too much exhausted for want of rest, and nearly every man was nodding as he rode along, reminding me of the old song, " Nid, nid, nodding." For the last hour previous to reaching the Amit River considerable delay was occasioned by waiting for the scouts, who were ordered to visit different plantations and obtain all the information they could respecting the situation of the bridge and whether any force was stationed there. Before reaching the bridge the scouts learned that a post of couriers was stationed during the day, and at night withdrawn, one half mile from the bridge, on the south side of the river. If this should prove to be the case, what a considerable advantage would be gained? Once across this bridge and all was comparatively safe. So thought Colonel Grierson, who was fully awake to the interests of his command. When within one mile of the bridge the roads became very muddy and rough. The column was halted, and the scouts were ordered to proceed to the bridge and ascertain if any picket was stationed there. Samuel taking the advance arrived at the bridge, dismounted and proceeded across on foot. The bridge was about two hundred yards in length, over a deep and rapid stream. He found it all right, and was not long in reporting this good news to Colonel Grierson, who gave the order "Forward!" and in a few minutes the horse's hoofs could be heard rattling upon the planks. It was a striking scene to witness the column crossing this long bridge at the hour of midnight. After crossing the column passed through a delightful country. The distance from the Amit to the Comit River is seventeen miles, and better roads are seldom traveled in the interior of any state. No alarm had been given in crossing the bridge. The couriers, who numbered ten men, were asleep at a house about half a mile from the bridge, little dreaming that the Yankee raiders were then within rifle-shot. They were not disturbed, and not until daylight did they learn what a rich prize had escaped their vigilance. For the first few hours every man was aroused, and all were congratulating each other on the success of the expedition. All felt that they were comparatively safe, and occasionally could be heard the booming of the mortars, which were throwing their ponderous shells into Port Hudson, all of which had a tendency to inspire the men with the prospect of soon meeting with our forces; thus we continued to move along, meeting with no obstacle.

SIXTEENTH DAY.

On crossing the bridge over Big Sandy Creek the scouts discovered a camp not more than two hundred yards from the bridge, but could not discover any sentinels, and upon approaching nearer saw two negroes, who were busy building a fire. Without being seen the scouts withdrew and reported to Colonel Grierson, who immediately ordered Lieut.-Col. Loomis to send forward two companies of the Sixth to open fire, while the rest of the regiment brought up the rear. Captain Marshall, company H, dismounted his men, crossed the bridge silently — being supported by Captain Lynch, with company E, mounted — and when within one hundred yards raised a tremendous yell, shooting and charging down through the long rows of tents, which must have somewhat startled the unconscious sleepers, who felt so perfectly secure as not to have out any pickets. Instead of finding a considerable force here, as was expected, there were only about forty men, principally convalescents, nearly all of whom were captured. The force stationed at this place numbered six hundred, (Williams' cavalry.) They had the day previous to this been ordered to push forward to Brookhaven and intercept the Yankees. Colonel Grierson at once ordered Colonel Prince to move forward on the advance, while the Sixth stopped long enough to destroy the camp and garrison equipage, and secure the prisoners, one of whom escaped and was afterwards captured, and related his experience that night by stating that he rushed from his tent, reached his horse, sprang upon his back, and away he went, bare-backed, with nothing on but his shirt and drawers and socks; he never stopped until he reached home, some sixty miles distant. The only casualty that happened while capturing this place was the wounding of one rebel.

We will now follow the Seventh, who are in the advance, going at a lively pace, over a good road, which began to show some signs of dust. The morning was beautiful, with a clear sky and a bright sun. The country had the appearance of being very level—on our right somewhat low and swampy, for several miles on our left fine and extensive plantations. After proceeding about a mile and a half a single horseman was seen, by two members of company A, to emerge into the road about two hundred yards in their advance, and between them and the scouts. The road was so straight and level that most any moving object could be seen for the distance of two miles. As soon as he came into the road he was ordered to halt, but did not feel inclined to obey orders, and using his spurs away he dashed, hotly pursued, exchanging a few shots. In a few minutes he overtakes our scouts, whom he takes for some of his own men, and brandishing his revolver over and around his head excitedly says, "Get out of here, boys; the road is full of 'Yanks' in our rear!" "Yes," says one of the scouts, as they closed in around him, "and you are right among them now." Imagine his surprise. His name was Hinson, and a Lieut.-Col. of cavalry. He had heard the firing in the direction of the camp that morning, and was on his way to give notice to a picket-post between them and Baton Rouge. After proceeding about three miles Samuel Nelson, who was somewhat in advance of his companions, met a man walking, a citizen, and asked him if there were any soldiers around. He replied that there was one at the next house, about a quarter of a mile further, on the right-hand side of the road. Samuel pushed ahead and stopped in front of the house. Dismounting and stepping up to the door, which was wide open, he confronted a female, who very politely invited him to enter. On stepping into the room he saw a soldier and three females seated around a table, enjoying a meal. The lady invited him to partake of their hospitality, which invitation he very readily accepted, and while eating had a very lively conversation with the "reb," from whom he learned that there was a company stationed on the road about four miles from there.

After Samuel had got all the information he wanted from the "reb," he asked him where he belonged. He answered that he was a lieutenant, and his command was at Natchez. Samuel then said, "You may consider yourself my prisoner." The Lieutenant, feeling very indignant, replied, " I am an officer, sir, and will start for my command in the morning; besides, sir, you have nothing to do with me, if you are a conscripting officer." At this one of the women spoke and said, "He ain't no officer and can't conscript you." Samuel, turning to the officer, said, "Do you know who you are talking to?" "I suppose you are a soldier, sir," replied the Lieutenant. "Yes, sir," said Samuel, "and a live Yankee, and you may just consider yourself my prisoner." At this the ladies burst forth in a chorus of voices, "It ain't no such thing; you can't fool us; don't believe him; he ain't nothing but a common soldier." Just at this time a squad of company A appeared in front of the house, to which he pointed. This changed the aspect of affairs; they all at once comprehended the meaning of the blue coats, and with tears and screams they all commenced hugging the Lieutenant, exclaiming, "Oh, my dear, they will kill you, they will kill you." Samuel quieted their fears by telling them that not a hair of his head should be harmed, and giving the Lieutenant in charge of the orderly-sergeant of company A, again took his place in the advance, though not before reporting to Colonel Grierson the information he had obtained respecting the force ahead. Nothing occurred until the column had arrived within half a mile of the Comit River, at which place the force spoken of was expected to be found. The scouts were ordered to advance cautiously and reconnoitre the ground, and find out the position of the camp. Owing to the situation of the ground the scouts could approach to within three hundred yards of the camp without being seen, the enemy not having out any vidette on that side, and as yet no report had reached them of the Yankees coming that way. The scouts then halted, and Wood volunteered to go and reconnoitre and see what he could discover. Just then a soldier was seen coming up from the creek, and approaching the scouts said, "How are you, gentlemen; have you come to relieve us?" "Yes; the company will be up in a few minutes." "It's about time you come to relieve us; we've been here now four days, and are just about out of rations." The scouts told him they would soon be relieved. In the meantime Wood returned, having obtained all desired information. The camp was situated along the east bank of the stream, shaded by timber, just at the end of the lane, and could not be approached only by charging down the road, which was fenced on either side. After the scouts had reported to Colonel Grierson the command moved forward slowly until within three hundred yards of the camp, when the following companies were ordered to proceed: company A to flank through the field on the left, while companies D, E and I kept the road, the former commanded by Lieutenant Bradshaw, the latter by Captain Ashmead. They charged most gallantly upon the unsuspecting foe. So complete was the surprise that the rebels, forgetting everything, tried to seek safety in flight; but a very few of them escaped, and not more than a dozen shots were fired. The confusion was indescribable— shot-guns, saddles, camp-kettles, rifles, old blankets, coats and hats scattered in all directions, while men and loose horses were stampeding from all quarters. It did not take long for our men to flank the woods and pick up the stragglers. One man, a member of company I, found sixteen rebels hid in a hole that the water had washed out by the bank of the stream. They all surrendered to him. While the Seventh was thus engaged gathering up their booty the Sixth was ordered in the advance, so as to save time. It was now about nine o'clock, A.M., and in half an hour's time the Seventh followed the Sixth, having captured forty-two prisoners belonging to Stewart's cavalry, together with all their horses and equipments, without sustaining any loss or damage. In order to cross this stream the command had to move up its bank about a half mile and ford it. All those owning large horses had the advantage—they could ford it without swimming, while the small ones had to resort to the latter extremity. After proceeding three miles the whole command stopped to rest and feed, the first for man or horse for the last thirty hours, having traveled eighty miles night and day, with scarcely a halt, and it is to be remembered that nearly the whole command was asleep on their horses while marching the greater portion of the last night.

The command was now within six miles of Baton Rouge, and all felt quite safe. The raid had been one grand success. A kind Providence had smiled upon our efforts all through our perilous journey, and finally crowned it with victory. Nearly eight hundred miles had been traveled in sixteen days, passing through fourteen counties, and through the interior of the State of Mississippi, destroying a great amount of government property, besides the destruction of railroad property, and effectually cutting off communication in various directions, preventing supplies from reaching Vicksburg and Port Hudson, drawing out a force from Jackson, at a time when General Grant was making a rapid flank movement on that place, and on the last morning surprising two camps, capturing and bringing in four hundred prisoners, not including the six hundred that were paroled and left on the route at different points, besides eight hundred horses and mules, and some five hundred negroes that followed us, a large number of cattle, and a considerable train of vehicles of various descriptions. But what must be considered the crowning glory of the expedition is the fact that during the entire march, and more especially the last forty hours, men and horses hungry and jaded though they were, not a murmur was heard from the lips of either officers or men. Our loss did not exceed twenty men.

While feeding and resting a company of the First Louisiana Cavalry, Union forces, came out from Baton Rouge, the report having reached there that a large force was crossing Comit River and advancing towards that place. This company was sent out to reconnoitre. Picture their astonishment when they learned whose command it was, and where it came from. It was some time before they could be convinced of the fact.

Our prisoners felt quite jubilant. They allowed that a force had to come all the way from Tennesse purposely to capture them; they considered it an honor to be taken by Illinois troops. Altogether they were a jolly set of fellows—the most of them living in Louisiana and Mississippi, and men of wealth. Their captain, at the time their camp was taken, escaped by climbing a tree, where he remained concealed by the Spanish moss, which abounds in that section of the country, and presents a beautiful sight, hanging in long clusters from every limb.

About eleven o'clock the command took up its line of march in the following order: first, the Sixth Illinois; second, the battery; third, the prisoners; fourth, the Seventh Illinois; fifth, the negroes, with the led horses and mules; and lastly, about thirty vehicles of every description, from the finest carriage down to a lumber wagon of the poorest description. The line extended about two miles. It really presented an interesting sight, one to which neither pen nor pencil can do justice.

After being formed, and when within four miles of Baton Rouge, the column was met by Captain Godfry, First Louisiana Cavalry, who escorted us into the city. For one half mile before entering the city we were met by citizens and soldiers, both white and black; male and female, old and young, rich and poor, paper collars and ragged urchins; everybody's curiosity was at its highest pitch. The streets were densely crowded, and amid the shouts and cheers of thousands, the waving of banners and flags, interspersed with music, the tired soldiers, all covered with dust, marched through the principal streets, around the public square, down to the river, watered their horses, and then proceeded to Magnolia Grove, two miles south of the city, a most delightful spot, shaded by the magnolia, whose long green leaves encircle a beautiful white flower, which fills the air with its rich perfume.

It was just at sunset that the command entered this grove, and that night, for the first time in sixteen days, they slept soundly under federal protection. Among the sleepers were the scouts—except those left behind—now relieved of their dangerous double-dealing duty, which rendered their death certain if they had been taken prisoners and discovered. They had given full satisfaction to the command, and I trust will make a favorable impression upon the mind of the reader. Their names are as follows:

R. W. Surby, Regimental Q. M. Sergeant, Seventh Illinois, commanding scouts; C. B. Weeden, corporal Co. E, do; L. H. Kelly, Co. E, do; Wm. Buffington, Co. B, do; Samuel Nelson, Co. G, do; Arthur Wood, Co. B, do; Isaac E. Robinson, Co. B, do; George Stedman, Co. C, do; Uriah Fowler, Co. H, do.

They were armed in guerrilla style, with a variety of arms—three Sharpe's carbines, four shot-guns, one sporting rifle, four sabres, and nine revolvers; had captured eighty-four prisoners, with their arms and equipments, and destroyed over two hundred shot-guns and rifles.

The evening found the men so exhausted for want of sleep and rest that the moment they had stripped the saddles off their horses they laid down, and it was almost impossible to arouse them, to partake of coffee and refreshments, prepared by the One Hundred and Sixteenth New York and the Forty-eighth Mississippi infantry regiments, who made their appearance, bringing with them their own cooking-utensils and provisions. This act on the part of the officers and men of those regiments was noble and kind, and will always be remembered by the Sixth and Seventh Illinois cavalry.

On our entrance into Baton Rouge it was difficult to distinguish the prisoners from our own men, who had, while on the march, exchanged their close-fitting jackets for citizens' coats—the same with regard to hats and pants; this, together with the dust that covered them, made it impossible to distinguish them apart, and as the column marched along the following remarks were heard: "Why, see how many prisoners they have!" A group of negroes was seen on one corner of the street, in which an old darkey was heard to say to one of his brethren, "Hush, child; you must look at dem peoples with respect; dey am de great warriors, wat come from de Norf; dey trable widout sleep, and stop de railroads, and cut up the track; I hear massa say so dis mornin'."

While on our route we were looked upon by the people with wonder and astonishment, and our courteous and kind manners seemed to surprise them considerably. There were undoubtedly instances where some unprincipled men would enter private dwellings, while away from the control of their officers, and pillage. Such things could not well be controlled, as the column was almost constantly on the move, and subsistence had to be procured from the country through which we passed. It was seldom we found a scarcity. Horses had to be pressed whenever and wherever found, and in many instances double the number were left for those taken, of exhausted animals, which, with a little care, would soon become as servicable as those taken. It would sometimes arouse a feeling of regret to witness the attachment displayed by the faithful old horse, who, on being turned loose by the road-side, to wander where he pleased, would be seen following up the column, and when it stopped he would lay down in the road to rest, and as we started again could be seen occupying a place in the ranks, where he would remain from morning to night, faithful in the discharge of his duty.

After a few days' rest the command began to wander around. They being privileged characters, were permitted to go where they pleased, and it was amusing to see to what extent they would carry their jokes. At one time they took possession of the Provost Marshal's office, turning him out of doors. One day about a dozen men went into a saloon—the proprietor having stepped out for a moment. Without waiting for him one of the men jumped over the counter and inquired of his comrades what they would have, and thus they treated each other until the proprietor arrived. He was refused admittance. For redress he applied to the Provost Marshal, who recommended him to shut up shop, that he could not do anything with those raiders. At another time some of the men entered an ice-cream saloon, and were rather noisy, when the Provost Marshal was sent for. The men got "wind" of it, and taking the soda fount charged it with gas and placed it in position opposite the door. The Marshal made his appearance, and would have received a salute had not a friend outside advised him of the danger. He very readily compromised with the men. Occasionally they would get into a fight, just for the fun of the thing. Passing an eating-house one day three of the men were attracted by hearing loud and angry words. Their curiosity must be satisfied. They entered the house and discovered two eastern officers engaged in a fist-fight. The landlady was trying her utmost to prevent the quarrel, and as our men entered entreated them to stop it if they could, as such a proceeding would injure the reputation of her house, which was of unquestionable character. Western troops are noted for their gallantry, and in less than no time the two officers lay sprawling in the street.

It is customary in Baton Rouge, when an auction is to take place, also for concerts and other entertainments, to send a negro around with a banner with the advertisement, and a bell, which he rings, and cries out at the top of his voice. As one of these was coming up the street one day a squad of the Sixth and Seventh made a charge, capturing the bell and banner. They proceeded on through the streets, crying out "Concert to-night, at Magnolia Grove, by the Sixth and Seventh Illinois cavalry." Some of the citizens were sold that evening. Providing they ever do conclude to give a concert, I have composed the following few lines for their benefit:

SONG OF THE RAIDERS.

The Sixth and Seventh you all know,
  Du da, du da,
Together on the raid did go;
  Row de du da da,
Colonel Grierson was in command,
  Du da, du da,
And in Baton Rouge did safely land,
  Row de du da da.

  CHORUS—
Are you going to march all night?
Are you going to march all day?
I'll bet my money on the Sixth and Seventh,
Who'll bet on the Southern Grey?

It was in April, 1863,
  Du da, du da,
That we left the State of Tennessee;
  Row de du da da;
The course we took on the map you'll see,
  Du da, du da,
Down through the State of Mississippi,
  Row de du da da.

  CHORUS.

We were accompanied part way,
  Du da, du da,
By the brave old Second Iowa;
  Row de du da da;
When at Clear Spring they were left to range,
  Du da, du da,
And fight their way back to La Grange,
  Row de du da da.

  CHORUS.

GRIERSON RAIDS.

With the railroad we did play "whack,"
  Du da, du da,
Burning the cars upon the track;
  Row de du da da;
We'd march all day and then all night,
  Du da, du da,
And only stop to have a fight,
  Row de du da da.
   CHORUS.

The people thought it very strange,
  Du da, du da,
To see so many from La Grange;
  Row de du da da;
They looked with wonder and surprise,
  Du da, du da,
To see so many from Illinois,
  Row de du da da.
   CHORUS.

When Port Hudson did surrender,
  Du da, du da,
We were there to see the "rebs" knock under;
  Row de du da da;
The 116th New York are bully boys,
  Du da, du da,
Kind hearted and full of fight besides,
  Row de du da da.
   CHORUS.

And now, kind friends, we'll bid adieu,
  Du da, du da,
Hoping to see this war soon through;
  Row de du da da;
How joyful then will be our song,
  Du da, du da,
As our wings of peace will glide along,
  Row de du da da.
   CHORUS—
 Are you going to march all night?
 Are you going to march all day?
 I'll bet my money on the Stars and Stripes,
  On Freedom and Liberty.

The following is characteristic of the good feeling existing between the Sixth and Seventh. One day one of the men, in roving around, discovered two men fighting. Stepping up to them he said, "How is this, Sixth and Seventh? you must not fight each other in this style." At this announcement the combatants eyed each other a moment, when one says to the other, "Do you belong to the Seventh?" "I do; and you to the Sixth, do you?" "Well, I reckon I do," was the reply. This was sufficient, and like two brothers they started, arm in arm, to the nearest saloon, to pledge anew their friendship for each other, allowing it was all a mistake.

About this time several of the officers, with Colonel Grierson and Prince, went on a visit to New Orleans. On their arrival in that city they were received by the citizens, who displayed considerable interest, complimenting them for their bravery and success, and as a token of their admiration for their gallantry, the one was presented with a horse and equipments, the other with equipments.

This state of things was not permitted to last long. The Illinois cavalry had their reputation up for being fighting men, and work was now laid out for them. The bombardment of Port Hudson had commenced, and a movement was to be made against the place by a land force. On the twelfth day of May the cavalry was ordered to move in the advance to Port Hudson. Some considerable skirmishing took place with the advance, until within eight miles of Port Hudson, at which point our forces, under General Auger, camped, and remained some time before advancing again. During this time the cavalry was not idle. A scout was made, which reflected great credit both upon the officers and men concerned. Captain Godfry, of the First Louisiana Cavalry, with one company, Captain Angley, of the Sixth Illinois, with one company, and Lieutenant La Grange, of company A, with twenty men, were sent from Alexandria eight miles to the rear of Port Hudson. When in the vicinity of the latter place, they learned of there being a force of rebels there, numbering ninety men. The three commands then separated, each taking a different road, with the intention of surrounding them. Captain Angley had succeeded in drawing the rebels after him, and falling back to a suitable position held them in check, while Lieutenant La Grange, learning of their situation, charged down upon them in the rear, completely surprising them, killing two and capturing nineteen prisoners, with their arms, horses and equipments, without sustaining any loss.

A few days after this the entire force was ordered to advance, which brought on the engagement at Plain's Store, noted for its stubbornness. Major Whitsit, of the Sixth Illinois, with companies A, K and L, were sent up to the railroad from the store, meeting the enemy—Colonel Miles' Legion—and commenced the engagement, falling back to the reserve, the enemy following closely. When the battle became general the Forty-eighth Massachusetts and One Hundred and Sixteenth New York behaved most gallantly, the latter regiment doing most of the fighting, the cavalry affording good support, dismounted. The fight lasted seven hours, when the enemy was driven from his position, leaving their killed and wounded on the field, which numbered one hundred, besides sixty prisoners. Our loss was fifty-four killed and wounded.

The next day General T. W. Sherman, of the east, arrived from New Orleans, with a long train of heavy artillery. On the following morning the Sixth and Seventh were ordered out, at an early hour. After riding about an hour they met the advance of General Banks' force, which had come up the west side of the river from New Orleans, and crossed to Bayou Sara. The first meeting which then took place between General Banks and Colonel Grierson was very warm and friendly. On the twenty-first of May a demonstration was made by our forces against the enemy, who were in position outside their works. It was here the One Hundred and Sixteenth New York distinguished themselves, repulsing the enemy, charging and driving them inside their works, while a Massachusetts regiment threw down their arms and run. The cavalry being ordered to dismount and support the New York regiment caused much surprise in the stampeders; they had never heard of such a thing as cavalry fighting dismounted.

On the twenty-fourth of May our forces advanced to within one mile of the fort. Some heavy skirmishing was done in the advance. Several attempts had been made by our forces to discover two steamers said to be concealed up the bayou, or Thompson's Creek, but were unsuccessful. Colonel Prince, by order of Colonel Grierson, left with detachments from each company of his regiment, proceeding to the creek, where he captured two fine passenger steamers, the Skylight, also a small ferry-boat. These boats lay within three hundred yards of the rebel batteries. So quiet and unexpected was the expedition that they were completely surprised, and knew nothing of it until the boats were run up the creek out of range of the guns. Colonel Prince was highly complimented by General Banks, who pronounced it one of the grandest feats of the campaign. The next day Lieutenant Lee, of company F, with four men, took a yawl belonging to one of the steamers and quietly dropped down the creek, passed close to the rebel works, entered Alligator Bayou, which they crossed, landed, and footing it through a neck of timber hailed the steamship Hartford. A yawl was lowered and they were brought aboard, and reported the capture of the boats, which the Hartford had been watching for at the outlet, to prevent their escape. Lieutenant Lee was highly complimented and kindly treated by the officers of the boat, and three cheers were given for the Illinois cavalry.

The men had considerable sport while camped in the rear of Port Hudson shooting alligators, with now and then a skirmish with Logan's or Wirt Adams' cavalry. In the meantime our forces were encircling and drawing nearer the enemy's works, the cannonading was growing more fierce and terrific each day, and sharp-shooting was practiced to some extent. Many of our cavalry could be seen each day on their way to the rifle-pits near the Twenty-first Indiana Battery, where they would dispose of fifty or a hundred cartridges before returning, firing at the distance of six hundred yards.

It was on the last day of May that the enemy charged one of our siege-guns, but we easily repulsed them. By the middle of June our forces had nearly two hundred guns in position, and the cannonading was most terriffic. The heavy siege battery manned by the Twenty-first Indiana, Colonel McMiller, proved most efficient. So accurate became their aim that the rebels dared not place a gun within their range. On the fourteenth of June our forces, commanded by General Sherman, made a desperate charge upon the enemy's works, and were repulsed with some loss. Captain Skinner, of the Sixth Illinois, with companies E and D of that regiment, was escort for the General. Their loss in horses was seventeen. The General had two shot from under him, and was himself carried off the field wounded. A braver or more gallant officer never led troops into any engagement.

It was on one of these occasions that a certain Massachusetts regiment refused to enter action because their time would be out in a few days. They were nine months' men. Previous to starting for their homes there was a great demand for trophies, and our cavalry could sell them almost anything for a good price. Many of the men took advantage and sold out, even to their old jack-knives, stating that they were captured on the raid.

The weather was now becoming excessively hot, and it was a severe task to both horses and men to labor through the heat of the day. In many instances scouts had to be postponed and conducted through the night. The large green flies and mosquitoes were very troublesome. The country abounded in blackberries, which afforded the men a luxury. Sugar could be obtained in abundance at the different plantations. Frequently the men approached the gun-boats, when some hearty old tar would hail them and inquire if they did not want to come aboard. They had a very exalted opinion of the cavalry, and looked upon them as true heroes. Regardless of the excessive heat, change of climate, and constant scouting, our men experienced but little sickness, and would find some kind of amusement to while away the spare hours. Musical instruments of various kinds could be found in camp, and the most noted among the players was Colonel Grierson, who could produce most perfect music on nearly all instruments. He possesses a natural talent for music. On several occasions after retiring has he arisen from his bed on hearing a violin, and finding it out would have all the negroes collected, and then such a variety of dances the reader can better imagine than I describe—jigs, breakdowns, and the original plantation dance, with its chorus of voices. There could be seen Sambo in all his glory—the genuine African.

There are several fine plantations and beautiful residences in the rear of Port Hudson and above it, particularly that of Mrs. ——, a sister of Jeff. Davis

While on a scout Colonel Grierson had occasion to call and pay his respects to this lady, who received him rather coldly. Not knowing who the Colonel was she very uncourteously left him and his adjutant alone in the drawing-room. In the room was a splendid piano. A request was made through the Adjutant for the ladies to play, which they declined. The Colonel was not to be bluffed in this way, so seating himself before the instrument he soon filled the room with the notes of a very difficult but popular air. This had the desired effect of bringing all the ladies to the room. They were very inquisitive to know who the player was, that he would not be any ordinary man to produce such beautiful music. Upon hearing his name they evinced much surprise, and apologised for their rudeness, they became extremely sociable, particularly with Adjutant Woodward, who is a great favorite with the ladies; of very prepossessing appearance, (good looking,) and knows how to play the agreeable; he is unassuming and gentlemanly in his manners, and not fond of display, as the following will show. He was the only officer on Colonel Grierson's staff, Acting Adjt.-Gen., and was of incalcuable service. His judgment was consulted on all occasions. After the successful termination of the raid, he wrote the official report, in which he was so delicate as not to mention his own name.

A scout was sent out to Clinton, La., consisting of the following troops—the Sixth and Seventh, the Fourth Wisconsin mounted Infantry, accompanied by

Captain Godfry, Captain Eaton of the First Louisiana Cavalry, and Lieutenant Perkins of the Mississippi Cavalry. This expedition left within four miles of Port Hudson, marched twenty-eight miles, met the enemy in force, fought three hours and retreated in good order, on account of ammunition being exhausted, arriving in camp about three o'clock the next day. The day following an expedition consisting of cavalry, infantry and artillery returned to Clinton, but the enemy had disappeared, leaving in our possession one hundred convalescent soldiers, which were paroled by Colonel Prince. An extensive cotton factory was destroyed.

An attempt was made by the "rebs" to capture a boat, used for keeping supplies on at Springfield Landing. Captain Cohn, of the Sixth, and Lieutenant Maxwell, of the Seventh, were on board at the time, and rallied what few men, that were scattered about, which did not exceed twenty, and repulsed the "rebs," who numbered sixty men, driving them away.

Company E, of the Sixth, while on picket at the crossing of the Jackson and Clinton road, four and a half miles in rear of Port Hudson, was attacked by a superior force of the enemy. Sargent Fayer was in command of the company at the time, and so placed his men as to hold the enemy in check while he sent a courier to camp, who returned with reinforcements, and the enemy were driven off. One battalion of the Fourteenth New York Cavalry, at this time, was stationed as picket on the cross-road and railroad.

They had just received some clothing and three boxes of Colt's army revolvers. One hundred of the enemy attacked them, capturing several prisoners, nearly all their horses, their arms, clothing, and four wagons.

About a mile from this post was a hospital, in which were at this time about three hundred sick and wounded, with two companies of infantry acting as guard, six ambulances, a quantity of hospital stores, and one hundred stand of arms, all in charge of Surgeon ——, who surrendered the whole to a Confederate officer and four men. In the meantime news had reached camp. Lieutenants Maxwell and Caldwell, of the Seventh, immediately collected about twenty men, principally convalescents—the regiment being absent on a scout at the time—and started for the picket-post, where they arrived only to find the enemy gone with their booty. They then started for the hospital, arriving in time to prevent its capture by the enemy, who had sent for reinforcements. The surgeon was very indignant, and insisted that he had surrendered the place, and would not permit the forces at his command to interfere. He soon found he had those to deal with who knew how to act, and with revolvers in hand Lieutenants Caldwell and Maxwell threatened to shoot the first man who refused to raise a musket in defence of his own liberty and Uncle Sam's property. Colonel Grierson, with his command, soon after made his appearance, who reprimanded the surgeon for his cowardly actions, but he was too late to pursue the enemy, they having sometime the start; they made good their escape, with the property taken from the Fourteenth New York Cavalry.

I will now draw the attention of the reader to those who were left wounded at Wall's Bridge, Mississippi. They had not been forgotten. Several efforts had been made by Colonel Prince to send a party with a flag of truce to learn their condition. Madame rumor was busy with her tongue. At one time she reported that Colonel Blackburn was dead, and that Sergeant Surby had been recognized as one of the scouts and was hung. It was about the last of June that permission was granted to proceed with a flag of truce, the rebel General Gardner furnishing the party with the necessary papers of protection. J. B. Hartley, company A, and A. G. Leving, veterinary-surgeon of the Seventh Illinois, started on their mission. They were to proceed to Clinton, Louisiana, where they were furnished with an escort of two Confederate soldiers, who accompanied them through. On the afternoon of the second day they reached Mr. Newman's plantation, and found Mr. N. at home, but were disappointed in not finding any of the wounded. They were told that the Colonel died, after suffering intense pain for seventeen days. A member of company G had also died from his wounds. The remaining two wounded men, together with the nurses, had been sent to Osyko Station. Mr. Newman expressed himself highly pleased and satisfied, stating that he had been paid most liberally by all parties concerned, and also that the dead had received a decent burial, all of which was gratifying news to the friends of the deceased. On the morning of the fourth day the flag of truce returned, having made the trip without meeting with any accident or trouble on the road.

At one time Colonel Prince made an effort to be detached with his regiment from the Sixth Illinois without consulting Colonel Grierson, his intention being that of remaining in the Department of the Gulf. General Banks thought well of him, and appreciated his military genius, but the idea did not meet the approbation of the officers, all of whom opposed it with the exception of one, besides Colonel Grierson did not approve of it, and told the officers and men that he would take them back to Tennessee. Colonel Prince, in making this effort, thought it was to his interest. As a military man he has few superiors, and is perfectly conversant with the tactics. The following is one of his ideas, suggested to General Banks, and by him and his chief engineer approved and carried into execution —that of collecting the sugar hogsheads from the neighboring plantations and constructing a lunette fort and tower of observation. This work was commenced by digging a trench within three hundred yards and following up to within forty-five yards of the enemy's works, when the main work was commenced as follows; thickness at the base, fifteen feet; length, forty feet; height, twenty feet; with wings extending from each flank, serving as rifle-pits. From the top of this a fine view was obtained of the enemy's river works, and was about to have been mounted with four guns, when the fort surrendered, which would have commanded an enfilading fire on both the enemy's flanks, which could not have been returned in the same manner by them. This work was frequently commented on, and General Gardner's chief-engineer remarked, that had it been completed, it would have proved very destructive to them.

When the news of the surrender of Vicksburg reached the command at Port Hudson, the rejoicing was beyond describing. On the eighth day of July General Gardner surrendered Port Hudson and its garrison to General Banks. It was then that the cannon pealed forth in thunder tones, volley after volley from the gunboats and land batteries in honor of the great victory achieved. The last stronghold on the Mississippi river was wrested from the traitor's clutch, the "father of waters" once more carried its entire length, proudly floating the banner of liberty. The next day a portion of our force marched into the fort, and then in the presence of cavalry, infantry, artillery and marines, the "rebs" grounded arms; this was a proud moment for the Illinois boys. General Gardner requested to see Colonel Grierson, who came forward and was introduced to him. He complimented the Colonel very highly, saying, that he was both glad and sorry to see him, glad to see so brave and gallant an officer, but sorry to see the one who caused the surrender of Port Hudson, he having cut off his communications and supplies, thus starving him into a surrender.

A few days after this the Sixth and Seventh embarked

for Memphis, Tenn., amid the cheers of friends and the deafening roar of artillery. Accompanying and under guard, were the Confederate officers of the garrison, General Beall and staff occupying the same boat with Colonel Grierson and Colonel Prince. On our arrival at Vicksburg the boats were detained several hours, during which time Colonel Grierson had an interview with General Grant, who received him with marked courtesy, displaying a high appreciation of his services. On the arrival of the command at Memphis, they disembarked, rejoicing that they had returned safely back again to old Tennessee, shortly after which a re-union took place between the raiders and those who were so unfortunate as to be left behind. They consisted mostly of convalescents and men who were on detached service, and doing duty at the time the expedition left, together with those who returned as an escort from near Pontotac, Miss., all of which did not spare them from a nickname conferred upon them by the raiders—" Quinine Brigade;" the meeting was warm between old comrades, and a thousand and one questions were asked, and a large mail was distributed, letters which contained word from the loved ones at home. Mails had been a scarce article while in the Department of the Gulf.

The brigade was once more thrown together, and the meeting between the Second Iowa and the Sixth and Seventh Illinois was of the most friendly character. The respect that these three regiments entertained toward each other is only what brave and unprejudiced minds are capable of; the confidence reposed in each other is generally portrayed on the battle field. I do not think I vary from the truth when I say the Second Iowa is the best drilled regiment in that branch of the service; in the department of the Mississippi, their fighting qualities were unquestionable, and with such a intrepit commander as Colonel Hatch they are invincible in an engagement. He knows how to get into a fight and how to get out again. The part they performed on the raid was of the greatest importance. You will remember that this regiment left us and we proceeded alone, I will now give you their account of their journey back to La Grange. About five o'clock, April 21st, the column moved at the junction of the roads leading to Columbus, West Point and Louisville. At this point Colonel Grierson and Hatch separated, warmly shaking hands and mutually wishing each other God speed in their hazardous duties. In compliance with orders from Colonel Grierson, Colonel Hatch was to proceed with his regiment (about five hundred men and a section of artillery belonging to company K, First Illinois Light Artillery,) and make a demonstration toward Columbus, Miss., striking West Point; destroy the railroad bridge over the Okatibbayhaugh River; thence moved rapidly southward to Macon, destroying the railroad and government stores, and thence to find his way north to La Grange by the most direct route. After the departure of Colonel Grierson, Colonel Hatch sent a detachment of his regiment with orders to follow the former about four miles, then counter march back for the purpose of obliterating the tracks of Colonel Grierson, then moving south; at the same time the Colonel ordered the pieces of artillery he had to be wheeled from the timber into the road four different times, so that the marks would correspond with the four pieces of artillery in Grierson's command; this done, Colonel Hatch moved rapidly until reaching Palo Alto, where he halted to feed and rest an hour. It was now about twelve o'clock. The enemy had been concentrating their forces several days previous, anticipating a movement on Columbus; their scouts had counted the entire column under Colonel Grierson; knowing the exact number they accumulated what they thought a sufficient force to overpower and capture the whole command. Colonel Hatch had not separated from Grierson more than three hours, when the rebels who had been following in the rear made their appearance at the junction of the roads, and after patrolling a few miles in the direction that Colonel Grierson had gone, concluded from the counter marching that the main column had returned and gone toward Columbus. Under this impression they started in hot pursuit, and just as Colonel Hatch's command had finished their noonday meal they were most furiously attacked by a force under General Dolsen, consisting of Smith's partisan regiment, Bartoe's regiment and Ingis' battalion; on they came, confident of an easy victory, but the brave Iowa boys were not the least daunted. Company E and G quickly formed, and as the "rebs" came within easy range, poured a deadly volley from their running five shooting rifles, which quickly checked their speed and sent some of them to their long home. They now fell back out of range and formed in two columns, moving down on both flanks. In the meantime Colonel Hatch quickly formed in the edge of the timber, where his devoted little band could be completly concealed by trees. With a portion of his force dismounted behind a barricade and breastwork constructed out of fence rails and logs; while the little two pounder was placed in a position to command the front, a sufficient force was placed on either flanks to protect the rear. In order to make the charge the "rebs" had to cross an open field; on they came the second time, yelling like demons. Colonel Hatch had cautioned his men not to fire until the command was given. When within easy range the order "fire" was passed along the line. At the command up rose two hundred men armed with the revolving rifle. Volley after volley was poured into the rebel ranks in quick succession, playing a tune more loud than charming, while the well manned cannon nobly supported the base. The rebels (who had boasted at a house near which they made the attack that they would take our cannon in three minutes,) did not appreciate this song and broke back in all directions. Colonel Hatch immediately ordered a charge which completely stampeded the entire command, driving them back full three miles, capturing thirty prisoners, besides about twenty-five killed and wounded men left on the field, and wonderful to tell not a drop of federal blood was spilt. From that time until dark it was a constant skirmish, the enemy still believing that they were engaging Grierson's entire command.

Colonel Hatch now shaped his course northward, crossing the Hooka River, and drawing the enemy's force immediately in his rear. On nearing the Tippah River it was discovered that the enemy were strongly posted on the opposite side to protect the ford. The Colonel at once turned into a large swamp through which the river run, and after proceeding a few miles pressed in an old negro to act as guide. It was now near midnight and very dark. The guide led the command by a blind path to a ford crossing the river, one which had not been used in years. A place was found where a large quantity of floating timber had collected and was lodged against some trees; over this the men constructed a foot bridge, stripping their saddles off and carrying them over to the opposite side. The bank on the side where they entered the stream was about six feet high; the horses were pushed off this bank, one at a time, and compelled by long poles, used as whips, to swim to the opposite shore, where men stood hip deep in water to assist the animals up the bank which was too steep for them to climb unassisted; in this way the entire command crossed the river without any loss. The cannon was taken to pieces and drawn over the bed of the stream by means of ropes. After crossing the command moved several miles before daylight, leaving the enemy, who were guarding the ford far in the rear. On the twenty-second the command took but little rest. Detachments were sent in various directions to hunt up droves of horses and mules, which had been run into the low bottom lands to avoid capture by our forces. The men sent out for this purpose were very successful. At four o'clock the command reached Okolona, a place on the Mobile and Ohio railroad, charging into town, driving out the enemy's cavalry and state troops, burning the barracks for five thousand troops, destroying a large quanity of ammunition, quartermaster's stores and considerable Confederate cotton. The command moved five miles northwest from town and camped for the night.

The twenty-third was spent hunting horses and mules. The enemy was again discovered trying to overtake the column. Citizens were collecting from all parts of the country armed with shot guns, hunting rifles, &c., constantly firing on the flanks of our troops, but taking care to keep at a respectful distance. Detachments were sent in various directions, which had the desired effect to so completely puzzle the enemy that they could not arrive at our real intended movement. In order to check the main force following in the rear, the bridge over the Chiroppa Creek was destroyed. The command camped for the night near Tupelo.

On the morning of the twenty-fourth Colonel Hatch sent Major Coon with six companies off to the left, to pursue another route and form a junction again near La Grange; while he, (the Colonel) with the remainder of the regiment and the plunder, consisting of thirty-one prisoners and over two hundred horses and mules, led by seventy negroes, took the Birmingham road. The rebels, who were constantly watching their movements, thought this their time, and just as the head of the column reached the latter named place the rebels attacked their rear in force. The Colonel quickly detached a sufficient force to guard the prisoners and train; this done he had just sixty-five riflemen whom he could dismount, and fourteen sabre-men whom he placed on the flanks, mounted, and the little cannon manned by Corporal T. H. Walker, Sixth Illinois Cavalry, and four men from the same regiment; with this small force the enemy was repulsed three times. The Colonel retreating slowly, concealing his men at all favorable points, letting them approach to within short range, when he would pour a withering fire into their exposed ranks with his revolving rifles, aided by the two pounder which did excellent service. The enemy suffered terribly, while the loss on our side was very small. In this way the attack was kept up for about six miles, when the enemy evidently became tired, and with exceptions of a little annoyance from guerilla parties they were not troubled by the enemy from that point to La Grange, where they arrived safe with all the plunder on the morning of the twenty-sixth.

The loss sustained by the Second Iowa Cavalry on this important trip was but ten men killed, wounded and missing. They left La Grange with seventy rounds of ammunition per man; on their return they had but two rounds left to the man. They captured and destroyed over three hundred shot-guns and rifles—mostly Enfield—killed and wounded not less than one hundred of the enemy, brought safely into camp two hundred horses and mules—besides re-mounting nearly the entire command—together with fifty-one prisoners, and about sixty negroes, who followed of their own accord.

Too much praise cannot be awarded Colonel Hatch for the skillful manner in which he handled his men against far superior numbers. His fight at Palo Alto —diverting the enemy from Colonel Grierson—did undoubtedly give the latter some thirty-six hours start of all incumbrances.

And now, while the command is resting, camped in the suburbs of Memphis, I will take the reader down to Wall's Bridge, Amit County, Mississippi, and tell what disposition was made of us who were left wounded at Mr. Newman's plantation, and with it bring my history of our journey to an end.

CONCLUSION.

After receiving my wound I made my way back to the rear of the column, when with the assistance of a few comrades I was helped from my horse and laid upon the ground. They assisted me in changing my dress for that of the Federal army, and securing my side-arms, horse and equipments. I was then carefully laid into an ambulance, and conveyed to the plantation along with the rest of my wounded comrades. I remember of being carried through the front into a back room, joining the kitchen, and laid upon a pile of unginned cotton, which Hughes, Roy and myself occupied, the Colonel remaining in the front room. I had not lain many minutes before it occurred to me, for the first time since receiving my wound, that l had considerable Confederate money in my possession, and acting on the impulse of the moment I concealed it by poking it down under the cotton, together with my pocket-knife, match-safe, and three dollars in silver and a breast-pin. Shortly after this I heard considerable talking in the adjoining room—the one in which the Colonel lay. The cause was soon explained, by seeing the door-way filled with Confederate soldiers. We excited some curiosity, and with few exceptions were treated with respect by them. Some threats were made against the Colonel by a Confederate officer, who drew his sabre, threatening to plunge it through him. The Colonel told him that he did not expect to live long, and as he had done nothing but his duty he would not ask for mercy at his hands. The Southern "chivalry" was prevented from putting his threat into execution by the timely interference of a superior officer, who reprimanded him severely. These soldiers proved to be the advance of Colonel Miles' command—better known in that region as Miles' Legion—having just arrived from Osyko Station, and in pursuit of Colonel Grierson. I could plainly see the column from my window as it moved along. It consisted of about three hundred cavalry, two thousand infantry, and one battery of artillery—four and six pound rifled guns. They felt confident of capturing the "Yanks," and did not appear to be in any hurry, stating that a force had been sent out from Port Hudson, and that they would intercept our forces when they attempted to cross the Amit River.

Colonel Grierson had now five hours the start, and I knew that he would not let any grass grow under his feet. We were visited by the Colonel while his command was passing. He informed us that he had instructed the nurses that they should pay every attention to the wounded. He treated us with kindness, and I shall never forget his kind manner and venerable form. He was afterwards captured at Port Hudson, and related his interview with Lieut.-Col. Blackburn, and the wounded men of our command, upon this occasion.

After they left I felt some anxiety about the command, fearing they wauld be cut off from crossing the river. Mr. Newman, the proprietor, had been pressed in by our command and taken as far as Greensburg. The women, being left alone, at first felt very much alarmed. Their fears were soon quieted by the arrival of some of their neighbors, who assisted them. They were all very kind, and did everything in their power to alleviate our sufferings. During the evening Mr. Wall, of Wall's Post Office, made his appearance, and evinced much desire to provide for our wants. He seemed to think we ought to have the assistance of a surgeon from Osyko Station, and without any delay started that evening on his mule, rode eleven miles, and returned that night, bringing with him an army surgeon, who displayed considerable skill in dressing the Colonel's wounds. He had to leave the next morning, being ordered to Port Hudson, and would not receive any compensation for his trouble, saying that it was his duty, and his government paid him for his services. Mr. Wall was another man of the same principles, but he complained bitterly, and regretted the loss of his saddle-horse, which our command had taken from his stable. It seemed to me that it was in my power to replace his loss by offering him the value of his horse in money. I felt influenced to act thus by the kindness and interest he had displayed in our welfare. Desiring to see him he was sent for. On his arrival I asked him how much he valued his horse at and he said five hundred dollars. I told him he should receive that amount for it—that it would be paid to him by Mrs. Newman. My reason for not paying him then was that I did not wish to show them where my money was concealed; no one had known of my having it except my comrades. As the reader will want to know how much money I had, and how I came by it, I will explain. The amount was twenty-five hundred dollars, nearly all in Confederate fifty-dollar "graybacks," the remainder in notes of smaller dimensions. The money was handed to me by a member of the Seventh Illinois, who found it at Newton Station, floating on the water, as previously mentioned. The next morning, at about ten o'clok, Mr. Newman arrived, having been released by our command. It was a timely arrival, for many of the citizens were under the impression that he would be murdered, and had in circulation a rumor that our command had murdered Captain Scott, and many were the threats muttered against us, which they were prevented putting into execution by Mr. Wall, until the appearance of Mr. Newman, who, by his statement, dispelled all evil intentions. He also brought the joyful news that the command had safely crossed Amit River, which was confirmed a few hours later by the arrival of a courier, who was on his way to Osyko Station. He stated that the force sent out from Port Hudson consisted of two regiments of infantry and one battery of artillery, and when Colonel Grierson crossed the bridge the rebels were within five miles, waiting for daylight, so as to proceed—something Colonel Grierson did not wait to consult in cases of emergency. We all felt elated over the good news.

And now the question arose, what disposition would be made of us? We were all wounded in a manner that would not admit of our being moved. It was in the afternoon of the second day that a squad of cavalry arrived from Osyko Station, being sent as guard, with orders to bring us all to that place. They had a rickety old ambulance, which they intended to put us all into. Dr. Yole explained matters to them—that it was impossible to move any of the wounded except myself. After parleying awhile they submitted, and I was carried out and laid in the ambulance. As I was carried through the Colonel's room I could not but notice how pale and haggard he looked. He was suffering intensely. I bid him good-bye, hoping that we would meet again. Previous to leaving the room I saw Mrs. Newman, and having confidence in her I handed her twenty-three hundred dollars, my pin, miniature, pocket-knife and silver, keeping one hundred dollars myself. I requested her to pay Mr. Wall five hundred for his horse, and I would devise some way to get the ballance. Dr. Yole, Le Sure and Douglas were ordered to accompany the escort on foot, which made them puff, on an eleven mile march, they not being used to infantry tactics. The Colonel was left without any medical attendance, though every care and attention was bestowed on him by Mr. and Mrs. Newman.

About six o'clock we arrived at Osyko Station and

halted in front of headquarters. I was surprised to hear and see the rebel Colonel Richardson, from Tennessee, who took particular delight in heaping abuse upon the Sixth and Seventh cavalry, by saying everything that was mean and unbecoming a gentleman. He has since met with his reward, by being shot while attempting to make his escape from the Union forces. From this place I was moved to the depot, where I rested all night, very comfortably, on a cot. The next morning a soldier made his appearance, followed by a little girl, who carried a pitcher of coffee, some nice ham, biscuits, and tender beefsteak. It was really inviting, and my appetite being in a good condition I did ample justice to it. This soldier was actuated by a noble impulse. He had come voluntarily from his dwelling, and brought me a breakfast prepared by his wife. He had once been a prisoner, was taken at Fort Donelson, and was kindly treated by our army, and had not forgotten it. I am sorry that I have forgotten his name.

At an early hour I was put on board the train, on my way to Magnolia Station, ten miles north. Previous to starting I learned that the Doctor and Le Sure were permitted to return to the Colonel, on their parole, while Douglas was retained and would be sent to Richmond. On my way to Magnolia my boots and coat were stolen from beneath my cot. On my arrival at the latter place I was taken from the cars and carried to the hospital, up the first flight of stairs, and put into a large-sized room, in the north end of the building, fronting the street, on the east side of the railroad, with a piazza in front; the room was a very pleasant one. The building was built for a hotel, and used as such until the breaking out of this war. It was capable of accommodating about four hundred guests. Connected with it was an extensive livery-stable, bowling-saloon, billiard-rooms, bathing establishment, &c. Before the war this was a place of much resort from New Orleans, it being only ninety miles distant, and having a healthy location, surrounded by the beautiful magnolia trees in full bloom. A clear stream of water, abounding with fish, afforded sport for the angler. Magnolia Station did not contain more than two hundred buildings of all classes, a few stores, two hotels, and an extensive tannery, busily engaged manufacturing leather for the government.

I had not been here long before my wound was attended to by the principal surgeon, Dr. Huford, formerly from Baton Rouge, whom I found very kind in his treatment, but stern in his manner. He had some three hundred patients under his charge, and was assisted by Drs. Stebbling and Biggs, formerly of Kentucky. I shall never forget the kindness extended to me by those gentlemen. They would frequently visit my room, where I was alone, and sit and talk for hours at a time. This was very considerate in them, and a great privilege enjoyed by me. It was here I lay in suspense many a long hour, busy with thoughts of home and friends. Contrary to what I anticipated I had not been searched, and was in possession of the following articles: one pair drawers, one pair overalls, one pair of socks, two shirts, and one hundred dollars in Confederate money—no hat, coat, boots, pants or jacket. The second day after my arrival my drawers, shirts and socks were washed, after which I felt quite comfortable. A black man was assigned to wait upon me, and I received every attention. The landlady—I have forgotten her name—furnished me with books to read, and occasionally would bring me in a fresh magnolia, which, placed in water, would keep the room sweet for several days.

Though the ladies of the South are to be admired for their graceful forms and manners, they indulge to excess in one habit—that of dipping snuff—which looks strange enough to Northern men. The hospital-steward was very kind, calling frequently to see me. My fare, though scant, was clean and properly cooked, which consisted of corn-bread, molasses, mush, sassafras tea, and almost invariably the leg of a goose for breakfast, baked, no dressing, sometimes tender as a spring chicken, then again tough enough to make a good whip-cracker; however my appetite was sufficient for all I could get. In the course of a week I was able to dress my own wound, by the aid of a glass, washing it every morning and evening with warm water and castile soap, keeping it constantly wet with cold water. I did not have occasion to take a single dose of medicine. The ball, in passing through my thigh, had just missed the main artery and bone, and the Doctor said I would soon be able to go about on crutches.

I had permission to write a letter home, which the Doctor told me would be forwarded through the lines, subject to military inspection. I felt rejoiced at this, and wrote a suitable letter, handed it to the Doctor, and I supposed it was on its way and would soon be in the hands of my friends. I was doomed to disappointment. In a few days it was handed to me, with the unwelcome news that no more letters were allowed to pass the lines. I felt sad and lonely; this was my last and only hope of getting news home. My death had been published in the Jackson Appeal, and if one of those papers should get into our lines it would be copied, and my friends would think me dead. I was in suspense, but not forgetful of a kind Providence, that had spared me thus far. I put my trust in God, and tried to wait patiently.

In the meantime I was not forgetful of my wounded comrades, of whom I made daily inquiries—at one time hearing the Colonel had died, the next it would be contradicted. It was impossible to get a correct story. Finally I succeeded, through the exertions of the steward, in hiring a man to go out to Mr. Newman's and learn the truth, at the same time to bring in a portion of my money. On the third day after leaving he returned, bringing the sad intelligence that after seventeen days of intense pain and suffering the Colonel had died, also the man Hughes; that they were buried on the plantation, and that Roy, Le Sure and the Doctor had reported to Osyko; that my property had been delivered over to Le Sure. This was a sad disappointment to me. I feared I would not see my comrades again before they were sent to Richmond. Again the hospital-steward showed his kindness, by going on the train to Osyko Station and seeing the sergeant-major, who sent back word that he would pass next day, on his way to Richmond. I was now able to move around on crutches, and had been up and down stairs several times. The sergeant-major made his appearance next day, and handed me my breastpin and four hundred and fifty dollars, the balance of the twenty-three hundred which I left in the hands of Mrs. Newman. The five hundred had been paid to Mr. Wall, according to promise, and the remainder was used towards defraying the expenses of the wounded and nurses, burying the dead, &c., everything being scarce and consequently very expensive. It seemed as if the hand of Divine Providence directed the use of this money for this special purpose.

I was soon able to walk around, with the use of a cane, and was permitted to promenade the streets. I had a pair of shoes made, very common ones, for which I paid sixteen dollars. I also purchased some clothing, paying for a common felt hat thirty dollars, a light summer coat forty dollars, a pair of pants, half cotton, twenty dollars—cotton socks one dollar and thirty cents. I make mention of this that the reader may know how scarce and expensive articles were at that time in Dixie. The following prices were given me by the hospital-steward: flour one hundred and fifty dollars a barrel, none in market; coffee five dollars a pound, none in market; sugar three dollars a barrel; molasses three dollars a gallon; bacon one dollar and a half a pound; eggs one dollar and a half a dozen; chickens, live, twelve dollars a dozen. The two first named articles I had not seen in the hospital. I was now allowed the privilege of eating in the dining-room, with the non-commissioned officers, also of visiting the different wards. Among the patients I found one federal soldier, belonging to the navy. He had one leg amputated just below the knee. His name was William Hawkins. He served at one of the guns on the Indianola, when she was sunk by the rebel batteries at Port Hudson, where he received his wound and was taken prisoner. I found him a very intelligent person. We could sympathize with each other, were company for each other, and time passed more rapidly and agreeably.

It was very amusing sometimes to listen to the various reports respecting the army and battles, which, according to their statements, always resulted in their favor. There was a telegraph office at the depot which brought them daily news from Jackson, Mississippi. That, with the Jackson Appeal—which could tell the biggest lies, for a small paper, of any one published— were the only sources we had to obtain news. They took particular pains to report to me, which was very kind of them. At the time that Hooker withdrew from Fredericksburg, Virginia, they received the news that he lost forty thousand men in killed, wounded and prisoners, that he was completely routed, and his army flying in all directions. A few days later and General Lee occupied Arlington Heights, and threatened to shell the city of Washington. The next report was that Grant had lost at Vicksburg, in storming the works, eighty thousand men, and owing to the excessive warm weather, and disgusting stench arising from the bodies, they had to be burned. They were confident of capturing his whole command, and had his supplies cut off. Following this was a report that Kirby Smith had crossed the Mississippi River, attacked Banks in the rear, and captured nearly all of his command; and lastly, that a Texas regiment of cavalry had met Colonel Grierson, wounded and taken him prisoner, together with nearly all of his command. You can imagine my feelings on hearing such reports. I could not contradict them, nor did I choose to believe all. I could occasionally hear, after night, the reports of our mortars, as they were throwing their ponderous shells into Port Hudson, eighty miles distant. I knew in that quarter, at all events, our forces still existed. Vicksburg was their boasted Gibralter.

The month of May was now drawing to a close, and I was able to move around quite lively, feeling anxious to be sent North. My wishes were soon gratified. On the second day of June I was notified by the Doctor that he would send me to Jackson on the morrow. I felt rejoiced at the thought of going towards home, and knowing that my friend Hawkins desired to accompany me I sought an interview with the Doctor, and after considerable talking he consented to send him along, as

I could be of some service towards assisting him. In the meantime I purchased two watches from inmates of the hospital, paying for them two hundred and fifty dollars. I thought this a good investment, knowing that the Confederate money would not be of any use inside of our lines. The morrow came, and with it the train. At one o'clock Hawkins and myself went aboard, and were soon leaving Magnolia far in the rear, where I had remained just one month. Upon arriving at Summit Station I was told that we could not proceed further by railroad, as it had not been repaired since Grierson's command destroyed it. Here was a space of twenty miles which we must walk, or hire a private conveyance, paying fifteen dollars each. I at once procured passage for Hawkins, the Sergeant who was guarding us, and myself. It was here I again experienced the benefit of that money. After proceeding about half way we stopped at a house, where we stayed all night. We had not been here long before we were joined by other passengers. I at once recognized the plantation and the proprietor as one on whom I had called with a squad of men, and taken two horses, while the command was destroying government property at Boyachitta, one mile distant. The planter did not recognize me, and I did not take the trouble to relate to him the circumstance. We were provided with a good bed and supper, for which I paid one dollar and fifty cents. The next morning at four o'clock we started for Brookhaven, arriving there at eight o'clock, just in time to take breakfast at the hotel before leaving on the train. While passing through Hazelhurst I saw several faces that were there when we rode in so gallantly. The most familiar were those of the landlady and her daughter, at the hotel. I felt as though I would like to speak to them, but circumstances did not permit.

Aboard the train was an Englishman, who held a captain's commission in the rebel army. He amused me very much, not only by his foppish appearance, but by his ridiculous actions and the interest he took in watching me. I could not move but what he would tell the guard to keep his eyes on me. He belonged to that class of Englishmen who interfere with other people's business.

About one o'clock we arrived within two miles of Jackson. The train could not run further on account of the road being torn up by Sherman's forces, at the time they occupied the place. Here were quite a number of private conveyances. After obtaining one for my wounded friend I started for the city on foot with the Sergeant. I had a very good opportunity of seeing the Capitol of the State, and was surprised to see so much of it left standing, having been told that our forces had destroyed the principal portion of it. The first place I was introduced to was the Provost Marshal's office, where I had to wait some two hours before being examined. While so doing I took occasion to hand Hawkins fifteen dollars, thinking he might need it, and we might be separated, which proved to be the case, he being examined and sent away the same evening, with a number of others, to Richmond. They allowed him to keep his money. I bid him good-bye, not expecting to see him again. My turn came, and unfortunately for me, being neatly dressed, I was looked upon with suspicion, and ordered to strip myself to my shirt and drawers, which I did not hesitate to do. They then proceeded to search the pockets, lining, &c., appropriating to themselves my watches, papers, and all my money, except about twenty dollars, my pocket-knife and miniature pin, which they allowed me to keep—very considerate in them. I also had in my possession two letters from Doctors Stebbling and Biggs, which they requested me to mail after reaching our lines. They were not sealed, and contained nothing but what was of a domestic character. I felt sorry about those letters, for I had been kindly treated by those two gentlemen. The search ended, and they found nothing to implicate me. They expressed some disappointment in not finding any Lincoln greenbacks. I thought this rather queer proceedings for the head military authorities of Jackson. I soon found I was not the only one subject to this treatment—others also suffered. The name of this specimen of "Southern chivalry," who appeared to be the star actor in this military drama, was J. C. Winnin. I think I will remember his face, and if I am ever so lucky as to meet him again will ask him the "time of day." From the Provost Marshal's office I was sent to the guard-house, a one and a half story frame house on Main street, where I lodged with about twenty-five others, and remained for thirty-six hours before receiving any rations, which, when they did come, consisted of a scanty supply of unsifted corn meal and refuse bacon—nothing else; no cooking utensils of any description, and nothing but cistern water to drink, on the top of which could be seen pieces of bacon floating. I had not been here long before the lieutenant of the guard ordered me into a private room, and ordered me to undress, while he gave the garments a thorough examination. He found nothing. My pocket-knife seemed to please his fancy, which he kept, and it was only through my earnest entreaties that he allowed me to retain my miniature pin, for which I thanked him. The money he had no use for—greenbacks was what he was after. Among the prisoners were two citizens, who claimed to be residents of Memphis, Tennessee. They were very kind to me, inviting me to their table, which they had furnished from a hotel close by—a priviledge not allowed soldiers. Thus I fared very well, until the third day, when we were ordered to be in readiness to leave at nine o'clock next morning. At the appointed time we were found in line, twenty in all, and marched two miles, crossing the Pearl River, and taking the train on the Jackson and Mobile railroad were soon comfortably seated in a passenger car. Our guard consisted of one sergeant and six men—old soldiers—who treated us with kindness and respect. Before leaving Jackson we were not provided with rations, nor did we receive any until we arrived at Selma, Alabama.

The first place of any importance was Meridian, then the Tombigbee river, where we took a boat for Demopolis and again resumed the railroad, arriving at Selma the next afternoon. Remained all night, and received three day's rations of hard tack and boiled salt beef, (a very good article). We were kindly treated by the Provost Marshall, and looked upon with some curiosity by the citizens, as well as a show of sympathy and respect. Not being allowed the privilege of the streets I had no opportunity of viewing the place, but the small portion I could see impressed me favorably; the extensive buildings, fine roads, level sidewalks, shaded by beautiful trees, all looked neat and business like.

The greater portion of this State, through which we passed, appeared to be under good cultivation, and the crops looked very favorable. Corn appeared in abundance on all sides. The next morning we were marched down to the river, where we took deck passage on board a steamer for Montgomery, Ala. Before leaving Selma I saw what was said to be the keel of a boat on the stocks intended for a gunboat. One had been completed a short time before and launched. Our trip up the Alabama was very pleasant indeed; not being confined to close quarters, we enjoyed a fine view of its high banks, shaded by trees. In due time we arrived at the capitol of the State, where we remained a few hours. Taking the train we proceeded to West Point on the Alabama and Galine railroad, where we remained all night in a close building. What little money I had upon leaving Jackson I had spent for something to eat, which I shared with some of my comrades who were in feeble health, two of whom belonged to the Fourteenth N. Y. Cavalry; our rations at this time becoming rather scant, I concluded to sell my coat, which I offered to the guard, for twenty-five dollars; he took it, at once paying the money. I derived more benefit from this money than I would have done by the use of my coat, by purchasing a few luxuries which benefited my health, and at the same time assisted my feeble companions who were not so fortunate as myself. The guards were very accomodating, allowing us many privileges. At an early hour next morning we left on a train arriving at Atlanta, Ga., where we were conducted to a guard house, a few blocks from the depot, at which place we had the pleasure of staying three days. We were put into a small room in the second story of a frame building which was surrounded by a high board fence, while several guards were patrolling their beats around us. Upon being put into this room I found it already occupied by about forty prisoners, the most of them citizens belonging to East Tennessee, who had been dragged from their homes and thrust into this filthy, loathsome room, because they loved the good old Union better than secession. It was a sorrowful sight to look upon the bent forms and wrinkled brows of these old men, whose heads were silvered by the frosts of seventy winters, and many were still older. After living a life of honest industry, enjoying the privileges and blessings of a free and independent country, to be at last separated from wife and family by lawless hands and cast into a prison, there to subsist on a scant supply of corn bread and salt beef. For what? because they still continued to love the good old flag that had protected them so long. Our fare at this place consisted of a small piece of corn bread, about three inches square, twice a day, with a limited supply of salt-beef. Upon a table in the centre of the room (the only piece of furniture it contained,) stood a pail of water and one cup—this was the only drink we had. Every man had been searched and every pocket-knife taken possession of by the jailor, a most brutal and unfeeling specimen of humanity. No one was permitted to look out of the window into the street; if he did violate this unreasonable order he ran the risk of being fired upon by the guard below, who was watching for the chance. One innocent citizen was shot dead a few days before our arrival for the above offence—the blood stains were still fresh on the window sill. From this place we were conducted to the depot by a new guard, where we took the train for Augusta. As we left Atlanta I was surprised to see so many locomotives and cars; they were making this their depot for supplies for their army, which explained for the large amount of rolling-stock seen. I did within my heart wish that our cavalry could make a dash into this place and destroy this property.

Our trip through Georgia was not unpleasant considering our circumstances. The new guard were home guards, and were not very strict; and we were allowed to look out of the windows; so we had a good view of the country, and I noticed that wheat was the principal crop, which looked very well. On our arrival at Augusta, which was in the night, we changed cars, and just at daylight crossed the bridge over the Savannah river, a very pretty stream. We were now in South Carolina, and in due time we arrived at Columbus, the capitol of the State, through which we were marched, giving us a good opportunity of seeing a large portion of the business part of the city, as well as the suburbs. I must say it is a beautiful place, displaying good taste and abundance of wealth. From this place we were conveyed in freight box-cars, which at that time I thought very cruel, (but since have experienced the same treatment in my adopted State of Illinois, from Alton to Springfield, when returning home on furlough, as a veteran, with the regiment to which I belonged, after serving my country two years and eight months,) I came to the conclusion it was not so bad after all. From Columbus we went direct to Chesterville, soon passing out of the hot bed of secessionism. This was the only State we passed through that we received any taunts from the citizens, many of whom seemed to take delight in spitting their venom upon us. On one occasion they remarked how meanly we were dressed; that there was no uniformity about our clothes; and I took pains to tell them the cause—that when taken prisoners our captors made an exchange with us—our boots, pants, hats, and sometimes our coats or jackets; thus the cause of our appearing so ragged and offensive. This did not sit well, and some of them were for breaking the d——d Yankee heads. The crops in this State did not look so well as through Alabama and Georgia, though we passed through some very delightful country.

The first place of any importance we arrived at in North Carolina was Charlotte, thence to Salisbury, Greensboro, Raleigh, Goldsboro and Weldon, the last place bordering close upon Va, and fortified to some extent, though few troops were stationed there at that time. Our trip through this State was not unpleasant. The country through which we passed was not prepossessing in appearance. One incident occurred while passing through this State worthy of note. While stopping at a wood station to wood up, I saw an individual approaching our car, who, as soon as he came up, inquired, in North Carolina accent, if any of us had Confederate money we wished to exchange for Lincoln greenbacks. I inquired how much he had. He replied five dollars, and would give it for five dollars in Confederate money; that he had carried the d——d abolition money long enough, and nobody wanted it out here. I hauled out my pile, amounting to eight dollars, and handing him five received the greenback, which looked natural enough, and made one feel sort of good. The question arose in my mind, how will I keep it hid from the searching eyes of the Richmond officials. We had been informed by the guard that we would all be strictly searched and examined immediately on our arrival at Libby prison. An idea occurred to me how I might save my greenback, which I put into execution. I had remaining, tied up in an old dirty handkerchief, a few hard biscuits that I had bought. I borrowed a knife of one of the guard, and unperceived by them I cut a square piece out of the side of one of the biscuits, and scooping a hole out in the centre large enough I concealed my money together with my miniature pin; plugging up the hole again, I took care not to break into those biscuits which were hard and dirty. On our arrival at Petersburg we were delayed a few hours, and then, "On to Richmond," nineteen miles distant. When about half way between those two places we came in sight of the rebel fortifications, which are expected to protect Richmond. The works are very extensive, extending some eight or ten miles, and two to five miles in breadth, and, if well defended, will take an immense army and hard fighting to get possession of.

I will here take occasion to make some remarks respecting their railroads. Those over which I passed, as a general thing, were pretty well used up—track very rough, and rolling stock out of repair. They could not average more than fourteen miles per hour. The most substantial track was in South Carolina. On the afternoon of the fourteenth of June we arrived at the capitol of the Southern Confederacy, being ten days on our way from Jackson, Miss. We were marched down through the main street where every idle spectator could gaze at us, which we returned in full. We were soon introduced to that hospitable mansion, "Libby Prison," so familiar to so many of our brave boys; and where, by close confinement and cruel treatment, many a brave heart has beat its last within its walls, whose spirit gone forth to a just God will be avenged. We were formed in line fronting the prison, and almost the first man I saw was Sergt.-Major Le Sure, and the next, Dr. Yole. I felt pleased at seeing my old companions and longed to speak to them, which was not permitted just then. We were ordered into the building, and formed in line through a narrow hall, when the search commenced, passing through the entire line, finding but little plunder beside canteens and haversacks—the two latter they invariably kept. Upon presenting my biscuits they were looked upon with contempt. I felt satisfied with the result and still continued to freeze to them. The next proceeding was to take our names, rank, number of regiment to which we belonged, what State, &c. We were then paroled, signed an article of agreement, and swore not to do so and so until duly and lawfully exchanged. After this, we were told the joyful news that we should be sent away to City Point with a batch that was to start in the morning; for this, I felt really thankful. From the hall we were conducted to another apartment, up two flights of stairs, into a large room crowded with Union soldiers. The first thing we heard upon entering was the cry of "fish, fish, more fish;" at first I could not imagine what it meant; I thought they were receiving rations, and I began to anticipate something good to eat; imagine my disappointment when I discovered that we were the object of all this noise and confusion. The prisoners had adopted a rule—that of keeping a man on sentry at the stairway—and when any new prisoners arrived to cry out "fish, fish," which sentence would be taken up and repeated by nearly every one in the room, while they would flock to the stairway, expecting to see some old friends and comrades. The size of this room was sixty by forty feet, with no ventilation except what came from three heavily barred windows at each end. It contained no article of furniture whatever, and was crowded with about three hundred and forty men. At the lower end, and about the centre was a small closet, six by four feet, in which a pipe entered coming up from the canal below; this afforded drinking water, as well as wash room and water closet. You may well blush, but such are facts. Picture to yourself this room at night, the floor covered with human frames, inhaling such impure air. The stench that then arose was almost suffocating, enough to cause disease and sickness. Besides the soldiers there was other company, and plenty of it, well known by the name of "graybacks" in the army. Our rations consisted of a limited supply of flour bread, a small piece of boiled salt beef, and a mixture called Confederate coffee, which was anything but agreeable to the taste or appearance. Before retiring that night we were notified that we would start next morning at three o'clock and for every man to be awake and ready, that no one would be permitted to take his blanket with him. I laid down, not to sleep, but to think of Libby Prison, and how thankful I should feel that a kind Providence had favored me thus far; then I pictured home and all its inmates, who were anxiously waiting to hear some word or news concerning me; perhaps they thought me dead, if so, what a sweet disappointment my presence would create; and thus, I fancied in thought until sleep closed my eyes. At an early hour next morning everybody appeared to be awake; all was excitement and confusion, but we did not have to wait long before a guard appeared at the stairway and gave the order to move out until we reached the street and then form fours. We soon arrived at the depot, some five hundred in all, taking the cars to Petersburg, then changing and making a short run we were soon at City Point. I perceived there were no officers aboard, and upon inquiry, was told that they would not be exchanged for a long time. I felt sorry for them, and was glad that I was not an officer. While waiting at Petersburg a few hours I saw several strangers in a sly way offering four dollars in Confederate money for one in greenbacks. Upon reaching City Point, toward the neutral ground for exchange of prisoners, our sight was greeted by the old flag, whose stars and stripes were floating defiantly and proudly from the mast-head of the steamer New York. Cheer after cheer rent the air, and tears could be seen trickling down the cheeks of more than one brave hero, whose heart was full to the brim with gladness at once more beholding the emblem of liberty.

> Like the symbol of love and redemption its form,
> As it points to the haven of hope, and the nation;
> How radiant each star, as the beacon afar,
> Gives promise of peace or assurance of war.
> How peaceful and blest was America's soil
> Till betrayed by the guile of the traitor demon,
> Who lurks under virtue, and springs from his coil,
> To fasten his fangs on the life-blood of freedmen;
> Then boldly appeal to each heart that can feel,
> And the flag of our country shall in triumph remain,
> To guide us to victory and glory again.

From the cars we all rushed to the river, and after taking a good wash in its bright waters, feeling much refreshed, were ordered to form twos and march aboard of Uncle Sam's boat, and as we stepped upon its clean white deck the first thing that we saw, which was served out to us, was a large slice of fresh bread and boiled ham, and a large tin-cup full of real old Java coffee. Wasn't it good? If you doubt it, just ask any soldier who has been in Libby Prison until half starved. Who would not fight for such a government as we possess? What a contrast! Just view the picture. There are landed at this very spot three or four hundred Confederate prisoners, fresh from a Northern prison. They look clean, healty and strong, are well dressed; each man is in possession of a blanket, and a haversack, which is filled with good rations; he is fully prepared to enter immediately into active service. On the other hand here comes a few hundred Union prisoners, fresh from Libby Prison or Bell Island; their garments are ragged and dirty—robbed of their own clothes, they receive old garments of every description—their steps are weak and tottering—their forms are wasted away to mere skeletons—their spirits broken. They are no longer fit subjects for the battle-field—close confinement in a filthy room and starvation has brought them to this condition. They carry no blankets, haversacks or rations. This is Southern chivalry, Southern hospitality —and as the war is prolonged the more barbarous is the treatment inflicted upon their prisoners. The inmates of Libby Prison, the inmates of Bell Island, God help them! they deserve the pity and sympathy of all Christians.

As we left City Point I bade farewell to Southern hospitality. I have no desire to taste its sweets again. As we glide swiftly down the stream how refreshing the breeze! how sweet is liberty! We were allowed to range over the boat at pleasure, which was guarded by a portion of the few that remained of the famous Ninth New York Volunteers—Hawkins' Zouaves—a noble, manly set of men, neat in attire and perfect in discipline. They treated us with every kindness, particularly M. E. and J. L. Fitzgerald, company K. The officers of the boat were also unremitting in their attentions.

The scenery along the James River presents some beautiful landscape views. As we came in sight of Fortress Monroe we could see our gunboats—the two extremes, the old man-of-war Constitution, three decker, carrying —— guns, and near by could be seen the little iron-plated Monitor, apparently not more than twelve inches above the water, with a round turret, carrying two ponderous guns. As we came opposite the fort the boat anchored and a yawl was lowered, which conveyed the Captain to the fort to report to the commander of the post.

While lying here I could see at a distance the immense Lincoln Gun, capable of throwing a one hundred pound shot six miles with great accuracy. Who would have believed it twenty years ago? In the meantime I had not forgotten my biscuit, and cut it open in the presence of a gaping crowd, who looked with perfect astonishment when they beheld the pin and greenbacks extracted. They allowed it was genuine sleight of hand. After a few hours delay the order was given to weigh anchor, and with steam up we started for Annapolis, Maryland, arriving there the next afternoon in time to march up to the camp of parole. We were formed in close column and ordered by the Major commanding for each man to answer to his name as it was called, and he would assign troops from different states each one by themselves; this being accomplished a short address was made by the Major, stating that those who desired clothing to report to the quartermaster department and they would be furnished it, also a quantity of soap, and every member was advised to visit the bay close by, where they could indulge in a salt-water bath. I assure you there was some scrubbing done just about that time, after which a new suit of clothing throughout was put on, which made us look once more respectable. Of rations we had plenty and good, and were allowed the limits of the town as long as we did not abuse the privilege. It was quite refreshing to visit the oyster stands down near the water's edge; and indulge in some fresh from their native brine.

Annapolis is the capital of the State, a delightful location, surrounded by beautiful scenery. A very extensive Naval Academy is established here, but since the war broke out the buildings are used as hospitals. A more appropriate place could not be selected. The streets present a very odd appearance, radiating from the State House. A large number of the buildings are of the old style of architecture, and the old State House still remains, in which Washington used to give to the world his noble sentiments.

Among the many soldiers that were here on our arrival I was pleased to find some of my old comrades—Sergeant Vaughn, who accidentally wounded himself near Union Church, Corporal Douglass, from Osyka, and friend Hawkins. After remaining here about ten days an order was read at roll-call for all Western troops to be in readiness, at an early hour next morning, to take the road for Baltimore. Starting at the time appointed we crossed Chesapeake Bay, having a very pleasant trip. It was amusing to watch the schools of porpoises roll leisurely over and then disappear. It was about two o'clock when we arrived in Baltimore, and at once marched up to the Soldiers' Association Hall, where a good table was supplied for us, and lodgings for the night. The next morning we left by train on the Pennsylvania Central Railroad, over a good track, making excellent time. We soon found ourselves winding around the hills, through ravines, woodlands, and over streams, with mountain peaks in the distance, which we were fast approaching.

And oh! how the heart did beat with joy to witness at almost every house the waving of handkerchiefs and star spangled banners. It was one continual display of patriotism. To me it was the first demonstration of the kind I had seen for fifteen months. The next day we arrived at Pittsburg, Pennsylvania, after a pleasant ride through a fine agricultural country, presenting a variety of beautiful scenery, where we were conducted to Union Hall and partook of a sumptuous dinner, served by the fairest daughters of Pittsburg. From here we proceeded in separate parties, those belonging to the Army of the Cumberland being sent to Camp Chase, Ohio, and those belonging to the Mississippi department being sent to Benton Barracks, St. Louis, Missouri. After arriving in Illinois I soon discovered that the train would pass within ten miles of my home. I had been absent about two years. The temptation was so strong that I naturally dropped off, and in a few hours afterwards was joyfully received by my friends. I immediately reported by letter to the commanding officer at Benton Barracks, and by keeping a strict watch I received the first notice through the public prints of an exchange, and at once started for Memphis, Tennessee, joining my regiment at Colliersville, on the C. and M. Railroad, October 13th, 1863, after an absence of five months and thirteen days. There was a general greeting of old friends, particularly with the scouts, who I found occupying the same position they held previous to the raid. They had met with no reward, and it was some time before I was permitted to resume my former duties; but regardless of position let all who love freedom, justice, and their country,

  Strike for the Union! let her name ever be
   The boast of the true and the brave;
  Let freedom's bright star still shine on her brow,
   And her banner the proudest to wave.
  Strike for the Union! shall the heroes that fell
   In graves all unhonored repose,
  While the turf on each head and the sword by each side
   Has been stained by the blood of the foes?

    CHORUS.—Three cheers for our land of the free,
     Three cheers for our noble and true,
    For freedom, right, and liberty,
     Our flag of the Red, White and Blue.

  Strike for the Union! for liberty's sun
   In darkness and gloom has not set;
  Her bright beams still shine, like a light from above,
   And will lead thee to victory yet.
  Strike for the Union! for her weapons are bright,
   And the heroes who wield them are strong;
  Let her name brightly glow on the record of time,
   And hers be the proudest in song.

    CHORUS.—Three cheers for our land of the free.

  Strike for the Union! we will honor her name,
   For the glorious deeds she has done;
  The laurel will twine on each patriot's brow,
   And shout when the battle is won.
  Strike for the Union! it must never be said
   That her banner was furled to a foe;
  Let those stars ever shine in bright glory above,
   And the pathway to victory show.

    CHORUS.—Three cheers for our land of the free.

The following is a roster of the officers of the Sixth and Seventh Illinois cavalry regiments, on their arrival at Baton Rouge, May 2d, 1863:

SIXTH.

FIELD AND STAFF.

Col. B. H. Grierson, commanding.
Lieut.-Colonel, B. Loomis.
First Major, M. H. Starr.
Third Major, C. W. Whitsit.
Assistant-Surgeon, A. B. Agnew.

NON-COMMISSIONED STAFF.

Sergeant-Major, D. S. Flagg.
Q. M. Sergeant, T. Legget.
Com.--Serg't, Wm. Pollard.

FIRST BATTALION.

Captain A. D. Prince, Co. A.
Captain W. W. Patterson, Co. B.
Captain D. Angley, Co. C.
First-Lieut. Chas. Howard, Co. C.
Captain I. Cohn, Co. D.
First-Lieut. H. Daily, Co. D.
Second-Lieut. L. V. Allen, Co. D.

SECOND BATTALION.

Captain John Lynch, Co. E.
First-Lieut. E. Ball, Co. E.
Second-Lt. H. W. Stewart, Co. E.
Captain G. W. Sloan, Co. F.
First-Lieut. W. H. Dove, Co. F.
Second-Lt. G. W. Newell, Co. F.
Captain W. D. Glass, Co. G.
Second-Lt. S. L. Woodward, A.A.
Captain S. L. Marshall, Co. H.
First-Lieut. D. Manling, Co. H.

THIRD BATTALION.

Captain L. B. Skinner, Co. I.
Second-Lt. D. L. Grimes, Co. H.
Captain F. Charlesworth, Co. L.
Second-Lt. J. W. Hughes, Co. L.

SEVENTH.

FIELD AND STAFF.

Col. Edward Prince, commanding.
Adjutant, George W. Root.

NON-COMMISSIONED STAFF.

Veter'y Surg'n, A. G. Levering.
Hospital Steward, Charles Hall.

FIRST BATTALION.

Captain Charles Hunting, Co. A.
First-Lt. J. J. La Grange, Co. A.
Second-Lt. D. V. Rhea, Co. A.
Captain G. W. Trafton, Co G.
First-Lieut. J. Gaston, Co. G.
Second-Lt. Wm. Stiles, Co. G.
Captain W. H. Reynolds, Co. D.
First-Lt. D. W. Bradshaw, Co. D.
Captain J. K. Fleming, Co. K.
First-Lt. J. W. Maxwell, Co. K.

SECOND BATTALION.

Captain William Ashmead, Co. I.
Sec'd-Lt. S. H. Richardson, Co. C.
Captain I. M. Graham, Co. E.
First-Lieut. N. G. Wiley, Co. E.
Second-Lt. I. M. Caldwell, Co. E.
Captain S. A. Epperson, Co. L.
First-Lieut. W. W. Porter, Co. L.

THIRD BATTALION.

Captain A. W. McDonald, Co. F.
First-Lieut. C. F. Lew, Co. F.
Second-Lt. James Breze, Co. F.
Captain B. C. F. Johnson, Co. M.
First-Lieut. Charles Stall, Co. M.
Second-Lieut. Henry Nicholson.
Capt. Milton L. Webster, Co. H.
Second-Lieut. S. A. Kitch, Co. H.
Captain Henry Forbes, Co. B.
First-Lieut. William McCausland.
Second-Lieut. Jos. O. Ram, Co. B.

Charles Hall, hospital-steward, was the only medical attendant of the Seventh Illinois that accompanied the expedition, and he deserves much praise for his unremitting care and attention to the wants of the suffering during the raid and while at Baton Rouge.

Biographical Sketch.

RICHARD W. SURBY.

RICHARD W. SURBY, was born May 23, 1832, in Kingston, Upper Canada, of English and Scotch descent. While very young his parents removed to the frontier of Niagara, where he remained until he attained the age of fifteen years, he then left home to seek his fortune, relying entirely upon his own exertions. Being possessed of a roving disposition, he visited New York city, Philadelphia, Boston, Cincinnati, St. Louis, Chicago, New Orleans, and various other places of note. While absent from home his parents died, leaving four younger brothers who had no experience of the world abroad and relied upon him for help and advice, which he has always given, proving himself a true brother. For a number of years previous to the breaking out of the rebellion he was employed in the service of the New York Central Railroad Company, and the Great Western Railroad Company, of Canada, where he gave good satisfaction. His sober habits and industry won him many friends.

In the fall of 1860 (accompanied by his much esteemed friend C. B. Griffin), they left Niagara Falls on a hunting tour, visiting the Northwestern States, until late the following spring, when they visited a friend residing in Edgar Co., Ill., where they remained a few months. About this time the excitement of the people was intense, caused by the assault made upon our flag at Fort Sumpter by a traitorous crew. Though comparative strangers in that section of the country, they at once enrolled their names upon the list to serve their country for the term of three years in the cavalry service; they resolved to link their fortune together, bound to each other by the ties of pure friendship—

> Which is not of that changeful form
> That makes the most of earthly things,
> But in the coldest bosom warms,
> And round the heart it closely clings.

Previous to leaving Camp Butler, Ill., he was appointed second duty sergeant. October, 1862, he was appointed Quartermaster Sergeant of the regiment, which position he filled with honor to himself and the command. Until his re-enlistment as a veteran, in the spring of 1864, at which time he was the choice of the regiment for their future quartermaster, receiving a unanimous vote of all officers and men present. For services rendered on the raid he was tendered a position by General Grierson, which offer he did not accept, choosing to remain and preferring a promotion in his own regiment, if so fortunate as to obtain it.

He has participated in seven general battles, besides numerous skirmishes. He had three brothers serving in the Union army, all of whom enlisted at the first call, and have served their country faithfully. Benjamin Surby, Fourth New York Heavy Artillery, lost his left arm at the battle of Fredericksburg, Va.; he has been discharged the service with a pension. Joseph belonged to the Eleventh Illinois Infantry, mustered out at expiration of his term, (three years.) James, formerly member of a cavalry battalion attached to the Thirty-Sixth Illinois Infantry, now consolidated into the Fifteenth Illinois Cavalry regiment, has re-enlisted as a veteran.

The following statement is inserted with the hope that it may meet the notice of some person, who may be able to give some information respecting his father's family. He has never in all his travels met any person answering to his name. He has a very limited knowledge of his parents' history, previous to their arrival in America, and gives the following as being correct:—His father was born at Seven Oaks, Kent County, England. When but sixteen years old he left home and enlisted in the army, and was a short time afterwards bought out by his father; he left the second time and enlisted where he remained for twenty-one years. After the arrival of his regiment, the Sixty-sixth infantry, in Upper Canada, from which place they were ordered to the West Indies; he preferred remaining in America and bought his discharge. Previous to his departure from England his name was changed to the present one, the original was Southby. His grandfather paid a large sum of money to have it re-established; a portion of the family retained it. His father had a brother John who owned a wholesale basket establishment in the city of London. It is the impression of the family that their father loaned his brother a considerable sum of money while on a visit from America, a few year's previous to his death.

OPERATIONS

OF THE

SECOND BRIGADE

OF THE

FIFTH DIVISION CAVALRY CORPS,

MILITARY DEPARTMENT OF THE MISSISSIPPI.

ILLUSTRATED; ETC.

BREVT. MAJ. GENL. EDWARD HATCH.

Biographical Sketches.

BREVET MAJ.-GEN. HATCH.

AMONG the many distinguished men that this war has produced, and brought before the public, is Edward Hatch, whose reputation is less from the position that he holds than from the splendor of his military talents. His character is free from the excesses and vices that often tarnish a military life. He is just and upright in all that pertains to his duty as a soldier, or in that which renders him a friend in private life. He was born on the 22d of April, 1831, in Bangor, Maine. He was the son of Nathaniel Hatch, a lawyer in that place, distinguished for his abilities.

Edward choosing a military life was placed by his father in the military school at Norwich, Vt., where he excelled in mathematics and every branch pertaining to the army. After three years of unceasing study the bent of his inclination, together with his roving disposition, led him to ship before the mast, on board a trading vessel. He went to sea, and after numerous adventures on the Atlantic and Pacific coasts returned home, satisfied that the briny deep was not the place for him. His father being engaged in manufacturing lumber in Pennsylvania placed him in charge of his mills, where he acquitted himself satisfactorily. With his experience and indomitable will he embarked heavily in the lumbering business, without any capital, illustrating the old proverb "that where there's a will there's a way." In the winter of '51-2 he succeeded in getting a large quantity of his lumber down the west-branch of the Susquehannah—a task that no one else succeeded in that year—and returning home paid all his liabilities, leaving a surplus on hand. At this time he became interested in a manufacturing establishment in Norfolk, Va., in which he has not been as fortunate, the rebels having confiscated his interest.

In the early part of 1854 he made a trip to the Western States, spending a summer with the Indians on the plains, where he met with numerous adventures. In the autumn he returned, and on his way east he stopped and passed the winter with the lumbermen on the head-waters of Black River, Wisconsin.

Early in the year 1855 he moved with his family to the West, locating at Muscatine, Iowa, continuing his lumbering business. As an illustration of his indomitable perseverance and self-reliance, to overcome every obstacle, I will tell, as related to me, how in the winter of '56 he succeeded, under the most unfavorable circumstances, in getting about one hundred and thirty million feet of lumber, that had lodged in the river, and been accumulating for two years, though many attempts had been made by others, but they failed to secure it. With Hatch, success demonstrated the wisdom of his plans; it was deemed by all impracticable.

At the breaking out of the war he was in Washington, and immediately tendered his services to the Government, deeming it his duty to protect the flag. He shouldered his musket and joined an independent company, raised in the city, and composed mostly of men holding office under the government, for the purpose of guarding the White House and other public buildings. He was shortly promoted to a lieutenancy In the month of April, '61, he obtained his discharge, and at once returned to his home in Iowa, where he took an active part in raising the Second Iowa cavalry regiment, in which he was appointed captain, and passed through the regular grades of promotion to the colonelcy of the same. He was commissioned Brigadier-General April 28th, 1864, and was made a Major-General by brevet December 15th, 1864. He has been engaged in the following battles and skirmishes: New Madrid and Island No. 10, March, 1862; Farmington, Miss., May 9th, 1862; Boonville, Miss., May and July, 1862; Iuka and Corinth, Miss., September and October, 1862; had the advance of the army commanded by General Grant down the Mississippi Central Railroad, December, 1862; checked and held the enemy at Coffeeville, Miss.—who numbered two to one—several hours; took an active part in the Grierson raid, in which he fought against vastly superior numbers, April, 1863, at Palo Alto and Birmingham, Miss.; was at Jackson, Tenn., July, 1863; at Colliersville, Tenn., November, 1863; at Moscow, Tenn., December 4th, 1864, at which place he was severely wounded, being shot through the right lung, from which he suffered greatly, but having an iron constitution he recovered sufficiently to accompany the expedition on its sixty-four days' march. He participated in several hard fought battles, displaying rare military genius.

In stature he is about five feet ten inches, well proportioned, of a florid complexion, dark hair slightly tinged with grey, a high forhead, a full blue eye, beaming with intelligence, and when in battle or excited they shine like meteors, a Roman nose, a well shaped mouth and chin, thin lips, denoting firmness; his upper lip displays a heavy dark mustache; his dress is neat and very plain—no guady display. He possesses a cool, collected mind, that sees things at a glance, is a splendid horseman, very active in all his movements, full of energy, and is noted for being the last man to sleep when on a march, and the first one up in the morning. He has always practiced visiting the camp of his command at revillie, which not one general or brigade commander in one hundred does. He is a strict disciplinarian, loved and respected by his troops, and requires no more of his officers and men than he performs himself.

BREVT. BRIG. GENL. DATUS E. COON.

BREVET BRIG.-GEN. COON.

DATUS E. COON is a fine example of our American self-made men. Beginning life in an humble sphere he has, by straightforward integrity and well directed efforts, won for himself the position he now occupies. As a citizen he was upright in principle, courteous in conduct, and by his manly bearing in every transaction of life commanding the respect and esteem of all who formed his acquaintance. As a soldier and officer he has proved himself energetic and trustworthy in camp, vigilant and watchful on the march, and brave and collected in the field. Wherever his command has been—whether in the camp, bivouac, or saddle, whatever the position assigned him—he has always been at his post, enduring the hardships and fatigue required of him as a soldier and patriot. In appearance he is a little above the medium height, and well proportioned—has a clear grey eye, brown hair slightly sprinkled with grey, and a heavy beard, usually worn with a military cut. He is a native of New York State, and was born in the town of Decatur, Madison County, in the year 1831. During early childhood his parents moved to the western part of the State, and settled in Cattaraugus County, where his father cultivated a small farm until the spring of '46, when he again moved to the town of Little Genesseo, Allegany County.

In the year 1849, in company with his parents, he followed the tide of emigration westward and settled in the State of Wisconsin. He received the ordinary education from the public schools, but he desired a more liberal one. His father's circumstances would not allow him to leave home, and he stayed with him, working upon the farm, until his services were no longer required by his parents. He then, with their approbation and "God speed," with his worldly effects tied in a handkerchief, started to seek the good or ill the world had in store for him. Following the plan previously decided upon he entered the Milton Academy and remained two years, paying his way by swinging the cradle in the harvest field in summer, and the axe in the forest in his vacations; but notwithstanding these disadvantages, so closely did he devote his time, that at the expiration of his term he was far in advance of many of his fellow-students who had enjoyed liberal school advantages.

In the year 1853 he went to Iowa, in the capacity of school-teacher, which profession he followed for two years, carrying forward and perfecting himself during the time in the various studies he had taken up while at the academy.

In the spring of 1845, through the earnest solicitations of his friends in Delaware County, Iowa, he entered upon the publication of a country paper called the Delhi Argus, which proved so profitable that after eight months' publication he was enabled to pay all obligations incurred there, and to start early in the spring of 1856, at Osage, Mitchell County, a paper called the Democrat. As an editor he was a zealous friend and unflinching advocate of the policy he once determined upon. The weak-kneed policy and administration of President Buchanan he warmly denounced, causing a warm controversy between him and his former democratic friends, which proved of so serious a character that he disposed of the Democrat and established an independent sheet in the town of Mason City, Iowa, called the Cerro Gordo County Republican, which carried the colors of Stephen Douglas through the presidential campaign of 1860.

When the country was called to arms in the spring of '61, burying politics and party in the service of his country, he responded to the call by raising a company of men for the Second Iowa Cavalry. He arrived with his men in Davenport —which was the rendezvous of the regiment—on the 17th day of April, and was assigned to it as company I. He was duly elected captain by his men, but in the organization of the field and staff of the regiment he was appointed and commissioned second-major and assigned to the command of companies A, C, G, and H, which were designated the second battalion. He commanded this battalion during the spring and summer of 1862, was present at the capture of New Madrid and Island No. 10, and with his regiment accompanied the Army of the Mississippi on its first demonstration upon Fort Pillow, and then at Pittsburg Landing, where it arrived a few days after the battle of Shiloh.

During the advance upon Corinth his regiment was actively engaged in ascertaining and developing the position and strength of the enemy. He led his battalion at the battle of Farmington, where the Second Iowa Cavalry made a desperate sabre-charge upon twenty thousand of the enemy's infantry, for the purpose of diverting their attention while General Payne's division, which was in a critical situation, could be withdrawn. He distinguished himself for his bravery and gallant conduct on that occasion. He accompanied Colonel Elliott, on his raid to Booneville, Mississippi, and assisted in destroying an immense amount of rebel stores at that place, and by cutting General Beauregard's communications, aided in no small degree in hastening the fall of Corinth.

The exploits of the Second Iowa Cavalry procured Colonel Elliott the position of Brigadier-General. In the summer of '62 Lieut.-Col. Hatch was promoted to Colonel, and the First-Major to Lieut.-Col. Major Coon was then First-Major, and as such took command of the regiment in August, 1862, Col. Hatch having been assigned to the command of a brigade, and the Lieut.-Col. being on detached service. During the advance of General Grant to Coffeeville, Miss., in the fall of '62, he commanded the regiment, and acquitted himself creditably in the several engagements of that expedition. Actively as the regiment was engaged during the spring, summer and fall of '63, it never left camp without Major Coon accompanying it, and usually in capacity of commander. During that summer there was hardly a county in Northern Mississippi or Western Tennessee but that he scouted through, at the head of the gallant Second Iowa.

In the spring of 1864 Colonel Hatch was promoted to Brigadier-General, and the regiment re-enlisting Major Coon was commissioned Colonel of the veteran regiment, and immediately assigned to the command of a brigade, composed of the Second Iowa, Sixth and Ninth Illinois Cavalry, and designated the Second Brigade, First Division Cavalry Corps, District of West Tennessee. This brigade was with General A. J. Smith, on his expedition to Tupelo, Mississippi, in the summer of 1864, and the able manner in which Colonel Coon handled it assisted very materially in bringing the expedition to its successful termination.

In the fall of 1864 his command was transferred to the Department of the Cumberland; the Seventh Illinois and Twelfth Tennessee cavalry were attached to it, and the whole re-organized and designated as the Second Brigade, Fifth Division Cavalry Corps, Middle Department of Mississippi. Of this gallant brigade I need say nothing—it speaks for itself, and is probably one of the finest in the service, owing its discipline and efficiency, in a great measure, to the military ability and untiring exertions of Colonel Coon. He is no carpet-knight, or parlor warrior, but has gained the confidence and esteem of the men of his command by his constant attention to and faithful performance of the duties devolving upon him. During the three and a half years he has been in the service he has never had a leave of absence, and unless on duty has never been absent from his command, upon any pretext whatever. He has been in every engagement in which his regiment has participated, from the time of its organization until now, and, without exception, has always acquitted himself well. Few officers can show a cleaner record of faithful service than he, and few have better merited their country's approbation.

THE SIXTY-FOUR DAYS' MARCH.

By order of Maj.-Gen. Washburne, commanding the Department of West Tennessee, Brig.-Gen. Edward Hatch, commanding first division cavalry corps, was ordered to hold his command in readiness to march, with ten days rations, and, if possible, form a junction with the United States forces then operating up the Tennessee River, as far as Eastport, Miss. The division was composed of the following troops: The first brigade, commanded by Colonel Oliver Wells, Twelfth Missouri Cavalry, and consisting of the Seventh and Third Illinois and Twelfth Missouri cavalry regiments; the second brigade, commanded by Colonel Datus E. Coon, Second Iowa Cavalry, consisting of the Sixth and Ninth Illinois and Second Iowa Cavalry, and company K, First Illinois Light Artillery, Captain J. W. Curtis, commanding, the whole numbering about twenty-four hundred men, rank and file. The expedition was fitted out at White Station, on the line of the Memphis and Charleston Railroad, within seven miles of Memphis, Tennessee.

September 30th, 1864. The column moved out on the Germantown road; the rain fell in torrents for two hours. When within one mile of Germantown they turned north and crossed Wolf River, at Pattine's plantation; the crossing was upon a poorly constructed bridge, which delayed the wagons and artillery until after dark, and caused much trouble in passing through the heavily timbered bottom on the opposite side. The command was in bivouac by eleven o'clock, seven miles north of Germantown.

October 1st. Left camp at daylight, the first brigade in the advance—passed through Macon at 12 o'clock, and took the Sommerville road, camping three miles from the former place.

October 2d. Moved out of camp at four o'clock, reached Sommerville and took the Boliver road, arriving at that place at four o'clock P.M. Here a heavy detail from the Second Iowa was sent to assist the Seventh Illinois in constructing a bridge across the Hatchie River—they were sent six hours in advance the evening previous. At eight o'clock, A.M., the bridge was completed, and the whole command crossed over and went into camp, except the Seventh Illinois, which did not cross until the next morning.

October 3d. Moved out of the Hatchie bottom at daylight, taking the Mt. Pincton road, southeast of Jackson, crossed the Forkadeer River at sunset, and camped at eight o'clock in a heavy rain.

October 4th. Left camp at three o'clock, A.M., and reached Miffin, Henderson County, fed horses, prepared coffee and rations, and moved at ten o'clock, taking the road leading down the valley of Beach River, leaving Lexington to our left and north some eight miles. Camped at Jones' plantation, three miles from Scott's Hill; rained all day.

October 5th. Moved at daylight, passing Scott's Hill, taking the Decaturville road, at which place we arrived at two o'clock, P.M., and halted one hour to feed. At sunset reached the Tennessee River, opposite Clifton, Hardin County, having crossed a very impracticable, rocky, picturesque country. At Clifton we found the gunboat fleet and transports, under command of Maj.-Gen. C. C. Washburne.

October 6th. Arrangements were made early this morning to cross the river, by means of the transports City of Pekin, Kenton and Aurora. At two o'clock the command was all over, and in accordance with orders from Brig.-Gen. Hatch it moved out in direction of Waynesboro, on the Nashville pike, for twelve miles, and camped for the night on a beautiful hillside.

October 7th. We left camp at an early hour, moving towards Waynesboro, passing through that little place at ten o'clock, A.M., which is the county-seat. The command stopped and fed on the plantation of Mr. W. C. Barnes, a very respectable man. Waynesboro is 41 miles from Florence, 44 miles from Pulaski, and 92 miles from Nashville. The country is mountainous, rugged and barren, covered with vast and unknown forests, and filled with beautiful trout streams, whose clear waters gleam like pearls in their rocky basins.

It is not very thickly settled, owing to its sterility. The roads being in good condition we made good time, and camped within seven miles of Lawrenceburg.

October 8th. Resumed our march this morning at three o'clock, amid the most intense darkness. We took the wrong road and were led some five miles out of the way. We halted at nine o'clock for breakfast and to feed. Reached Lawrenceburg, the county-seat of Lawrence County, at one o'clock—a dilapidated, ancient looking place, and after a short rest moved out on military road leading to Florence, Alabama. When three miles out we took the road leading down the valley of Shoal Creek, through the most picturesque of countries, and camped for the night on its bank, ten miles from Lawrenceburg.

October 9th. Left this encampment at daylight, returning to the military road, and moving in the direction of Florence. Reached Baugh's Mills, and received orders to camp for the night. At this place we learned that Forrest had crossed the Tennesse River and escaped unharmed.

October 10th. At four o'clock this morning we were again in motion. On arriving at Wilson's cross-roads we changed our course and moved toward Waterloo, passing to the north of Florence some six miles. We reached Waterloo at four o'clock, P.M., and camped.

October 11th. Remained in camp until four o'clock, P.M., when the command moved down the river some ten miles, with the hope of finding the gunboats and fleet, and procuring rations for the men. To make this more certain Major C. C. Horton, commanding the Second Iowa, was sent in advance with his regiment to the fleet with dispatches. Unfortunately the fleet had left a few hours previous to the arrival of our cavalry opposite Eastport, Miss.

October 12th. The command left camp at four o'clock, A.M., moving in the direction of Savanah, and at two o'clock, P.M., was snugly encamped one mile below that place.

October 13th. There being no visible signs of procuring rations for the command, who had been subsisting on the country at a poor rate some three days, we still remained in camp. Brigade commanders applied to General Hatch, who gave them permission to send out detachments of men, under suitable officers, and procure corn and wheat and have it ground at the neighboring mills. This supplied a scanty amount for the next four days.

October 14th, 15th and 16th. During this time each day was industriously spent at the mills, by parties grinding wheat and corn, while others scoured the country to procure bacon, salt, &c., to make it palatable. In great anxiety they waited for the boats, until the evening of the 16th, when orders were received to move in the morning.

October 17th. At seven o'clock, A.M., we moved out on the Waynesboro road a distance of some ten miles, when we turned toward Clifton, at which place we camped, having marched thirty miles, over a very rough road, and having to forage off the country, which is a very disagreeable necessity, and cuts both friends and foes most cruelly.

October 18th. On arriving at Clifton no boats were in sight. The "grand rounds," on a large scale—some 150 miles—had been made, and we returned to the starting point, very hungry, ragged, and tired. During the afternoon, while unwelcome feelings were causing us to cast about for some means of subsistence, the steamer Duke came in sight, to the great satisfaction of the whole command. Our fine hopes were soon blasted, for we learned that it only had short rations of hard-bread and meat, which was equally distributed among the different regiments, the balance to be gathered from the country, during the absence of the steamer to Johnsonville.

From the 18th to the 27th of the month the officers and men were industriously employed in shoeing horses, and making necessary preparations for an active campaign. Owing to the scarcity of blacksmiths and tools scouting parties were sent out in the country to press in sufficient to supply the deficiency. Only a few were obtained, and many horses were shod by the use of the common pocket-knife and a hatchet. The horses improved, as forage was abundant.

While camped at Clifton, Tennessee, it was not an unusual occurrence for the rebls to make their appearance on the opposite side for the first few days, and considerable sharp-shooting was practiced by the men. At last both parties entered into an agreement not to fire upon each other, and a lively conversation ensued between them across the stream. Taking advantage of circumstances, Major Graham and Dr. Briggs, both of the Seventh Illinois Cavalry, procured an old canoe, hallooed over to them, asking if they would receive company. The rebels assented, and promised not to fire upon them, or detain them. Away they went, and upon landing were greeted by the "Johnnies" most cordially, who appreciated the visit highly, complimenting the Major and Doctor, and more particularly the good old Bourbon, a bottle of which the Doctor presented to them. Among the rebels was a surgeon by the name of Green, belonging to a Texas regiment, with whom the visitors had a very lively and agreeable conversation. The surgeon, on receiving the bottle, mounted himself upon a stump, and attracting the attention of the men on the opposite side, displayed the bottle and hallooed across to them to give three cheers for Old Abe, which was heartily responded to; then turning to his visitors drank to the success of Old Abe, (a remarkable circumstance, but true,) after which the parties returned, much pleased with their visit, the main object of which was to obtain information respecting three soldiers belonging to the Third Illinois Cavalry, who had been sent down the river in a skiff, some ten days previous, to ascertain the whereabouts of the gunboats. Their not reporting to their command in a reasonable length of time led to the supposition that they had been captured by the enemy. No information was gained concerning them.

October 29th. Left Clifton at three o'clock, P.M., taking the Nashville pike. Camped three miles out.

October 30th. At nine o'clock we moved towards Waynesboro, as far as Lincoln Creek, twenty-four miles from Clifton, and camped.

October 31st. Resumed the march this morning, reached Lawrenceburg, and camped one mile beyond.

November 1st. Left camp at six o'clock, A.M., and reached Pulaski, eighteen miles distant, and camped for the night.

November 2d, 3d and 4th. During these three days the time was occupied in procuring clothing and rations for the men, while shoes were being fitted on the horses, and preparations made for a heavy campaign. On our arriving at Pulaski we found two divisions of the Fourth Army Corps, under command of Maj.-Gen. Stanley. General Croxton's cavalry command was below, toward Florence. While here a brigade of cavalry arrived, consisting of the Fourteenth and Sixteenth Illinois and the Eighth Kentucky regiments. The Twenty-Third Army Corps, commanded by Maj.-Gen. Schofield, was reported to be *en route* for this place. Railroad trains arrived daily from Nashville, bringing supplies.

November 5th. Left camp with three days rations, marching from Pulaski southwest toward Florence. We were joined there by General Croxton's command, who were ordered to report to General Hatch. Our forces were reported to be at Shoal Creek, where the enemy was also reported to sustain his pickets. During the afternoon of this day heavy cannonading was heard in the direction of the Tennessee River, which gave undoubted evidence of Hood's advance into Tennessee. The command camped for the night on Sugar Creek. A beautiful sunset was witnessed, for the first time in three days, it having rained constantly. This gave the men more life, and raised their drooping spirits.

November 6th. Pushing out of camp before daylight enabled us to reach Lexington, Ala., before eleven o'clock, A.M., where we halted for an hour, to learn the movements of the enemy. Getting no reliable information the command moved on to Baugh's Ford, on Shoal Creek, the Second Iowa Cavalry in advance. On arriving within two miles of the ford the advance met the enemy's pickets, driving them across the creek rapidly, when the whole command came in full view of a heavy line, extending along the bluff on the opposite side. By order of General Hatch a detachment of the Second Iowa, under Lieutenant George W. Budd, commanding company G, was sent for the purpose of destroying by fire a flouring mill, which was located above a factory. After a lively skirmish of nearly an hour the Lieutenant returned and reported that the mill was on the opposite side of the stream, and that the water was too high to admit of crossing, mounted or dismounted—besides the enemy were some three hundred strong, and a large number posted in and about the mill, rendering the position almost impregnable, to say nothing of the difficulty of crossing the stream. On learning these facts the General directed a withdrawal of the whole command, except the Second

Iowa, which was sent to remain and hold its position until further orders. At 9 o'clock, P.M., the command went into camp, in a most unpleasant rain storm.

November 7th. Daylight found us with mud and water under foot, and a drenching rain still falling. Information obtained stated that Hood's forces were located between here and Florence. The Second Iowa was withdrawn to feed. At one o'clock Colonel Coon was ordered to take his brigade and make a demonstration upon the enemy's pickets, the Ninth Illinois, Captain Wm. C. Blackburn, commanding, in advance. A persistent and heavy skirmish took place, when the enemy were driven from the bluff on the opposite side. The regiment reached the ford, but the creek was too much swollen to admit of crossing, the water carrying horse and rider down the stream. During an hour spent in skirmishing, and an unfruitful effort to cross and destroy the mill, it was ascertained beyond doubt that the enemy had reinforced the pickets heavily, and that Shoal Creek was much higher than at any day previous. The second brigade was withdrawn, falling back to Slutt's Cross-Roads, and camped for the night. It had rained all day.

November 8th. The whole command remained in camp this day, with exception of detachments sent out to reconnoitre, &c. This afforded the men an opportunity to vote for President, the result of which was that an overwhelming majority was given for "Honest Old Abe." At two o'clock, P.M., the detachments sent out in the morning returned. They all reported, as the three days previous, that the stream could not be forded. An effort was made by the Second Iowa to construct a raft to cross to the mill, but failed for want of material. During a skirmish of an hour the rain fell in torrents, and soon night came on, closing all operations for the day. The second brigade was withdrawn to a point near the bivouac of the previous night. Major C. C. Moore, Second Iowa, was immediately sent out, with a detachment of one hundred men, to the rear of the enemy on the Tennessee River, with instructions to strike the river ten miles below Florence.

November 9th. During the night Colonel Coon received orders from General Hatch to move out early in the morning with his brigade, and make another demonstration on the enemy at Baugh's Ford. At nine o'clock the ford was reached; the road was nearly impassable from mud and water. They found the enemy's pickets heavy and well posted on the opposite side—the stream still too high to admit of fording from either side. The brigade withdrew during the afternoon and camped at Wadkin's House. It rained nearly all day, but cleared away at sunset. In the meantime Major Moore, Second Iowa, returned with his command safe, having passed around in rear of the enemy's line, a distance of forty miles, and striking the Tennessee River ten miles below Florence, making a distance, in going and returning, of eighty miles travel in twenty-four hours. The object of this expedition was to bring in some men of General Croxton's command, who had been three days previously sent down the river from

Bainbridge to destroy the enemy's pontoons at Florence, which was not accomplished. They were to complete the work of destruction and meet this party below, but after diligent search and careful inquiry the Major returned.

November 10th. Remained in camp all day, the first pleasant day since leaving Pulaski. Owing to the very inclement weather, bad roads, &c., the whole command was again entirely destitute of rations. Two mills were taken possession of, and a regular system of foraging off the country was adopted, which, with the most careful management, could but poorly supply the men. Orders were given for the whole command to be ready to move upon the enemy next morning.

November 11th. The division moved out, the second brigade advancing on the Baugh's Ferry road, the remainder of the force moving on the Huntsville, Bainbridge and military roads. It was not long before each command was engaged, skirmishing with the enemy's pickets. The Sixth Illinois, Major Chas. C. Whitrish, commanding, had the advance of the second brigade, and were deployed as skirmishers, dismounted, forming a line from the main road up the stream to the mill, while a section of artillery was put in position on the military road. The skirmishers soon drove back their pickets, while the artillery caused their reserve, at first in plain sight, to scatter to the rear. A company of mounted men were, in the meantime, to try the ford on the main road and ascertain its condition for crossing. After a thorough trial it was found too deep, even for mounted men. The Second Iowa, Major C. C. Horton, commanding, succeeded in finding a crossing, nearly one-fourth of a mile below the main crossing. Col. Coon dispatched an orderly to the Major for him to cross as rapidly as possible, which order was obeyed, in a most gallant manner, by company G, of that regiment, with Lieutenant Geo. W. Budd commanding, in the advance. The first battalion, Major Gustavus Schwitgar commanding, was soon over and engaging the enemy in a brisk skirmish, when Major Horton reported the ford impracticable for the passage of more troops, owing to the quicksand and miry soil on the opposite shore, and that it was impossible to cross the artillery in any event. The Major was ordered to dismount the remainder of his regiment, place them in line along the shore, and recall Major Schwitgar. In crossing and re-crossing the stream the enemy kept up a heavy fire from a barricade some three hundred yards distant, on a high bluff. Another effort was made to cross at the mill, but failed. The Ninth Illinois Cavalry, Capt. Blackburn commanding, had been sent, on leaving camp, to make a flank movement to the right of their position, by crossing Shoal Creek above the pond and mill, and moving down on the opposite and west side of the stream. They now appeared in sight, fighting the enemy's pickets to such an extent that they fell back so far that the Second Iowa was enabled to cross by swimming their horses, which feat was accomplished in safety, with one exception—Lieutenant David Hilliars, commanding company A, who, by a misunderstanding of orders, took the wrong track, and being sorely pressed by a brigade of the enemy's cavalry, coolly took to the timber and hills, evading their main force, and after much difficulty succeeded in re-crossing Shoal Creek, and reporting with all his men in camp at dark. The cool, undisturbed manner of this officer in releasing himself from the snare of the enemy is at least highly complimentary. This evening the command camped again at Wadkin's House.

November 12th. Remained in camp all day. Issued a very light ration of meal ground at the mills.

November 13th. Remained in camp all day. Orders were received from General Hatch for the brigade to send heavy details to all the fords and main roads, and by felling timber to obstruct the passage of the enemy. This was done to enable the command to shift from right to left, and make an immediate attack. Forrest was reported crossing at Eastport to join the advance, with 15,000 men.

November 14th. Remained all day in camp. Details returned. All roads were effectually blockaded, in compliance with orders.

November 15th. The command moved out on the military road a few miles, toward Lawrenceburg, and camped at Wilcoxson's plantation.

November 16th, 17th and 18th. Still along the enemy's front, heavily picketing. The second brigade, Colonel Coon commanding, left the military road at eight o'clock, A.M., of the 16th, passed down the valley of Wolf Creek and crossed Shoal Creek at Wolf Ford, moved from the opposite side to Abberdeen, thence to Big Butler, and down to Little Butler, from which place it moved directly south toward Wilson's Cross-Roads. After passing a mill the advance of the Second found the enemy's pickets and dashed at them furiously, running them into their reserve pell mell, which created a stampede of the whole command, composed of General Rhoddy's brigade, which also ran back to their infantry camp in great confusion. Through the gallant conduct of Lieutenant Tiffoth, company D, Second Iowa, the command captured several prisoners, who informed us of many important facts touching the movements of the enemy. After forcing Rhoddy within the infantry lines the brigade retraced their steps, re-crossing Shoal Creek at Savanah Ford, and went into camp at Harris's plantation, three miles from Cowpen's Mill. General Hatch became satisfied that the enemy were constantly receiving reinforcements, and that Forrest had recently joined Hood, (on the 14th,) and that the location about the two Butler creeks was not the most safe place for the camp of a cavalry command.

November 19th. While the first brigade was watching the different roads, the second brigade, Colonel Coon commanding, was ordered to move across Shoal Creek, at Cowpen's Ford, for the purpose of camping on Butler Creek. On reaching the creek, some three miles west, they drove in the enemy's pickets. Captain A. R. Mock, of the Ninth Illinois, commanding battalion, was sent to patrol the Waynesboro road—the main column to move north to Butler Creek, while Captain J. W. Harper, with the remainder of his regiment—the Ninth—stood picket on the road running south toward Florence. Colonel Coon and escort remained at the cross-roads to see the train safely closed up. He had not been superintending the direction of the train quite an hour when an orderly informed him that the Second had met the enemy in force, and that Buford's division (rebel) was in the front on Big Butler Creek. At the same time Captain Harper reported the enemy pressing his pickets from the south, and had the appearance of being infantry. Leaving an orderly to close the column and sending another to inform Captain Harper that he must hold his position, at all hazards, until the pack-train and artillery had passed, as it was impossible, from the bad condition of the road, to halt or return by the same route, Colonel Coon rode rapidly to the Second Iowa, and found them engaged with a superior force. He at once sent an orderly with instructions for the train and artillery to turn up the valley of the Little Butler, accompanied by the Sixth Illinois as escort, Major Whitrish commanding, who was instructed to take all the spades and make a crossing on Shoal Creek, at all hazards, as this was the only place of escape from a well devised trap of the enemy. Great anxiety was felt for the command, as Buford, on the north, was pressing the Second Iowa hard in front, and flanking on the right and left with vastly superior numbers, while the Ninth Illinois were heavily pressed in the rear by a force from the south. During this time a

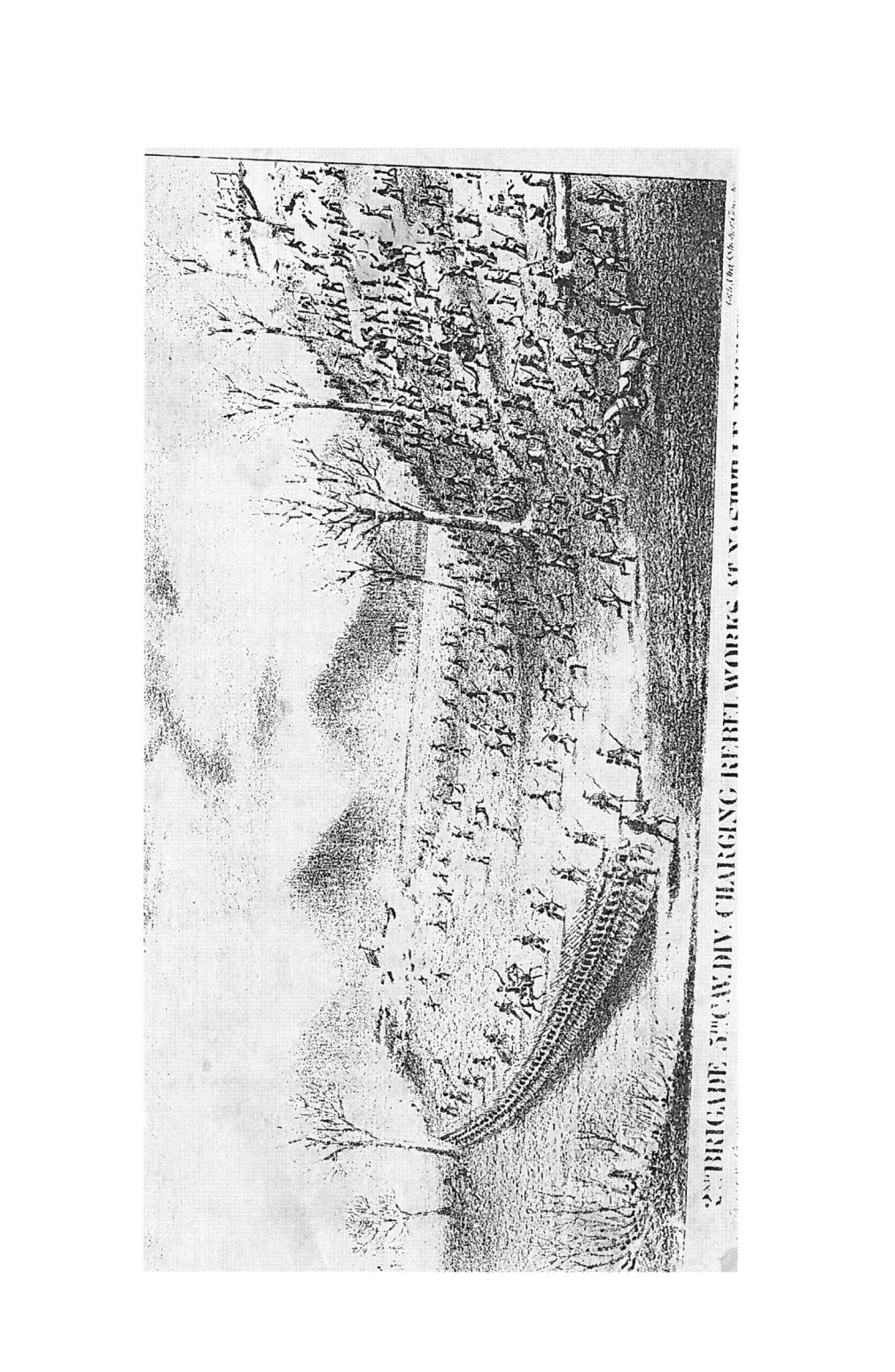

2ⁿᵈ BRIGADE 5ᵗʰ CAV. DIV. CHARGING REBEL WORKS AT NASHVILLE

messenger was sent to Captain Mock, informing him that unless he returned soon the last place left for his escape would have to be abandoned. As the Ninth Illinois came up they passed to the right and rear of the Second Iowa, down the Little Butler, and formed in line dismounted at the junction of the two rivers, where the high and abrupt bluffs on either side made the valley quite narrow. This made a good support for the Second when compelled to fall back. By this time the situation of the Second became critical, in consequence of the rapid movements of the rebel flanking column, which reached nearly to their rear on right and left. Seeing that it was impossible to hold the gap until Captain Mock could be heard from, Major Horton was ordered to fall back and form again in rear of the Ninth Illinois; each regiment then fell back alternately and formed lines for two miles, when they reached Shoal Creek and found, to their great surprise, the Sixth Illinois pack-train, artillery and ambulances all safe on the other side, and the regiment dismounted to cover the crossing. A lively skirmish was kept up by the rear guard while the command passed down the steep, miry bank by file, obliquely, one hundred and fifty feet. The mortification and apparent chagrin of the rebels, when they found their prey had unexpectedly escaped their snare, was made known by their hideous yells, such as rebels only can make. Pickets were carefully placed on all practicable roads, and the command encamped at dark at the same place it left in the morning, with the firm belief that

Butler Creek was by no means a desirable location to encamp. The day had been one of incessant rain.

November 20th. While the second brigade was engaged with the enemy, the first held a position a few miles below, and on the left of the Second, facing the enemy, while Croxton's brigade was posted yet further to the left of the first. The fighting devolved principally upon the second brigade. At three o'clock, A. M., the second moved out on the military road, thence to Bluewater Creek and camped, leaving pickets on the military road. Captain Mock, of the Ninth Illinois, reported on the military road, having traveled all night to reach the command. He succeeded in reaching the Waynesboro road, but in returning found himself and command completely surrounded by the enemy, and took to the hills by by-roads. By accident he came upon General Chalmers' division wagon-train, (rebel) made a charge on the guard, capturing several wagons and prisoners, and fifty mules, besides much plunder, which he could not bring away. While in the act of destroying the train he was attacked by a superior force and compelled to leave all and take to the woods again. By the assistance of Union men and negroes he was guided by circuitous routes until he reached the column. His loss was thirty men, most of whom were taken prisoners. In capturing the train, papers conveying important information were found, which must have been of infinite importance to General Thomas, as they detailed the movements about to be made, giving timely notice to all of what was to take place. Captain

Mock is entitled to much credit for the skill displayed in bringing out his command with so little loss. At sunset the pickets were driven in on the military road. Patrols who had been sent out returned, reporting the enemy advancing in force.

November 21st. The whole command moved at an early hour, on the Lexington road, the second brigade bringing up the rear. After resting a few hours at this place the whole force moved toward Lawrenceburg, the second brigade still guarding the rear. At five o'clock, P.M., the command reached the latter place and camped for the night. The day was cold, and much snow fell during the afternoon and night.

November 22d. The morning was cold and the ground frozen hard. About twelve o'clock the enemy commenced skirmishing with our pickets, and Captain Bandy, Second Iowa, with one battalion, was sent to ascertain their force. After skirmishing with them an hour he returned and reported the enemy three miles from town in force, and strongly posted on bluffs and behind well arranged rail barricades. At two o'clock the enemy moved up in heavy force, infantry, cavalry and artillery, and encamped in line, in plain view of town and our bivouac. The General commanding the division ordered the second brigade into line of battle. A brisk artillery duel was kept up for an hour between the enemy and company K, First Illinois Artillery. In the meantime a large dismounted force was displayed, showing all the characteristics of infantry. After holding the town until sundown the command was ordered to move out on the Pulaski road, Croxton's brigade in advance, while the second brought up the rear. The command withdrew in good order, though heavily pressed by superior numbers, and halted and camped seven miles east of Lawrenceburg.

November 23d. Left camp at four o'clock in the morning, and halted at Richland Mills to feed and issue rations. General Croxton's command was in the rear, heavily skirmishing with the enemy. At three o'clock, P.M., the command moved three miles toward Pulaski, took up the valley of Dry Creek, and camped five miles south of Campbellville.

November 24th. Moved out at six o'clock, A.M., the second brigade bringing up the rear, and arrived at Campbellville at 9 o'clock. The patrols reported the enemy moving on our left, with videttes standing on every high bluff in sight. General Hatch ordered the patrols strengthened. Had proceeded but a short distance when an orderly arrived and reported that a heavy column (supposed to be Buford's division,) was in front of the first brigade. The second brigade was withdrawn and fell back to the east side of town, and held the Linnville roads until the first division, then in a critical situation, could be recalled. The second had no sooner taken position than the enemy's infantry made its appearance in heavy force on the south and west side of the town. The General ordered battery K, First Illinois, to commence firing, at a range of one and a half miles; the effect of the cannonading was excellent, causing the whole rebel column to halt for at least one hour. During this time a flanking column of the enemy was discovered moving to our left, and threatening the Linnville road. The Second Iowa was immediately ordered to guard and check the movement, and they soon reported the force engaging them vastly superior to theirs. The Ninth Illinois was sent to their support. The position of these regiments soon became intolerable, as the enemy were undoubtedly moving their main column by the right flank, to get possession of the road in the rear. Upon learning this fact General Hatch ordered the second brigade to fall back and hold the road, regardless of the first. The enemy were strongly posted on the left of town, with a battery playing at one thousand yards. In the meantime the first brigade had succeeded, by flanking through the timber, passing over rugged and steep hills, and keeping up a bold front, in making a junction with the second. The Seventh Illinois, Major Graham commanding, made two gallant charges, driving the enemy before them in confusion. Two miles from Campbellville the flanking column and patrol of the second, from the left, were suddenly driven in. As the road turned to the left, through a narrow gorge, and just at the time General Hatch was passing, Captain E. B. Phillips, company M, Sixth Illinois, commanding his escort, discovering the rebels, charged in an instant with his company and saved the gallant commander from being captured. This gallantry of Captain Phillips is worthy of special compliment here, as well for his daring as the good results. Unfortunately the Captain received a wound in his left hand, which disabled him for the campaign. The Ninth Illinois, Captain J. W. Harper commanding, followed immediately in rear of the escort, and were immediately ordered by him to dismount and hold the gap, at all hazards. Captain Harper had scarcely dismounted his men when they received a heavy fire from a brigade of the enemy; not a particle daunted the Captain ordered his men forward until it became a hand-to-hand conflict. The Captain received orders to fall back slowly, their ammunition—sixty rounds—being nearly exhausted. The Second Iowa was formed across the gorge to protect them while they withdrew. The loss of the Ninth in this fight was thirty killed and wounded, in as many minutes; among them were four orderly sergeants. Much credit is due Captain Harper for the skillful manner and good order in which he retreated, although the loss was heavy. No sooner had the Ninth passed through the line of the Second Iowa than the rebel brigade came at a double-quick up the hollow, colors in front, and in another instant were in line of battle, when three hundred Spencer's in the hands of the Second Iowa drove them back in confusion; but a moment, however, intervened, when the rebels rallied. Major Horton, in the meantime, retired and mounted by battalions under fire, leaving one officer and five men on the field. The whole command then moved forward, Croxton in the advance, the second on the pike and the first to the left of the pike, while the rebels followed closely in the rear and on both flanks. At eleven o'clock, P.M., the command was in the rear of Columbia and inside the infantry pickets of the Fourth and Twenty-Third army corps, they being stationed there at that time.

November 25th. Crossed Duck River and camped three miles above the city. The advance of Hood's army was within a few miles of Columbia.

November 26th. At ten o'clock, A.M., moved out on the Murfreesboro road and camped eight miles east of Columbia. Hood's advance was engaged with our infantry. Rained constantly during the day and night.

November 27th. Remained in camp all day; raining very hard. The Seventh Illinois was assigned to the second brigade; Major John M. Graham, commanding the regiment, reported for duty. This transfer caused great rejoicing in the Seventh Illinois; they felt once more at home among their old comrades, with whom they had been previously brigaded. And now, kind reader, I will devote my pen almost exclusively to the benefit of the second brigade, Col. Coon, commanding. I do not wish to slight other commands, who have acted nobly and bravely, but space will not permit me to dwell upon the good merits of all.

November 28th. Rained until noon. At 2 o'clock Colonel Coon received orders to move immediately. While boots and saddles were being sounded the enemy opened with a volley upon the pickets on the Shelbyville road. By the aid of a glass the enemy could be seen in heavy force through the thin fog, about two miles distant. Captain Foster, commanding battalion of Second Iowa, was ordered to support the pickets while the command made preparations to move. By direction of the General commanding the artillery was sent to Hunt's Cross-Roads, on the Lewisburg pike, where the brigade erected a slight barricade of rails, and slept on their arms during the night.

November 29th. The brigade took up its line of march at four o'clock, A.M., passing Croxton's and Harrison's commands, and moving toward Franklin. The second brigade marched in the rear of the division to Mount Carmel, when it halted and fell in line of battle to the left of the pike. At 9 o'clock, A.M., General Croxton's command passed, heavily pressed by the enemy. The light rail barricade, previously constructed, served as a temporary breastwork, and enabled the second, then dismounted, to check the enemy's movements. But a few moments passed until the whole line was engaged in a heavy skirmish, which continued for an hour, when they were ordered to withdraw slowly, which was done by alternate numbers in line for two miles; the brigade was then ordered to mount and withdraw by brigade in line of regiments, each regiment in line of squadrons, in columns of fours. The enemy discovering this formation charged down the pike, in column of fours, on a small company of the Ninth Illinois, who were acting as rear-guard. The company did not halt, but continued to fall back, leading the enemy between the flanking column right and left, who opened upon them a raking fire, throwing them into confusion, and ending the pursuit for the day. The command arrived at Knowland's plantation, at twelve o'clock, and halted in line of battle until four o'clock, P.M., when it moved toward Franklin two miles, and turning to the right crossed Little Harworth River and moved north to the Knowlandsville and Franklin road, where the brigade camped for the night.

November 30th. The Twelfth Tennessee Cavalry, Colonel R. R. Spaulding, commanding, was this day assigned to the second brigade, and reported for duty. The day was a beautiful one. The positions on the roads were held in quiet until about three o'clock, P.M. The enemy had previously skirmshed General Croxton's command heavily, which was picketing the river, and at this hour compelled him to give back. The Confederate cavalry on their right made a general attack on the Federal cavalry on Schofield's left, and simultaneously with their main assault on the Federal works at Franklin, with the evident design of forcing back and flanking General Schofield's position. General Hatch formed a portion of the Twelfth Tennessee, a detachment of the Tenth Tennessee, the Third, Sixth, Ninth and Seventh in order from right to left, and facing a high ridge to the south, with the Second Iowa thrown across the Knowlandsville road half a mile east of and at right-angles with the main line, all dismounted. The fight was a very simple and brief one; heavy skirmishing well up with his right, and exchanged some pretty heavy firing. The General ordered his line to charge; he was then on the left with the Seventh Illinois, which wound up a long hill, in a direction to detach it by opening both flanks from its support, and upon gaining the brow of the hill unmasking a heavy line of dismounted men, carrying their stands of colors. With a volley and a cheer it charged them, driving them through their bivouac and across the river, and they were still retreating when this regiment was recalled. The regiments to the right joined in the advance, and carried the hill in their front, driving the enemy in most gallant style until they had recrossed the Little Harworth. Our cavalry on the Knowlandsville road was not attacked. The enemy's forces were estimated at from five to six thousand strong, and were said to be Buford's division of cavalry and mounted infantry. The entire brigade acquitted itself in a most creditable manner, and camped for the night on the ground occupied the night previous. From this date no operation of importance transpired, save the march to Nashville, occupying the 1st, when the command skirmished a little at Brentwood's, and the 2d, when it marched at five o'clock, and arrived in the vicinity of Fort Negley about eight o'clock the same morning. Until the 12th the time was diligently employed in re-furnishing the command. On the 13th it crossed the river and camped near the defence.

December 15th. By order of Gen. Hatch, pursuant to orders from Brevet Maj.-Gen. Wilson, commanding cavalry corps M. D. M., the division and brigade was marched at an early hour from camp, crossing the field on the right of the Harding pike, in the following order: The second brigade on the right of the infantry, commanded by Maj.-Gen. A. J. Smith, Sixteenth army corps, and on the left of the first brigade, with its regiments from right to left, the Twelfth Tennessee, mounted, Seventh Illinois, Second Iowa, Sixth and Seventh Illinois, dismounted, with horses led in the rear, and men carrying one day's rations and one hundred rounds of ammunition per man. The other cavalry extended the line to the Cumberland River on the right, and its movement was by a grand left-wheel against the enemy to double up his left, and by driving his center in to concentrate the Federal attack, besides opening a way to his rear, if it should be advantageous to use it. The rapidity of the movements of the infantry upon the left, and which constituted the movable pivot of the grand left-wheel of the cavalry, was so rapid that it was found impossible to accelerate the movements on the right. To keep up the entire line the various divisions and even brigades became separated, and even detached, and when the second brigade finally went into close action the first brigade on its right was detached some miles. It was down this opening that the Twelfth Tennessee, Colonel R. R. Spaulding, commanding, charged and captured some twenty wagons and teams, about forty-five prisoners, and a large amount of plunder, belonging to the rebel General Chalmers' headquarters. By one o'clock we had rolled back the enemy successively from the Charlotte, Hardin and Broad Street pikes, and approached some of the rebel redoubts, with the brigade line facing nearly due east, and much in advance of the infantry, which was moving down from the north. The brigade being formed on the extreme right of the infantry caused lively marching for the men, as the distance traveled by them was much further than that of the infantry; for three miles the marching was done on a double-quick. After a sharp artillery duel for an hour between the first redoubt and battery I, First Illinois Light Artillery, attached to the division, the brigade was ordered to charge the redoubts containing the guns. The regiments engaged in this charge were the Seventh Illinois, Major John M. Graham commanding, on the right, with the Second Iowa, Major C. C. Horton, and Ninth Illinois, Captain J. W. Harper commanding, in order on its left, and the Sixth Illinois, Lieut.-Col. John Lynch commanding, on the left of the brigade. In making this charge the right wing of the brigade—Seventh Illinois and Second Iowa—had an open field, with nothing to impede their progress save two stone fences, while the left wing—Ninth and Sixth Illinois—had a heavy thicket to pass through. At the word "forward," stone fences and thickets were very slight impediments in the way of this veteran brigade. At the distance of about eight hundred yards southwest of the work assaulted was another redoubt, mounting two guns, and filled with several hundred infantry; from this latter work, while moving eastward on the first, the Second Iowa and Seventh Illinois were exposed to a continuous shower of shells and musketry. The right of the Seventh Illinois, who were not more than four hundred yards from it, giving first their front, then their right flank, then their rear to this fire, without shrinking for a moment or firing a shot, was as proud evidence of good soldiership as ever displayed. The enemy in the first redoubt, discovering the movements, changed their little messengers (shells) to grape and canister, accompanied by heavy musketry from the infantry support behind their works. The men never halted from the time the charge was sounded until they had possession of the works, containing four Napoleon guns and seventy-five prisoners, besides a large number of small arms, thrown away by the enemy in their rapid flight. So eager were the men of each regiment to reach the redoubt first, that they became mixed up in such a manner that it is a difficult question to settle, or say who was first to reach the prize. All acted nobly, and all are entitled to the highest praise, under the circumstances, for their efforts to be first. The Second Iowa planted the first colors on the works; the others had none with them. General Hatch was among the first to reach the redoubt, and he is under the impression that Lieutenant Budd was the first officer inside the works, and consequently ordered him to take command of the guns and use them immediately upon the retreating enemy, which order was carried out with good effect. In the capture of this redoubt the infantry were behind time, though they afforded good support, and were fully as anxious to gain the prize as were the cavalry. After its surrender a major of an Ohio infantry regiment mounted the works, drew his sword and claimed the honor of capturing the fort for his regiment, but the cavalrymen standing around cooled his ardor. The rebel colors, which lay on the ground folded up, had been overlooked by our cavalry, and were afterward found by some infantry belonging to General McArthur's division. But few of the men lingered to view what they had captured—each and all were eager in the pursuit of the retreating foe, and were continually bringing them in by squads, numbering from two to forty. Major Forbes, Seventh Illinois, states that he met one sergeant and two privates in charge of thirty prisoners. The rally being sounded General Hatch ordered a charge to be made on redoubt number two, which had not ceased to fire its deadly missiles. With General Hatch and Colonel Coon at their head the men charged, and in less than thirty minutes after the order was given the works were in the possession of our brave cavalrymen. This redoubt was situated upon the top of a bluff, some two hundred feet high, and protected by strong earthworks. The colors of the Second Iowa were planted on the works by Sergeant John Hartman, of company F, color-bearer, who fell mortally wounded, and a braver man never faced the enemy. His last words were spoken to Major Horton, requesting him to tell his friends at home that he fell while performing his duty. During the charge the enemy kept up a brisk cannonading, accompanied by heavy musketry firing from the infantry within the redoubt. The long march previous, the charge on the first redoubt, and the short time given until the second charge, rendered it almost impossible for a cavalryman to move faster than a walk. So eager were the officers and men to reach the second redoubt that many fell to the ground exhausted. Lieut.-Col. John Lynch, commanding the Sixth Illinois, fell exhausted and was carried from the field. Many soldiers, when too tired to walk, crawled upon their hands and knees up the steep bluff to the foot of the redoubt. While the cavalry were rallying for the second charge General Hatch was apprised by Major Forbes, Seventh Illinois, of a very threatening movement of the enemy, who were concentrating a considerable force in a ravine in the edge of the wood, to the east of and at right-angles with the main pike, with the evident design of attacking the left of our main line, then moving westward against the second redoubt. The General at once comprehended the design of the enemy, and turning to the Major said, "Go into them, sir, with what you've got." The Major started for them at the head of about twenty-five men of his own regiment, and a few members of the Second Iowa cavalry and Fifth Minnesota infantry, not more than forty men in all; they charged and drove fully three hundred rebels from a greatly superior position, pursuing them three-quarters of a mile, and returned with ninety prisoners; meanwhile from the captured redoubt went up three hearty cheers for Uncle Sam. A rather amusing incident occurred while charging this redoubt, which was told me by an officer of high standing in this brigade. As the gallant General Hatch was charging up the hill, leading his command, his attention was attracted toward a cavalryman, a member of the Ninth Illinois, who was lying on the ground trying to crawl up the hill; but so exhausted was the poor fellow that it was impossible for him to go any further without some assistance. The General asked him what ailed him; he stated the fact, when the General told him to get hold of his horse's tail, and hold on, and he would help him up the hill, which was done. Another dispute arose as to who was the first to enter the fort, every regiment claiming the honor. The fort surrendered to Captain McCausland, and it was difficult to restrain the men from firing upon the rebels after they surrendered. Among some of the first to enter this fort was an infantryman, who had pushed ahead of his command and joined the cavalry, eager for the fun. He was a fine looking fellow, and with his bayonet fixed he kept close behind the Captain, and as the latter demanded the surrender of the fort exclaimed, "Go it Captain; I will follow you to h—l on a charge!" In this redoubt when captured were two twelve-pound guns, a large quantity of ammunition, over one hundred prisoners, including one surgeon, one major, and one captain. The infantry were behind time, unable to keep up with the cavalry, who did not keep very good order, while the former moved in solid column. It was very mortifying to them, and you could hear their officers calling upon the men to hurry up, and not let the cavalrymen take all the forts, which feat not only surprised them, but when it was reported to Maj.-Gen. Thomas that the cavalry had carried the first works, he replied, "Tut, tut, impossible, impossible, sir; such a thing as cavalrymen carrying forts by assault has never been heard of." However the General was convinced of the fact, by witnessing the brigade enter the second redoubt. The cavalry were soon in hot pursuit of the retreating rebels, leaving the fort and prisoners in charge of the infantry. It was now getting dark. Colonel Coon, mistaking two regiments of the first brigade for his own, had the honor of leading them to the summit of a third hill, under a most galling fire from the enemy in front and on both flanks, and holding the position until the infantry support came up, when they charged, driving the enemy before them and capturing three pieces of artillery. The Colonel says he will ever remember with pleasure the gallant conduct of the officers and men of the two regiments, which he had been told were the Twelfth Missouri and Eleventh Indiana cavalry regiments. At dark the brigade went into camp near the redoubts, on the Lewisburg pike.

December 16th. At ten o'clock, A.M., the brigade was ordered out to support General Nipe, commanding division of cavalry. After advancing one mile the brigade moved to the east of the pike, and formed a line dismounted, then moved forward in conformity to the infantry toward the Granny White pike. The steep hills, rising abruptly from one to two hundred feet high, and covered with a thick undergrowth, made it almost impossible to manœuvre troops, even when dismounted. The regiments were in line of order as on the preceding day, each upon a hill. After moving forward nearly one mile the whole line became engaged.

During the first hour the Seventh Illinois came upon a brigade of rebel infantry, strongly posted. A charge was at once ordered by Major Graham, commanding, who immediately after fell, wounded in the arm, and was carried from the field. The command now devolved upon Major Henry C. Forbes, who led the charge then in progress, and was ably sustained by the third battalion, under Captain McCausland, who, a few moments after, fell wounded—a young, brave and efficient officer, loved and admired by the regiment for his many noble qualities. The command moved up the hill in a direction perpendicular to the movements on the right, when the enemy gave way, throwing their guns in every direction and surrendering seventy-two prisoners, including a captain and four lieutenants.

The position thus gallantly taken was untenable for a single regiment. The enemy rallied upon discovering the small force that attacked them, and this regiment was obliged to withdraw, which it did in good order, bringing away the prisoners, and destroying the arms captured, by breaking and bending the barrels. Had the regiment been supported by any portion of the brigade they would have succeeded in making a large capture. The regiment lost fifteen men, killed and wounded, during the fight, including four officers. The same ground was passed over a few hours afterward by the remainder of the brigade, the enemy having evacuated the position.

During the afternoon the Sixth and Ninth Illinois, with the Second Iowa, were engaged firing at will on a fort some five hundred yards distant, while Battery I, First Illinois Light Artillery, played upon it from the valley below, which soon caused the enemy to evacuate. The line moved forward and the Twelfth Tennessee Cavalry charged and captured one hundred and fifty prisoners, eight stand of colors which were left in the hands of the infantry. The enemy were retreating in great haste on the Granny White pike. The brigade was ordered to charge them, if possible, before dark. Col. Spaulding, of the Twelfth Tennessee, took the advance, and had not proceeded more than a mile when he made a charge which threw them into confusion, and by the assistance of the Ninth Illinois, who were brought up dismounted, drove them from a strong position protected by a barricade of rails; the Twelfth Tennessee, Sixth and Ninth Illinois followed them to another strong position, a half mile distant, when a hand to hand fight took place and lasted an hour after dark. At this place Brig.-Gen. Bucker was captured by Captain Joseph Boyer, Twelfth Tennessee Cavalry, who received a severe blow on the forehead at the hand of the rebel General. In that personal contest Captain Boyer wrenched the rebel General's sabre from his hand, who in turn seized and took his; several cuts and points were executed by both parties, each one exhibiting skill in the use of their weapons; by a powerful and dexterious blow Captain Boyer succeeded in knocking from the General's hand his sword; the General then put spurs to his horse and tried to escape, upon which the

Captain drew his revolver and shot him through the arm, which resulted in his capture. It was in this melee, amidst intense darkness, that the two regiments of Twelfth Tennessee Cavalry (Federal and Confederate) met and mixed in mad confusion, neither knowing the other save by the usual challenge, "halt! who comes there?" Colonel Spaulding who was foremost in the charge was halted by two Confederate soldiers, who, on hearing his answer to the challenge grasped his horse by the reins on either side and demanded his surrender; the Colonel put spurs to his horse and with one bound the noble animal took himself and rider beyond danger. Private Barny Watson, Company G, Twelfth Tennessee, captured and brought away General Bucker's division flag, and was promoted to sergeant the same night for his gallant conduct. Majors Corwin and Bradshaw of the Twelfth Tennessee charged entirely through the rebel lines with their battalions and afterward returned by passing themselves off as belonging to the Twelfth Tennessee, (Confederate Cavalry,) and in great anxiety to meet the Yankees. The brigade encamped for the night on Granny White's pike, eight miles south of Nashville.

December 17th. Moved at daylight and continued the pursuit, following in the rear of the enemy's cavalry to Franklin, and thence to the Louisburgh pike, and crossed over to the Columbia pike. When three miles south of Franklin the enemy were met in force. The whole brigade was formed and charged, mounted, driving in the rebel left. The Second Iowa pressed their way round to the rebel left and rear, where they became engaged in a hand to hand fight, resulting in the capture of one stand of colors and several prisoners. In this engagement Sergeant John Coulter, Corporal A. R. Heck and private Black, of company K, Second Iowa, captured a stand of Division colors. The two latter were killed and the former severely wounded—but he succeeded in bringing away the colors. So desperate had been the conflict for these colors that two Federals and three Confederates lay dead within three paces of each other.

The firing in the rear, in conjunction with the brisk engagement in front, caused the enemy to fall back. General Hatch, with small detachments from the Sixth, Seventh and Ninth Illinois and Second Iowa, made a most gallant charge, which resulted in the capture of three more pieces of artillery, (formerly the famous Waterhouse Battery, of Chicago, captured from General Sturgis, by Forrest, near Gumtown, Mississippi, June, 1864.) The darkness of the night prevented further movements and the brigade went into camp, seven miles below Franklin.

December 18th. Continued the pursuit to Spring Hill, where a considerable force of the enemy were found. After firing a few shots, they fell back in confusion. The brigade camped three miles south of Spring Hill.

December 19th. Resumed the march to Rutherford's Creek, where the command dismounted and marched by the right flank. The Sixth Illinois succeeded in crossing the wreck of the burned railroad bridge, when the fragments floated away and the balance of the command were compelled to ford the stream some distance above. Moved two miles below the enemy's flank, the Sixth skirmishing until dark, when the command encamped for the night.

December 20th. At daylight were again in motion. Moved down Rutherford's Creek, about two miles, and constructed a crossing from the fragments of a railroad bridge, which the enemy had destroyed the day previous. This work was soon completed, and by twelve o'clock the whole command was across. The Seventh and Ninth were dismounted and deployed on foot, while the remainder of the brigade followed mounted to Duck River, opposite Columbia.

On arriving at Columbia they found that the enemy had crossed his rear guard in safety that morning, leaving a small party, with a piece of artillery, to guard the town, upon the opposite side. A brisk skirmish was kept up for some time, between the enemy's sharpshooters, who were lodged in the buildings. At the same time a light artillery duel was going on. General Hatch at once turned his attention toward the sharpshooters and ordered the buildings shelled, which soon caused an evacuation of them, and, also, an interview with General Forrest, who appeared with a flag of truce and approached the water's edge, requesting General Hatch not to shell the town, as he was doing more injury to his own men (many of whom lay in the buildings wounded) than theirs. General Hatch replied that he would stop the shelling if he—General Forrest—would withdraw the sharpshooters—which was done. At the conclusion General Forrest remarked to General Hatch that he hoped he would see him again. The General replied, that he hoped he would have that pleasure. During the skirmish the Seventh discovered where the enemy had abandoned four pieces of artillery, by tumbling them into Duck River. They were afterward taken out by the infantry.

December 21st, 22d and 23d were occupied pursuing the retreating enemy, continually bringing in prisoners, wagons, ambulances, caissons, small arms, &c. The road was literally strown with arms, blankets, knapsacks, cartridge-boxes, &c. One battalion of the Second Iowa, under Captain G. W. Foster, company M, was sent on the Shellbyville pike, in pursuit of a party of rebels who were reported escaping, with two pieces of artillery. The Captain succeeded in capturing them, after a day's march, and also found six ambulances and three wagons. The enemy, on the 23d, camped five miles south of Columbia, on the Pulaski pike. Prisoners reported that they had orders when they discovered Hatch's division pressing their rear not to fire but one shot before limbering up. It was a stated fact that if the enemy attempted to fire more than one round our men would charge and capture the guns. They asserted that they never saw such men; they did not seem to care anything about their artillery fire, but seemed to take delight in charging their guns, and would only stop to take aim and fire, not stopping to load nary a time—showing the superiority of the Spencer carbine.

December 24th. Brigade had some sharp skirmishing with Buford's division, and the rebel General Buford was wounded by the Seventh Illinois sharpshooters.

December 25th. Brigade marched in rear of General Hammond and Colonel Harrison's commands, passing beyond Pulaski, some six miles, where the enemy were found in force. Harrison's command being badly repulsed the Second brigade was ordered forward, dismounted. After a skirmish of an hour they drove the enemy from a strong position and camped for the night.

December 26th. From this date little fighting was done. The enemy had crossed the Tennessee at Bainbridge, badly defeated and terribly demoralized.

After a period of hard marching to Gravelly Springs, Alabama, the command went into camp, and remained three weeks, subsisting about two-thirds of the time on parched corn—owing to the scarcity of rations at the time. At the same time boats were constantly arriving loaded with forage, necessitating a great amount of fatigue duty. This, together with the inferior diet, caused much sickness among the men. However, General Hatch was not to blame for this gross neglect of the men, as he was subject to orders from superior officers.

During the stay of the command at Gravelly Springs, scouting parties were frequently sent out. On one occasion company A, Seventh Illinois Cavalry, Lieut.

CHARGE OF 2ND BRIGADE, 5TH CAV.DIV. ON REBEL FORTS AT NASHVILLE. 1864

J. I. LaGrange commanding, (to whom I am indebted for the following items,) states that, returning from Waterloo to Athens, a rebel deserter, John Mitchel, belonging to the First Missouri battery, came to us on the road, gave himself up, stating that he was tired of the war, and wished to get to his home in Missouri. He said that he had been in the rebel service nearly four years, and participated in every battle of any consequence in the west, commencing with the battle of Frederickstown, Missouri, and ending with Hood's defeat at Nashville, and that during all the engagements between the two mentioned, Chickamaugua included, he never saw men fight with the cool, calm, determined bravery of Hatch's cavalry. "Why, d—n it," says he, " you all must have been drunk or mad, for you paid no more attention to our batteries throwing solid shot, shell, grape, and canister at you than you would at a four year old boy throwing stones, and every stand our battery made—and it was kept contiually in the rear—we would never have an opportunity to fire over four rounds before you all would be upon us, and we would be compelled to limber up and get out at a gallop, to save our pieces. It is the first time during my four years of almost contiuual fighting that my old battery ever failed to repulse a charge, and she has been 'went for' frequently. And you can judge whether or not I have seen any service when I tell you upon the honor of a soldier, that I am the only man left out of a regiment of seven hundred that was organized in April, 1861. There was seven of us at the battle of Franklin, but upon going over the ground at daylight the next morning after the fearful and deadly charge of the day before, I saw (and the tears rolled down the cheeks of the noble fellow as he said it) my six companions lying stark and cold, and you now see before you, to the best of my knowledge, the only living representative of that seven hundred men. And now I am going home, satisfied that the South can never gain her independence, and to try and find the friends that I have not seen, or even heard from, for over three years."

The following order was issued, and read on dress parade, at the head of each regiment.

> HEADQUARTERS SECOND BRIGADE, FIFTH DIVISION, C. C.,
> GRAVELLY SPRINGS, ALA., M. D. M.,
> January 31st, 1865.

GENERAL FIELD ORDERS No. 2:—

The Colonel commanding takes this, the first opportunity, to express to the officers and men of this brigade his heartfelt thanks for their untiring energy and loyal, devoted patriotism to their country's cause, during the recent arduous campaign. He feels confident that the labors performed, and suffering endured, through rain, sleet and snow overhead, and mud underfoot, while at Shoal Creek, the retreat to Nashville; the cold, bleak weather at Edgefield, followed by the two days' battle at Nashville and near Franklin; the cold storm at Rutherford's Creek, and in the pursuit to the Tennessee River, are without parallel in the history of this war, while your record of gallantry and bravery has been more brilliant than that of any other cavalry brigade in the United States' service.

You have done what your noble department commander said could not be done with cavalry. When a staff officer reported that General Hatch's cavalry had charged and taken a Fort, he replied, "Impossible, impossible, sir! such a thing was never heard of."

When he and his staff rode forward rapidly to ascertain the truth of this report, arriving at the first redoubt in time to witness your taking the second, with no little astonishment.

You have won for yourselves and your respective States immortal fame; you have taught the army and the world the important lesson that cavalry can fight and charge breastworks, on foot, a fact heretofore almost unkown.

The acts of personal bravery during the campaign have been numerous, too many to mention here, but all present know who those men are, and you will do important service by relating, in the presence of "skulkers," the incidents of gallant conduct in the recent engagements.

The brigade now has a name truly enviable, and it is hoped that no officer or soldier will fail to lend his entire energy to render the record still more brilliant. Let our motto be: First in drill; first in disipline; unsurpassed in soldierly conduct, and, as of late, foremost in every battle.

By command of
DATUS E. COON,
Colonel Second Iowa Cavalry, Commanding Brigade.

JOHN H. AVERY,
Lieut. Ninth Ill. Cav., and A. A. A. G.

From Gravelly Springs the command moved to Eastport, Mississippi, and engaged in recruiting up, preparatory to another grand move.

In conclusion, I must say the campaign and labors of the brigade have been endured by the officers and men with unparalleled fortitude. They have been subject to all the privations that soldiers are heir to, and without eliciting the least complaint. An army made of such materials, veterans of nearly four years' standing, can accomplish what the world never before witnessed.

I would do an injustice were I to omit mentioning the important service rendered this brigade by company I, First Illinois Light Artillery, Lieutenant Joseph McCarteny, commanding, from the time it reported at Nashville up to the present, and especially in the battle of Nashville, on the 15th and 16th of December, and in every action and engagement the men and officers conducted themselves in a cool, brave and gallant style, always delivering their messengers to the enemy with astonishing accuracy.

The Regimental Surgeons, (of whom Dr. Riggs, Seventh Illinois; Dr. Burgess, Assistant Surgeon, Second Iowa; Dr. Agnew, Assistant Surgeon, Sixth Illinois; Dr. Jones, Assistant Surgeon Twelfth Tennessee; Dr. Price, Assistant Surgeon, Ninth Illinois; Dr. Corbusin, Acting Assistant Surgeon Ninth Illinois,) whose labors were unremitting during the tedious marches and on every battlefield, to the sick and wounded, and to their care many are indebted for life and limb.

During the charges on the first and second redoubts the Brigade Band, consisting of sixteen pieces, belonging to the Second Iowa and Sixth Illinois, played patriotic airs, which enlivened the men. They then did duty in carrying and caring for the wounded.

The following names comprise the field and staff of Brevet Maj.-Gen. Edward Hatch, commanding the Fifth Division Cavalry Corps, Military Department of the Mississippi.

SECOND BRIGADE. 245

Captain HERVY A. CALVIN, Twelfth Tennessee Cavalry and A. A. G.
Major E. T. PHILLIPS, Sixth Illinois Cavalry and P. M.
Surgeon J. S. HUNT, Third Illinois Cavalry and Surgeon in Chief of Division.
Captain J. P. METCALF, Second Iowa Cavalry and A. A. I. G.
Captain WM. B. BRUNTON, Second Iowa Cavalry and A. O. O.
Captain R. KEN. MARTIN, Eleventh Indiana Cavalry and A. A. Chief of Musters.
Captain F. W. BABCOCK, Sixth Illinois Cavalry and commanding escort.
First Lieutenant PAUL R. KENDALL, Twelfth Missouri Cavalry and A. A. Q. M.
First Lieutenant E. A. DEVENPORT, Ninth Illinois Cavalry and A. C. S.

The following names comprise the field and staff of Brevet Brig.-Gen. Datus E. Coon, commanding Second Brigade of the Fifth Division Cavalry Corps, Military Department of the Mississippi.

Major GEO. B. CHRISTY, Ninth Illinois Cavalry and Senior Surgeon of the Brigade.
Captain JOHN H. AVERY, Ninth Illinois Cavalry and A. A. A. G.
Captain GEO. W. BUDD, Second Iowa Cavalry and A. A. I. G.
First Lieutenant H. B. SUDLOW, Second Iowa Cavalry and A. A. Q. M.
First Lieutenant JAS. PRICE, Seventh Illinois Cavalry and A. O. commanding escort.

LIFE AND ADVENTURES

OF

CHICKASAW, THE SCOUT,

WHILE SERVING UNDER THE COMMAND OF

GEN'LS. SHERMAN, POPE, ROSECRANS, DODGE & GRIERSON,

During the years 1861, 1862, 1863, 1864.

L. H. NARON OR CHICKASAW THE SCOUT

Biographical Sketch.

CHICKASAW, THE SCOUT.

"CHICKASAW" was born in Newton County, Ga., and is of Scotch descent. He is about forty years of age, although he looks older. He is five feet nine inches in height, with a compact, muscular frame; a well shaped head, covered with a profusion of long gray hair, inclined to curl; a full, round blue eye; well shaped mouth, with thin lips; an honest, intelligent countenance, beaming full of generosity, springing from a heart that feels for others' woes. But mark the change. When speaking of wrongs inflicted, then the countenance becomes stern and resolute—the eyes are lighted up with a fire that makes guilty secessionists tremble to behold; there is an unflinching determination of character exhibited not to be terrified or thwarted in fulfilling a noble design, no matter how great the risk. He is the father of six children, the oldest of whom is fifteen years of age. His second wife and family are living in Illinois. He has been a resident of

Mississippi for twenty-one years, where he owned eleven hundred acres of land and six negroes. The negroes he inherited from his wife, but the land he acquired by the sweat of his brow.

He served through the Mexican war, belonging to the First Mississippi Rifles, commanded by Colonel Jeff. Davis, President of the Confederacy, participating in the battles of Monterey and Buena Vista. He carried a dispatch from the former to the latter place, a distance of sixty miles, in six and a half hours, when the communications were cut. He received, for this service, one hundred dollars, from Captain Brant, A. A. A. G., on General Wool's staff. He was lassoed, on the route, but escaped with his life, by cutting the lassoe with his bowie-knife.

At the commencement of this unholy rebellion, he was found to be an out-spoken, unconditional Union man, residing upon his own plantation, and surrounded by many wealthy planters, respected by all who knew him, and looked upon as one capable of exerting considerable influence. On many occasions he delivered stump speeches denouncing the bogus Confederacy. This difference of opinion soon created bitter enemies, until his life was threatened, and it was no longer safe for him to remain at home.

CHICKASAW, THE SCOUT.

The following narrative was furnished the writer by the hero of the story. He is better known in the Union army by the name of Chickasaw, and thousands can testify to his deeds while serving in the capacity of scout:

In the spring of 1861 I secretly organized three hundred Union men in Mississippi, with the promise of nine hundred more, making a full regiment. It was my intention, at this time, to place the regiment at the service of Governor Pettis, of Mississippi, for the purpose of enforcing the State of South Carolina to adhere to the Union. Some six weeks afterward an answer was received from Governor Pettis, saying he would accept their services to the gallows. During this time the State had seceded, and the Governor soon found it necessary to organize a vigilance committee, for the purpose of subduing the strong Union feeling then arising in that portion of the State. The manner in which this committee was formed was as follows: The Governor appointed the probate clerks of each county to act as presidents of the county committee, which consisted of twelve men; the probate clerks appointed five sub-presidents, to act in their respective districts, and take cognizance of all the acts and words of the people, and report the same to the president—probate clerk. The first proceeding of this committee was—under pretence that the Confederate Government needed all the arms in the county to be placed at the disposal of volunteers in the field—to issue an order for citizens to turn over, at the county-seat, all arms in their possession, which they would receive receipts for. A number, beside myself, refused to comply with the order. The committee then seized upon all the ammunition in the stores throughout the country.

Not long after this occurrence myself and thirteen others of my district were waited upon, by six of the vigilance committee, to learn our opinions, also why we did not comply with the order, and cited us to appear, on the following Friday, at the academy. This naturally caused considerable excitement. Some protested against going, while I advised them all to attend; and we did attend, with our fire-arms in our hands. When we arrived we found the president and his twelve men present, also the six who so kindly waited upon his. They announced to the president that we were there, and would answer for ourselves. We did not have any apprehension of danger, they all being our neighbors. The president then took his seat and requested us to state our views, and why we did not comply with the order. My friends then requested me to speak for them, which I did, making a speech of nearly an hour's duration, in which I stated we did not comply because it was unconstitutional to disarm peacable citizens, and that the order was not according to law, and did not originate from proper authority; also that it abjured the right and liberty of speech. We also protested that we had committed no offence against the laws, and that was not a proper tribunal if we had. I wound up by expressing my opinion in full, telling them that what I said was the sincere conviction of my heart; that their course would ruin themselves and their children, as well as mine; that we would be a ruined people—to which my friends added "Amen!" The committee then admonished us to desist from speaking against the Confederacy, and dismissed us, leaving us at liberty to return to our homes. Some three hundred persons were present during the examination, many of them armed, but all passed off quietly. I afterwards learned that some of the committee were very much dissatisfied with the result of the meeting, and allowed that the last d——d one of us ought to be hung.

Some two weeks after this one of my friends had business at the same town, and upon arriving there he learned that there was a company forming for the Confederate army. He was by some of said company assaulted and nearly beaten to death, and had to be carried home. This caused great excitement among the Union men, and many unguarded threats were made. Shortly after this the company in town were ordered to leave and rendezvous at West Point. The majority of them concluded that it would not be safe to leave behind them myself and friends, all of whom they threatened to hang, calling them d——d abolitionists. On the night they meditated this diabolical act I was notified by our friends, and my old friend J. M. T——, who had received such a beating, came to my house to know what he should do. I will here mention that at this time no citizen could travel a short distance without a pass from the president of the committee of his district, and no one could travel a long distance without a pass from the probate clerk of the county, with the county seal affixed to it, and no man suspected of Union sentiments could obtain it. I told my friend I thought the best thing he could do was to leave the country; he answered that he could not travel without a pass. I told my wife to stand picket while we repaired to the house, when I forged him a pass and furnished him a letter, requesting him, if he should succeed in reaching the North, to have it published; I also gave him my overcoat and twenty dollars. He then left, and I have never heard any word of him since, neither has his family, who now reside in Illinois.

The threats of hanging were now put in force; two of my best friends, more innocent than myself, were hung, but, thank God, I escaped. This naturally created great excitement, and some of the most resolute

Union men expressed their opinion that now was their time—they must fight. We met and consulted together, but our condition was such that it was not deemed advisable to commence fighting. We possessed but few arms and a scant supply of ammunition, with no prospect of obtaining more in the country, and no means of communicating by telegraph or railroad with our friends abroad. We considered our case desperate. Up to this time the Union sentiment was very strong in that section of country. The news now came that a great Confederate victory was won in Virginia—the battle of Manasses, or Bull Run. This caused a wonderful change of opinion. Union men felt dispirited, while the secessionists were inspired with a new energy, proclaiming that God was on their side, and victory must follow.

I am sorry to state that many professed Union men changed their politics and became sadly adulterated with the fire of secession. People were wild with excitement, and loudly proclaimed that every d—d tory must be hung. A number of my nearest friends, who at one time flocked together beneath my banner, afterwards joined the Confederate army, to save themselves (they say) from disgrace or the hemp. They betrayed all our future pre-meditated plans. This sudden and almost indescribable change caused a great re-action. The Confederate authorities became less vigilant, and, through policy, they extended their hand to the Union man. You perceive, my friend you were on the wrong side. We can forgive you for thinking differently, but now you must be convinced that God is on our side. Our cause is a just and holy one, and we will soon gain our independence.

This kind of feeling was very prevalent, and hundreds who heretofore kept back, now boldly came forward and enrolled their names on the muster-roll. This change of feeling, particularly among some whom I considered firm in their resolve, so wounded my feelings that I became, for a while, a silent spectator, kept secluded at home, and had but little to say, though many of my friends would visit and try to persuade me to retract, to once more attend church, and take my old seat, where I had so often knelt and prayed God that the Union might be preserved.

I lost all hope of raising a force or maintaining the Union at home. In the meantime two companies had been raised for the Confederate cause, and I was offered a commission which would place me in command of either one. I rejected the offer, telling them that I would not, on any consideration, aid by any act of mine the bogus Confederacy. Even good Union men were afraid to speak to each other. Previous confidence was lost and every man doubted his neighbor.

Such was the state of affairs in August, 1861. At that time I had a heavy crop on hand to which I at once turned my attention, gathering and housing it. The country was flooded by the New York Day Book, published in New York City and supported by Southern capitalists. Persons who would not subscribe for it, no matter what their politics, it would be sent to them for six months gratis. Though I tried to remain at home, it was impossible, and, occasionally, I found myself mixed up in a crowd of people, listening to some fire eater expostulating on Southern rights, and filling the minds of the ignorant classes with falsehood and a desire for vengeance.

It was at one of these gatherings, in October, 1861, that my last and final difficulty at home occurred, which was as follows: One of my nearest neighbors, Mr. J. L. J., myself, and quite a number of others, were seated in a drug store, in the town of A——, when I asked one captain J. W. what he thought now about the war, and could he now look the people in the face, after telling them that he would be willing to drink all the blood that would be spilt in this war, and would support all the widows and orphans? how were matters now? If reports were correct there was an army of one hundred thousand men, on each side, arrayed against each other, and a great battle had been fought, at Manassas, and some six or seven thousand human beings were reported killed and wounded. These remarks so inflamed my near neighbor, J. L. J., that, springing up from his seat, he said that no one but a d—n fool and coward would talk in that style. (He was considerable of a man and, at one time, noted for his fighting qualities.) This outburst of passion and insulting language fired me in an instant, and I told him there were those around who would testify that I was no coward, and for him to choose his weapons then and there. If he would not I said that he must take it back or fight me. This created quite a commotion among the bystanders and my friends flocked to me while his gathered on his side. Bowie knives and revolvers were freely and plentifully exhibited, and there was every appearance of a collision. His friends, however, advised him to take it back, which he did, and apologized, saying, that it was spoken in the heat of passion, and that he knew that I was no coward. This ended the difficulty for the present.

Mr. J. W. J. and J. W. were very wealthy planters, and had large families of children, and a long train of connections by marriage and intermarriage. They were so connected and so mixed up that they were sometimes puzzled to tell one from the other of these families of my district. The vigilance committee were largely represented. The news of the difficulty between myself and neighbor spread like lightning through the country, and the topic was that I had chalenged J. L. J. (more familiarly called Bull Dog Jack) to fight a duel. This caused a bitter feeling among his friends against me, and they swore that I could not reside in that country—that I must die.

I had in my possession two double barreled shot guns, which I loaded with buckshot and balls. They knew that I did not fear them, and were afraid to meet me on equal footing. I still continued to gather my crop, and, by this time, had forty bales of cotton put up, and twenty-five hundred bushels of corn housed. I should have previously mentioned that I had a brother who resided in my district. We did not agree on

THIS IS THE SPOT AND THIS IS THE TREE.

politics, nor did we quarrel. He belonged to the vigilance committee and had accepted a commission in one of the same companies that had been offered to me. Meeting him one day he enquired what I intended to do, advising me to see those people who felt so bitter toward me and make up with them—that it was out of his power to assist me further. I told him that when it became so pressing that I could not live at home I should go North. He laughed and said that it was impossible for me to go North; that the lines were closed—blockaded—and that it was out of the question for me to procure a pass. (I, however, had no apologies to make, having acted on the side of justice and right.)

A few weeks after this, on returning home one evening, about dusk, and while in my stable lot, putting up my horse, I found myself surrounded by a body of armed men, who ordered me to surrender. I recognized among them a few members of the vigilance committee. They at once ordered me to accompany them to the town of A——, stating that I should there appear before the vigilance committee. I asked permission to go to the house, but no, I must go with them. After proceeding about half a mile, we came to a halt, when one of them remarked here was the place and there was the tree, and all the committee that was required was here. This strange proceeding arroused my suspicions, and I said, gentlemen, this is not all the committee. One of them remarked that they would proceed to trial. I saw among them several of my most bitter enemies and, in my own mind, decided that action rather than words would save me from their revengeful appetites. They now proceeded to go through a mock trial. They stated that many of those present were legal substitutes to fill the place of those of the committee that were absent. Here I was kind reader (imagine yourself in the same fix) without a single friend near me—my wife and family at home not even knowing where I was. Those were trying moments, for I could guess their purpose—actions spoke plainer than words—but my unbounded love for the Union, and my trust in God, made me bold and resolute. I did not fear them, yet I could not see any passage for escape.

After hitching their horses, they gathered around me and asked me if I would tell them the truth, and I answered that I would. The speaker of the party, in a very persuasive tone, then told me to tell the truth, as I had but a short time to live. I answered, I would, so far as I knew. The first question was, "Are you a Union man?" I told them that I was and always had been. Following this were a number of other questions, all of which I answered truthfully. One of them then spoke and said: "We have heard enough, bring the rope." Another then asked me if I did not want to pray, and I replied that I had not waited till that late hour to prepare my soul to meet its Maker. (I will here remark that two of the party were professors of religion.) I then asked the question, "What are you going to hang me for?" (By this time the rope had arrived but two of them said, "Hold on boys, wait a a little longer"—at the same time gently pushing the rope back to prevent its being put around my neck.) They replied, "for treason." I asked, "For treason against what?" They said against the Confederacy. I replied that I knew no such power, and neither did the balance of the world. The latter sentence aroused their anger. A portion of them rushed at me with the rope, shouting, with loud oaths, "Let us hang him, let us hang him." I said stand back, gentlemen, I want to speak. Some of them desisted and said "Hold on, boys; don't be in a hurry; let us see what he has to say."

I then thought I saw a shadow of hope. My only salvation was to divide their opinions. I commenced by working on their sympathies—if they had any—but was interrupted by many questions. I tried to reason the case with them, but would occasionally use some expression that would arouse their anger, and again and again they would rush at me with the rope. Thus I continued: "Gentlemen, you say I have committed treason. All I have done is to speak my honest opinion, what I believe to be true. We differ in opinion and you are about to use physical force. You say you will hang me on this spot. Now, for instance, suppose I had one hundred armed men here to-night at my command, and you but twelve, and because my party and yours could not agree in politics, I should say, come boys, we are strong enough to hang them, let us do it. Is there any justice or reason in conduct like this?"

This seemed to have the desired effect, so far as

abating their anger was concerned, particularly that of the two who professed religion. Then they asked me on which side I intended to fight, and I told them that I did not want to fight at all. At this one of them said, "There is no use of talking in that d—n way, we have all got to fight, and he who will not fight is against us." The same speaker continued, "Suppose Governor Pettis orders every man to turn out and take up arms and fight for their homes, then what will you do?" This was a pointed question and I knew not how to evade it. I made the following comparison: "Suppose you tell me to knock down Mr. A. I tell you that I have nothing against Mr. A.; but you say that you shall knock him down, and if you do not I will knock you down. I will say knock away then, for I will be justifiable in knocking you." At this some of them remarked and construed the meaning of my language to be that I said I would knock down Governor Pettis, which was treason, and a great military offense, and swore they would hang me. They then rushed on me with the rope. I cried loudly, "Hold on, gentlemen, hold on; I want to speak; I want to reason with you." (Reader this was a tight place.) Through the influence of my religious friends, who cautioned them not to be in too much haste, but let him speak, they somewhat relented.

I then said, gentlemen, you asked me to tell you the truth. I have done so, and for that you would hang me. Now there are hundreds in this county who are of the same opinion as I am, and if they all tell you the truth you will soon hang all the good honest men you have, and nothing will be left but a batch of liars and rascals. I have taken an oath to support the Union, this government, which every man has to do who holds either civil or military office, and he who violates it is guilty of perjury. Now I have said all I have to say. I am here and you can hang me or let me go.

As I thus concluded, one of the church members proposed the following: "Now, sir; suppose the Northern army should come down here and commence confiscating our negroes and other property, killing our children and ravishing our wives, would you fight them?" I replied, I would, most certainly. He continued, then why not fight them now? They have commenced at it already, both in Baltimore and St. Louis. I said, gentlemen, I do not believe it—we have no proof of it. He then addressed his comrades with "Come, boys, I believe Mr. ——, is perfectly honest in his opinion, only he thinks the wrong way—which is ignorance in him. He may yet change his mind, and I trust he will, for the sake of his family, and save them from disgrace.

This speech somewhat cooled their anger, and, with the exception of a few, they decided to let me escape, this time, but reminded me that I was not safe, by any means—that they intended to kill me for the insulting language used by me at the store—as previously mentioned. I then asked if they would give me any show. They replied, "Yes, all you can get," and, with this last remark, they mounted their horses and left me alone, and if ever there was a fervent thank God spoken it was then. A mind so much relieved, a heart feeling so glad, I bent my steps for home, where I soon arrived, my family little dreaming of the solemn ordeal through which I had just passed, and the narrow escape I had for my life.

I refrained from mentioning it to my family, for several days, and but little was said about it through the community, but I have reason to think that the party concerned felt really ashamed afterwards for what they had attempted, not from any pity for me, but because they had set out with the determination of hanging me and failed to do so.

Matters went along very quietly with me for a few weeks, when I was cautioned by a few friends to be on my guard—that four of my most bitter enemies were riding about, carrying their guns, watching for an opportunity to shoot me. My wife had become acquainted with these facts, and grieved herself nearly to death. Her mind was in a constant fear of my safety, both night and day. She believed, however, that I was governed by the right principles, which was a great consolation to me.

I now took my two double-barreled shot-guns, and took to the woods. I had made some effort towards trading, and offered good chances for speculation, and my neighbors at once proclaimed that I wished to steal out and leave for the North, which caused a more vigilant watch to be kept over me. While living most of the time in the woods, I frequently saw my enemies, but not in any position to my advantage to attack them. They, in turn, would see me and would refrain from attack, on the same grounds.

Thus matters stood when I concluded to leave home. There was a few of my neighbors who had always remained true to me, and among them the following, who, upon learning that I was agoing to leave the country, decided to leave with me. It was in December when we started. I loaded up two bales of cotton and started a nephew—a young boy—with instructions to go to Grenada, and I would meet him there. I knew this stroke would draw the attention of my enemies, and while doing so I would be pursuing some other road. On the second day after starting the cotton, myself, my wife's brother, and my cousin, with two others, met at my house, I furnishing the party with the necessary funds, and, at ten o'clock at night, in the month of December, eighteen hundred and sixty-one, we started, mounted. My wife's brother and cousin going one route, by the way of West Point, on the Mobile and Ohio railroad, and to join me at Corinth, while myself and friends would go by way of Grenada. (None of us had passes.) That night we made about forty miles, arriving in Grenada a few hours after the cotton, which I sold for six cents, bought some family groceries, and sent back to my family. The balance I invested in gold, paying two for one, also disposing of my mule.

When the hour arrived to leave Grenada, my two friends, seeing the great risk and almost impossibility to travel without the proper passes, concluded to return home, and, with sorrowful hearts, weeping like children, they left me. While looking around in Grenada I chanced to meet with an old acquaintance, who was not acquainted with my politics. He procured me a pass to Grand Junction. I then asked the commander of the post, Captain L. Lake, for a recommendation to travel on. He replied that I did not require one. I took the first train, and in due time arrived at Grand Junction. I at once repaired to a private boarding house, and kept myself as much secluded as possible. Citizens were closely watched and every one was liable to arrest.

While here the news of the fall of Forts Henry and Donelson reached us, which gave me cause for much joy. Not long after this news I procured a pass for Corinth, through the influence of my landlord. On reaching Corinth I found many troops stationed there, and had some fears that I might be recognized by some of my acquaintances. I was disappointed in not meeting my brother-in-law and cousin.

After remaining a few days, I finally ventured into the Provost Marshal's office, and, after presenting my two passes, enquired if he thought it would be safe for a person to go up into Tennessee. He asked, "What regiment do you belong to sir?" I answered, "None sir." Whereupon he replied, "It will be safe for you to go into the guard house," and instantly ordered me under guard and sent me there. I tried to make some explanation, but he would not listen, and I was marched off. Upon being ushered into the guard house, I found some two hundred citizens, and learned that the most of them were there on the same pretext as my own case, that of not belonging to any regiment and not desiring to join any, and were, in consequence, suspected of being Union men. Every morning we were offered an opportunity to volunteer, and many availed themselves of the opportunity, but I still protested. I had been here some ten days when the news arrived that the Yankees were coming up the Tennessee river.

After remaining in the guard house twenty-two days in all, I was taken out and brought before the Provost Marshal, who told me to go home, and furnished me a pass to travel south. The next day firing was heard at Pittsburg Landing, and the news came that Yankee gun boats had arrived and were shelling a small fort, which they succeeded in capturing that day. I still remained in Corinth, feeling secure with the Provost Marshal's pass.

In a few days General Bragg's army began to arrive from Pensacola. Troops were coming from all quarters, and great consternation prevailed, for it was known that the Yankees had possession of Pittsburg Landing. I had now fully resolved to try and reach the Federal lines. Previous to leaving home I had promised my wife that when I reached the last outpost I would write her a letter, and, in writing my name, if I made the Yankee lines, I would extend a straight dash out to the margin of the paper. If I did not I would give it a circle, which would indicate that my passage was blockaded. I felt quite confident, extended the dash, mailed my letter, and at seven o'clock, P. M., I started.

The distance from Corinth to Pittsburg Landing is twenty-one miles. At break of day I found myself three miles above the Landing, near the mouth of Lick Creek, and in the bottom, overflowing with water and full of drift wood, which I could neither wade through nor swim in. I had been fired at by Confederate sentinels four times but, thank God, escaped. After much perseverance I succeeded in wading and swimming across to the north side. I then followed the course of the river one and a half miles, when I was hailed by the picket and conducted to Colonel Davis' headquarters, where I had not been many moments when up rode General Sherman. I was then called to his attention, by the Colonel, who told him that I had just arrived from Corinth. The General then ordered me to report to his headquarters, at the bluff, where I would find a double log cabin, and there to await his arrival. His quarters had not yet been established.

I had not long to wait before the general made his appearance, accompanied by Colonel McPherson, (the late lamented Maj.-Gen. McPherson. A braver heart and more noble mind was not to be found in the army.) I was then taken into a private room and closeted with the General and his Aids, when I was questioned closely, and answered all their questions honestly and truthfully. I stated to the General all my previous troubles, and, while so doing, could not avoid the shedding of tears. The General displayed much feeling and sympathy;

told me not to be discouraged, that I was safe, and to make his headquarters my home. After being provided with food, I sat down to think over the past—my family at home—my own condition. I once more felt like a free man, while over my head was the flag, with its beautiful folds floating in the breeze, under which I had fought in Mexico. I there, on bended knees, sent up a prayer to our Father for my safe deliverance.

Troops kept constantly arriving, and in two weeks from that time headquarters were moved to the front, two and a half miles from the river, near Shiloh church. On many occasions I had been questioned and consulted by the General respecting the country with which I was familiar. He appeared to have implicit confidence in me, and allowed me many liberties not permitted a private soldier. It was he who gave me the name of Chickasaw, by which I am so well known in his army. Beside myself there was a Tennesseean, by the name of McDonald, who resided between the Landing and Corinth. Mc. was a good Union man, but had to seek protection within our lines. He was very anxious to go and see his family, but the General would not give him a pass. I interceded for him and procured one for us both. I was to proceed as near Corinth as possible, and obtain all the information I could respecting the rebels, their designs, &c. This gave me an opportunity to send a letter to my family, through Mrs. McDonald.

We reported to the General next day, the reliable information that the rebels were in force at Monterey, and were advancing upon him. The General was not disposed to believe us, saying that the roads were in such a deplorable condition that it was impossible for an army to move.

It was on Tuesday before the battle that the General requested myself and McDonald to go out and obtain what information we could. At first I felt somewhat dubious about going, for I knew they were advancing. However, I started, and we succeeded, after making some narrow escapes, in returning, the next day, with the news that the whole Southern army was advancing upon him—as stated to us by Mrs. McDonald—that Generals Beauregard, Johnston, Breckinridge and Bragg's combined forces would, in a few days, pounce upon him and completely annihilate his army. It appeared to me that, upon communicating this news for the second time to the General, he still had his doubts. He acted quite unconcerned, and I could not perceive that any preparation was made to receive them, though some caution was observed.

At this time General U. S. Grant's headquarters were at Savannah, about fifteen miles below Pittsburg Landing. On Friday, General Sherman sent out a force of cavalry to reconnoitre. They returned with the information that the rebels were advancing. Another force was sent out that evening, and had proceeded but four miles when the enemy was discovered in force, and our cavalry made a hasty retreat under fire of a battery. This report fully convinced the General that the enemy was in force and near by.

About this time an incident occurred which created considerable amusement at headquarters. About two miles from our pickets, in the direction of Corinth, resided a lady, who possessed considerable personal attractions, so much so that a gentleman belonging to the General's staff might have been seen to frequently ride in that direction. About four o'clock considerable stir and commotion could be perceived around the General's headquarters. Each and everyone's attention was directed toward the above mentioned gentleman, who came dashing into camp, apparently much excited, and minus his hat. His head and face being covered with a profusion of hair, resembling in color a flaming torch, with eyes protuding to their full extent, gave him a ludicrous appearance, and he was greeted with a general roar of laughter. After procuring sufficient breath, he stated that, while enjoying a social chat with the above mentioned lady, he was made aware of the presence of a rebel force, and, with a hasty good bye, he mounted his trusty steed and, with lightning speed, he made for camp, hotly pursued by a score or more of rebels, who did not give up the chase until checked by the presence of our pickets.

The general had two clerks, S. L. Woodward and J. W. Bame, both young men, and gentlemen possessing considerable talent. They are now occupying worthy positions on the staffs of Generals Grierson and Dodge.

The next day was employed in drawing in the pickets and strengthening our lines. I asked the General if he did not think we were going to have a fight. He replied that we would soon have all the fighting we would want. I must here remark that, in my opinion, the General is a very extraordinary man, possessing some peculiar traits of character. An early riser—eating his breakfast before sunrise; of very temperate habits; seldom using profane language; a fine military appearance; plain in his attire; exercising his own judgment; governing his actions according to circumstances; approachable by all—the private can meet him with the assurance of receiving attention, and respect, as well as the officers, (though there were times when his temper was not mild.) I pronounce him a difficult man to read, but brave and good, possessing a high military talent, with a constitution adapted to the field.

An incident occurred, while camped within six miles of Corinth, in the timber, with no tents stretched. Upon rising, early one morning, he discovered one of his headquarters sentinels asleep. The General gently takes his carbine from him, and commences to walk the beat, which he continued to do until the sleepy sentinel awoke. You can picture his consternation when he saw who was walking his beat. The General approached and handed him the carbine, mildly telling him what a great military offense he had committed, and the penalty. He left him hoping he would never neglect his duty again.

Sunday morning brought with it an early attack by the enemy, rather sudden and unexpected. The General hastily mounts his horse, and leaves for the front just as a rebel battery of six guns is opened upon headquarters. The shot and shell were thrown with great precision, killing horses and mules, and ripping open the tents. It was my desire to accompany the General to the front, but, not having any horse or arms, I was ordered by him to remain and take care of headquarters. I succeeded in getting the wagons and some other articles away. In less than thirty minutes from the time the ball opened, the rebels were charging, three deep, and within forty yards of the General's tent. I thought it high time to evacuate, and made a hasty retreat for the river, with a salute of musketry in my rear—but, luckily, I escaped.

I will refrain from making any comment on this battle. Its proceedings have been placed before the public various times, by various writers. I will conclude it by saying that I acquitted myself with honor and credit, and was highly complimented by the General and staff. From this time forward I was treated with every respect by all who learned my character.

My next adventure was the storming of the Russell House, four miles north of Corinth, on the Purdy road. I volunteered my services, along with two companies of the Fifty-Fifth Illinois Infantry, and the Eighth Missouri Infantry, commanded by Brig.-Gen. Morgan L. Smith, who so gallantly led the assault. Some tall fighting was done, for about fifteen minutes, when our boys dislodged a whole brigade of rebels, and held possession of the place. Our loss was thirteen killed and twenty-eight wounded.

Nothing more of interest occurred concerning me

until the evacuation of Corinth, two days previous to which I was present at a council of war, held at General Sherman's head-quarters, near the Russell House. The following generals were present: Halleck, Grant, Sherman, Buell, Pope, Thomas, and others. A strong debate took place, and I distinctly remember that Generals Sherman, Pope and Thomas were in favor of immediately attacking the place. It was finally decided by General Halleck, commanding the forces, not to do so, and in two days afterward the evacuation of Corinth followed, by a safe retreat of Beauregard and his whole army. After this the army divided into three grand divisions, under Generals Sherman, Pope, and Buell. General Sherman moved directly across the country to Shuwallah, situated nine miles due west from Corinth, on the Mississippi and Charleston Railroad; General Buell directed his course toward the Tuscumbia Valley; General Pope moved directly south down the Mississippi and Ohio Railroad. I now inquired of General Sherman which way he was going, and he told me to Memphis. I then requested him to let me go and join General Pope, as I was anxious to move toward home, which thought was uppermost in my mind. The General appeared to be very unwilling to part with my services, but finally consented, and furnished me with a letter to General Pope, the contents of which I never knew. I set out on foot, and after traveling two days arrived at General Pope's headquarters, then stationed at Booneville, on the Mississippi and Ohio Railroad, twenty-five miles south of Corinth. I at once repaired to headquarters, and, without being introduced, walked into his tent and stood before him. He eyed me closely, with a look of contempt, and in a gruff tone said, "What do you want here?" I made no reply, but at once handed him my letter from General Sherman. The treatment I was about to receive here did not look favorable to me just then, and I regretted leaving General Sherman. After reading my letter the General looked up at me, and in a very modified tone of voice asked me what I proposed to do. I told him I was willing to do anything in my power for the advancement of the Union cause, and that I desired to accompany his army into Mississippi, for there was my home. He dismissed me, saying in an hour and a half to report to him, and directed me to where his orderlies were quartered, to get something to eat, which I very much needed. At the appointed time I reported to the General. He then told me he wanted me to make a trip down South far enough to learn where Beauregard had stopped with his army, and to report the same to him as soon as possible. This was a trying moment for me, remembering all the difficulties under which I left home, and knowing if caught in that country again my fate was certain death. I reminded the General of all this, upon which he said, "If all that General Sherman has said about you is true, then, sir, you are the man, and fully competent to perform the task." I at once consented, fully resolved to accomplish the undertaking, or die in the attempt. Two hours were given me to prepare myself and receive the necessary instructions. The General here provided me with a splendid horse and equipments, citizen's dress, and twenty-five dollars in specie. I started, but the day being so far advanced I went no further than the outpost, and remained all night with Colonel Haskell. At an early hour next morning the Colonel escorted me outside his pickets, and left me with hearty good wishes for my success. I was now alone in rebeldom. I shaped my course southwest, and was soon keeping company with fragments of the retreating army. They all appeared to be excited, and each one was looking out for himself, paying little attention to who was going north or south. After traveling this course some forty miles I turned south-east, striking the Mississippi and Ohio Railroad near Okolona. I there learned that Beauregard and Bragg had halted their army a few miles north of here, at a place called Tupelo. I remained here twenty-four hours, watching the trains and procuring all necessary information. I then took a northeast course for thirty miles, when I stopped and put up for the night at my brother-in-law's, some six miles from Gunntown, in Itawamba County, Miss. I was somewhat surprised to find my brother-in-law here, who was to have met me at Corinth. He was dressed in the Confedarate uniform. I asked him what that meant. He replied that while trying to reach Corinth he was captured, and in order to save his neck he had volunteered. He had joined my brother's company. He said he was as good a Union man as ever, and had feigned sickness in order to be left behind and captured by the Yankees, whom he knew were coming. He expressed a wish to accompany me back, but not having a horse he finally backed out, and allowed he would go and see his family first.

I found it very difficult to travel north. Every one wanted to know what my business was. After staying here twenty-four hours I shaped my course toward Booneville, through the woods. It was reported that the Federals had advanced to Gunntown, but I did not believe it, and so continued my course toward Booneville. Previous to taking my departure from my brother-in-law's I handed him a letter and some money to take to my family, in Chickasaw County. I had arrived to within about two miles of Baldwin, where I certainly expected to find our troops, but imagine my astonishment to see before me, and not more than two hundred yards distant, a Confederate picket. I at once wheeled my horse and shot into the woods on my right. They hallooed after me but did not fire. I made quick time for a short distance, and felt quite satisfied there were no Union troops in that place. I pursued my journey, very cautiously striking the railroad again, two and a half miles north of Baldwin. I here inquired of an old lady if she had seen any of our cavalry that day. She replied she had, and that they were going toward Baldwin. I asked if she had seen any Yankees, and she said she had not, unless I was one, and she thought I was. I told her I felt satisfied that she had never seen any, for they had a horn and tail like a billy-goat, and wheeling my horse I put spurs, leaving her to her own reflections. I then made good time toward Boonville, meeting with no interruption until halted by the Federal pickets. They took me prisoner and carried me to General Oglesby's headquarters. It was then after night. I informed the General who I was, and he dismissed the guard and ordered his cook to prepare me some supper, after which he informed me that General Pope had moved his headquarters to Corinth, and that he was going there next day, and I should accompany him. The General furnished me with a blanket and a place in his tent.

I had been gone just six days, and had completely circumnavigated the Confederate army. I arrived at Clear Creek, near Corinth, where I found General Pope and reported. He expressed himself very much pleased with my services, and told me the horse and equipments were mine, which I felt very proud to own, it being the first present I had received from the Union army, and I began to have a better opinion of General Pope. I had not been in camp more than twelve hours when he sent for me. On appearing before him he told me he wanted me to go to Columbus, Miss., and to start immediately, furnishing me with all necessary instructions, and promised that if I returned successfully he would make me a present of one hundred and fifty dollars. The money was no inducement to me, but I thought I could serve my country, and was willing to try. I started next morning, and about three o'clock in the afternoon reached Blackland, where I found a detachment of the Third Michigan cavalry, commanded by Lieut.-Col. Minty. They had had an engagement that day near Baldwin, and a portion of them were then out. Just about sunset Colonel Minty put me through his pickets, and wishing me good luck left me alone.

I again launched out into rebeldom, taking a southwest course. After traveling some fifteen miles that night—it being very dark—I suddenly found myself halted, and two men emerged from the woods in my front; at the same time two came in my rear. They asked me if I was armed. I told them I was not. One of them asked, "Are you a citizen, or who in h—l are you?" I replied that I was a citizen, but did not belong to that settlement. One of the party was about to ask me another question, when I interrupted him by saying, "Gentlemen, I hope I am among my friends." One of them said, "Who in h—l do you call your friends?" I answered, "I am a Southern man, and hope you are the same." One of them, taking me by the hand, said, "We are, old hoss; but where in h—l have you been?" I told them I had been up above, after a sick brother, who had been left when our forces evacuated Corinth, but did not succeed in getting him, for I found that the Yankees were too convenient, and that I was then hurrying away from them. I asked them to what command they belonged, and they told me to the Second Alabama Cavalry. I then wanted to know if I could remain with them all night. They said I had better get to the rear and stop at the next house, for they had been fighting that day with the d——d Yankees, and they believed that they would be along that road the next morning. After leaving them I took a different road from the one they had directed me to take, and pursued a more westerly course. I traveled some ten miles further that night. I learned that the army had flanked out considerably since my last trip, and it required more caution. Next morning I took the road leading to Ellistown, but before reaching it learned that a cavalry force was stationed there. I then tried to circle it, by leaving it on my left, but unfortunately struck the outer picket west of town. They captured and sent me a prisoner into Ellistown, where we arrived about noon. I was put into a room, where I found several citizens, who had been picked up the day previous. The majority of them were soldiers who were returning to their commands. The captain in charge told me we would all be sent to Colonel Chalmers' headquarters, which was about four miles southeast from there. Upon being brought before the Colonel I stood back, allowing others to be heard, the better to frame my story. While standing there I was a silent listener to some of the most damnable falsehoods ever uttered by human tongue. Some of these soldiers, upon being questioned by the Colonel, told him they had been left behind at Booneville and vicinity, sick and wounded, where many of their families resided; that when the Federals advanced they were concealed beneath beds, in old garrets and other places; that while in those positions they saw the d——d Yankees violate the persons of their wives and daughters, destroy their property, etc. You can imagine my feelings, and God knows how I wanted to tell them they lied. And yet these stories were believed, and men shed tears, and swore by the Almighty God that they would have independence or death. It was such lies as these, in many instances, that so inflamed the Southern people against the North, and made demons of them.

I then related my story to the Colonel concerning my sick brother, and he told me to proceed on my way home. I had not gone more than eight miles when I was again arrested and taken immediately before General Breckenridge, who was camped a litte north of Pontotac. He questioned me very closely, and I related the same story. He also told me to go home. I then made a sympathetic appeal to the General for a pass, telling him that it was impossible for me to travel without one. He asked me for my County pass, and when I could not produce one he threatened to send me to General Bragg, who, of all men on earth, I dreaded most—for in his command were about four hundred men who knew me and threatened my life. I was then very willing to leave without the pass, which he permitted me to do. It was now night, and, on reviewing my situation, I found that each time on being arrested I had been carried east, away from my intended route, until I found myself on the main road between my home and the main Confederate army. I felt some alarm about pursuing this road, fearing I would meet some of my old acquaintances. So I put up all night at a plantation, where I found five Confederate officers, with whom I entered into conversation, and listened attentively to their plans. I found matters quite different since my first trip. People were less excited and all were organizing and taking up arms, making ready for another great struggle. Every one throughout the country were ordered to report at places designated by the authorities.

Now that I was so near home, (within fifty-five miles, and nearly on my route to Columbus,) I fully resolved to visit it. Deeming it unsafe to pursue the main road, I traveled paths and byroads. Night overtook me within fifteen miles of home, near the head of the Yellow Bushy River. Some five miles further on I stopped at a house, to inquire about the roads, when who should I find in the proprietor but my own cousin. He recognized my voice and called me by name. He then asked me to alight, feed my horse and sup with him. He then told me he had that day been sworn into the Confederate army. After supper I took him one side and asked him not to make public my appearance in that country, for I had been wrongfully treated, and he promised me that he would not. I then proceeded on my way home, arriving just before day. What was my astonishment to find my brother-in-law, whom I had parted with near Gunntown, on my first trip, and returning to the Federal lines. He had arrived a few hours before me, and delivered the money and letter. You can imagine the astonishment of my wife on seeing me, and my joy at being with them all again, and viewing the familiar spot where I had toiled for so many years.

My horse was sent to a place of safety, to be cared for by a friend, so as not to raise suspicion. I also sent for some of my old staunch Union friends to come and see me immediately. I found some of them wearing the Confederate uniform. My brother, who was commanding a company, and lived only half a mile from my place, was then home, gathering up stragglers belonging to his company. The following day, my cousin, with whom I had taken supper before reaching home, came over into my settlement and, in the presence of a number of citizens, announced my arrival. Notwithstanding my wife's joy at my unexpected appearance home, as soon as it was known that I was there, she became alarmed, and wept bitterly, fearing I would be assassinated. My friends kept me well posted. The second night after my arrival, a friend called and told my wife that I would be hunted for the next day, by a pack of hounds, and that my brother would be with the party. I sent for my horse, fully resolved to leave immediately. At eleven o'clock that night I met my wife, in the middle of my plantation, and there, in the presence of Almighty God, we knelt together and prayed, and I believe it was heard by Him who "knoweth all things."

The next morning found me many miles from home, on my way toward Columbus. About noon that day, I met a young man who was out conscripting negroes, to work on the fortifications at Columbus, and from that time we traveled together, arriving at the place about three o'clock that afternoon, having traveled sixty miles in the last fifteen hours. I had no difficulty in getting into town, and did not part company with my young friend until after riding around and viewing all the works. After satisfying my curiosity I repaired to the Cady House, where a large concourse of Confederate officers were collected. That night they had a grand ball, while opposite the house was a large building which contained some six hundred prisoners—Federal soldiers and Union citizens. While the Confederates were dancing the prisoners were praying and singing patriotic songs. This occurred June 21st, 1862.

The next day I called on the Provost Marshal, where I found quite a crowd who, like myself, were applying for passes. I remained some time, watching and listening, the better to frame a story for myself. It required a voucher before a citizen could procure a pass to leave the city—of which I had none. Before presenting my case I was deeply interested, listening to the following conversation, between a colonel, commanding—if I remember aright—the Second Tennessee Infantry, who desired a pass to visit his wife, then residing in the vicinity of Tuscumbia valley. The Provost Marshal, Captain Gregory informed him that the Yankees were in the valley and would capture him if he went up there. The Colonel replied, d—n the Yankees; he felt no alarm about being captured; he saw friends from there every day; that he would dress in citizen's clothes and go all among them, and find out what they were doing; and that his wife had some eighteen recruits for his regiment, and that he must go. He was granted a pass and left.

I now presented myself, and was asked who would vouch for me. I replied that I was a stranger in the place; that I lived in Chickasaw County, Mississippi; had come here with a friend, to drive some cattle, who had left the day before, without notifying me. He said how do I know whether you live in Chickasaw, or somewhere else. I then produced my papers, showing him my cotton bills of sale and receipts for taxes. He then propounded some hard questions. I convinced him that I was acquainted with all the prominent citizens in that section of country, and told him he must know we had hung all the Union men in our county. Upon this he gave me a pass to go to Chickasaw County—just where I did not wish to go at that time. I had left the office and proceeded about sixty yards when I was halted and found myself a prisoner, and was conducted back to the Provost Marshal's office. I could not account for this proceeding, and, at first, thought that I had been recognized by some old acquaintance—in which case my life was not worth a cent. However, I did not show any signs of fear, but, with a bold, defiant look, confronted the Captain, and, handing him my pass, demanded what he wanted. After looking me in the eye, for nearly a minute, he said "Go, d—n it, go; I believe you are all right." I felt much relieved, and, without further delay, procured my horse and left the city, on the north side. After passing the pickets, I bent my course east, and, that evening, struck the road leading from Columbus to Tuscumbia.

I had proceeded about thirty miles when I overtook the Colonel, previously mentioned. He was seated in a buggy, dressed in full uniform. I entered into a conversation with him, and soon found that he had not recognized me while in the Provost Marshal's office. I was not long in working myself into his good graces, and, telling him that I, too, was on a visit to the valley, after a widowed sister, whose husband had fallen while gallantly fighting under Zollicoffer, at Mill Springs. I found but little difficulty while traveling with the Colonel, as but few questions were asked me. When within about thirty miles of old Russelville, Alabama, I framed an excuse and left him. I had not proceeded far when, crossing one of the branches of Big Bear Creek, I was arrested by a Confederate picket. From all appearances I began to think matters were going hard with me, one claiming my horse, and another my saddle. I felt very indignant, and demanded them to report me to their officers. I was then taken across the stream to a house near by, where I saw some two or three officers. I then called for dinner, and requested that my horse might be fed. I saw the officers had no notion of letting me pursue my journey further. Just as we had finished dinner, up drove the Colonel, whom I had left behind. He appeared rejoiced to see me, and our familiarity had the effect of changing the suspicions of the others, if any existed and I was not questioned any further, but at liberty to leave when I pleased. On calling for my horse, I discovered that my saddle was gone, and soon learned that one of the officers, a lieutenant, had taken a fancy to it, and stolen it, and sent me his saddle and a note, enclosing ten dollars, saying that he was well pleased and that I had better leave those diggings d——n quick.

Before leaving that place, in company with the Colonel, we were told that we would not find any more Confederate cavalry on our course, but we would be liable to be gobbled up at any time by the d———d Yankees. After proceeding some two miles with the Colonel, I framed an excuse and, pretending that my course lay in another direction, I left him, taking the direct road to Russelville, about twenty miles distant, which I learned was occupied by the Federals. In passing down the mountain into Russelville I met one of General Bragg's scouts, who informed me that he had to report that night to General Bragg, at Tupello, some sixty miles distant. (This was very early in the morning, and his horse was covered with foam.) He cautioned me how I was to proceed in the valley, as the Yankees were thicker than bees in June. I felt very much disappointed that I had no fire arms. I might have taken him prisoner.

I reached Russelville without any further detention, and found two companies of the Fourth Ohio Cavalry stationed there. I informed the Captain that an attack was premeditated upon him in a few days, (which I had learned at the house where my saddle was stolen.) The attack did occur with some loss to our side. I requested the Captain to send me immediately to Tuscumbia, which he did, under guard, arriving there the same evening, and reported to General Wood, commanding the Post. The General knew nothing about me. I told him I could capture a rebel colonel that night, if he wished it done. He consented and ordered a lieutenant and twenty men to accompany me. I had, while conversing with the Colonel, (my traveling companion) learned his destination. We started, and when within one half mile of the house, a charge was ordered by the Lieutenant. The clattering of the horses hoofs over the hard gravel road could be heard twice that distance. This was poor policy, and it betrayed the ignorance of the Lieutenant, who thought he knew it all.

Fortunately the Colonel had not arrived. After the house had been thoroughly searched, the women making sport of us the while, they turned their attention toward me, and commenced cursing me, and allowed that it was a d——d lie, and they believed I was a d——d rebel too. My feelings were considerably wounded. I then told the Lieutenant that if he would take my advice I would yet secure the Colonel. After some considerable argument he consented. I then had him withdraw his men one half mile from the house, and dismount, six or eight proceed on foot back again, and so conceal ourselves near the house as to see any person who might approach. Everything being ready we had not long to wait before a buggy was seen to drive up to the house and stop. Now was the time, and at a signal the men bounded forward and secured the Colonel before he had time to get out. I remained concealed, so as not to let him see me, but at a distance I could perceive that he had shed his uniform and donned a citizen's dress. He expostulated, denying that he had anything to do with the Confederate army. We finally reached headquarters. He still protested that he was no Colonel. The General approached me and asked me if I was certain that was the man. I told him I thought it was—that if I saw his face before the light I could tell, but I did not wish him to recognize me. The Colonel still protested, until the General was inclined to doubt my word, and told me as much. I then told him, in order to convince him, that I was no humbug, and that I would confront the Colonel. I then came forward, and stepping before him and saluting him said, "Colonel, how are you?" This was a nailer; the Colonel was dumbfounded, and you can well imagine his astonishment. He at once confessed, and turning towards me gave vent to his feelings by cursing me for all that was out, telling the General that I accompanied him from Columbus, that I was a d——d rascal, and ought to be hung.

This proved a disastrous, a painful affair for me and mine. The Colonel had learned my name and place of residence. In two months he was exchanged, and he immediately went to my county, and under the alien enemy act, entitled the "Sequestration Act," seized forty thousand dollars worth of property, leaving my family destitute. The next morning I was put on board the train, and under guard sent to Corinth, to report to General Pope. On arriving at the latter place I was informed that General Pope was about to leave for Virginia. I had just time to see him and bid him good-bye. He told me to report to General Rosecrans, and he would make everything satisfactory with me. I then reported to General Rosecrans, whose headquarters were at Bear Spring. I had been absent just twelve days, having spent two at home.

I now appeared before the General, telling him who I was, where I had been, and who sent me. He took down all the items, and then said to me, "As I do not know you, sir, I will want some proof." This was a stunner. I thought of General Sherman, but he had gone to Memphis—General Pope had left for Virginia. I told him that General McPherson knew me, and who was then in Corinth. He said he was going to Corinth that day, and taking down my proper name told me if General McPherson knew me that whatever he said would be all right. The General started, leaving me in charge of an orderly. He returned that evening, and early the next morning sent for me, telling me that General McPherson knew no such name, and that I must be an imposter. I told him I knew that the General did not know me, and that I would go with him to the General. General Rosecrans then said that General McPherson knew one Chickasaw very well, and would vouch for anything he said. I told the General

I was Chickasaw—that General Sherman had always called me by that name, but I hoped that I had lost it. The General then burst into a laugh, and said I must be the man, for I answered the description, and that should be my name. He then wrote me an order, and sent me to Captain Wm. Wiles, Provost Marshal at Corinth, for him to swear me into the United States' service as a scout, furnishing me the necessary papers.

It was now about the last of June. For the following month I was kept almost constantly riding, guiding scouting parties here and there, until the army moved toward Iuka. During this time an order had been issued to the effect that citizens who would report and take the amnesty oath would be permitted to bring in their cotton, for which they would be paid in gold. At that time the country was well settled around the town of Danville, and it was surprising to see them flock into Corinth and take the oath. There was one person around headquarters who was a cotton speculator, and who kept me, a considerable portion of my time, finding cotton. On one occasion two teams had been sent out, and were returning loaded with cotton, when about two miles west of Danville they were stopped in front of one H. L——'s house, where they were captured and wagon and cotton burned, and the mules and drivers taken south. Some time after we had arrived at Iuka one of the drivers, who had been captured, reported, having succeeded in making his escape. He said that Mr. H. L——, who professed to be a good Union man, was the person who burned the cotton, and told the guerrillas to be sure and have the Yankees killed, not to let them return. At this time our pickets stationed in that section of country were very much annoyed by being fired upon after night and several had been killed and wounded. This was then reported to General Rosecrans, who was then at Iuka, and sending for me, requested me to go to Danville, and by playing off sesech obtain all the information I could, particularly concerning this man H. L——. I selected six men, well armed and attired in citizen's dress. We started, arrived at Danville the same evening, and reported to the Provost Marshal, handing him a note from General Rosecrans, directing him to furnish me what assistance I required. That same night I set out with six men and advanced to within four hundred yards of Mr. H. L——'s house. I then ordered my men to conceal themselves, while I called on Mr. L——, whom I found at home. At first he was very shy and questioned me closely, but I answered all his questions with apparent satisfaction to him. I told him I was a member of Colonel Faulkner's command, and that he had sent me here to learn what I could respecting the Yankees. It was not long before he related to me all about the burning of the cotton, fully confirming the report of the driver. He also stated that he had planned and assisted, only a few nights previous, in shooting two of the Yankee pickets, and while his two sisters were preparing supper for me he wrote a letter to Colonel Faulkner, which I was to hand him. It contained the following statement: that all the citizens in that part of the country had taken the amnesty oath, not out of any pure motive, but for the purpose of selling their cotton, and that they all had arms, which they kept concealed, and if he would only come up in that country they would all flock to his support and help to clean out Danville.

I had now procured all the information I wanted, and bidding him good night we parted. I at once rejoined my men, and sent a portion of them to arrest him and take him to headquarters, which they did. The next day, as I accompanied him to Iuka, he at once recognized me, though I had taken the precaution to change my clothes, and begged me, for God's sake, to deal with him as easily as possible. He was duly examined, convicted, and sentenced to be shot, in five days from that time. In attempting to make his escape, on the third day of his confinement, he was shot dead by the guard. I felt sorry that I had any hand in this, still I honestly believe that he deserved his fate.

About this time hundreds of persecuted Union men were flocking into our lines from Alabama, Mississippi, and Tennessee, expressing a desire to fight the rebels. The General requested me to take charge of them and organize them into companies and regiments, and also to select such men as I chose for scouts, which I was to have full control of, and be his chief of scouts. Upon conversing with the refugees I learned that they wanted to become independent companies, and fight the rebels on their own hook. This the General would not permit. They then agreed to be sworn into the United States' service, if allowed to elect their own officers. This also the General objected to. They then became disgusted, and the majority of them disbanded and left, going in all directions. I think this was an oversight in our General. I am confident that, if granted the latter privilege, I could have raised a full brigade of good Union men, who would have been very valuable to the Government, operating in that section of the country.

A few days previous to the evacuation of Iuka I was sent out to watch a female, who had been coming into the lines almost every day and procuring passes. After following her about four miles I concluded to flank out and come in ahead of her. I succeeded in doing so, and being dressed in Confederate uniform I pulled up at a house, where I found two ladies. I inquired if they had a pass issued that day in Iuka. At first they seemed to doubt my character, but after alluding to General Price's army, and telling them that I was direct from there, they felt better satisfied, cautioning me not to remain long, as I was in danger of being captured by the Yankees. They also informed me that General Price was then advancing to attack Iuka, and they were expecting a sister back from there. At the same time, on looking up the road, she was discovered coming, with a Federal soldier by her side. This was unexpected, and I now must act; so keeping out of sight I waited until they came up, when I stepped out before the gentleman, with revolver presented, and demanded his surrender. He at once complied. The ladies then beseeched me not to kill him there—that they were placed in a very peculiar situation. I drew the soldier aside and managed to inform him who I was. At the same time, unperceived by us, another soldier, (Federal) who had been following his comrade, saw the proceedings, and managed to get behind the house, and was just in the act of drawing a bead on me when I detected him. Fortunately for me his comrade saw him at the same time, and motioned to him not to fire. He thought he had a good thing. This broke up any further conversation with the ladies, and we all returned to camp. The information which I obtained respecting Price's movements was of much value, for at that time it was the impression of Grant and Rosecrans that he was advancing to attack Corinth.

Another incident occurred a few days previous to leaving Iuka. The same old cotton buyer, previously mentioned, ordered me to take two of my men and go over to a certain house on Indian Creek, and there find a negro, who would show me where there were ten bales of cotton hid in the swamp. It was nearly dark when we arrived at the plantation. Riding into the middle of the cornfield we hitched our horses, fed them, and waited until dark before advancing to the house. At the proper time we started, and when near the house and still in the cornfield what was our surprise to see several men jump up and run like the old scratch. We retreated in an opposite direction at the same time. After awhile we started again, coming from another direction, when the first thing we knew up they jumped again, "lickety scoot," while we turned, increasing our speed in another direction. Again we concluded to try our luck, but still we could not account for those men being there, nor could we tell what they were. We could see that they had arms, and also that they outnumbered us, yet there was no firing done on either side. Making a large circuit we felt confident of reaching the house this time, when the first thing we knew they were right before us, running away as if the very old boy was after them. We now concluded to wait until daylight, at which time we approached the house, without seeing our unknown friends. Upon finding the negro he informed us that his master and three sons had returned from the army, and also a neighbor's son; that they dare not remain in the house for fear of the Yankees coming upon them; that they had been run to death all night by the sneaking cusses, but they had succeeded in getting away that morning and were gone.

While out one day, dressed in Confederate uniform, I met a healthy, robust looking young man, whom I concluded to conscript, telling him I thought he had been up here so long among the Yankees that he would soon spoil, and I would take him down to the army. I asked him if he knew where I could find some good horses. He replied that his aunt, living near by, had three horses, but would not sell them to the Yankees. I let him go, not paying any further attention to him, and, returning to Iuka, reported. On the next day, the old cotton speculator ordered me to take one man and visit the lady, and, if the horses would answer for cavalry purposes, to buy them. We started and had not been at the lady's more than one-half hour when I saw, passing the house, the same young man I conscripted the day before. He seemed to recognize me and hurried away. The lady now insisted upon our remaining to dinner, which she appeared to be very slow in getting. In the meantime she had sent for the horses, when, the first thing I knew, the place was surrounded by our infantry. The Sergeant commanding the squad appeared before me, pointing his bayonet to my breast, commanded me to surrender. Of course, I complied, not feeling the least alarmed, nor could I avoid laughing. Just then up came the horses, but, when I expressed a desire to examine them, they refused, saying that I would soon have other kinds of horses to examine. We were soon ordered to move forward. I told the old lady not to part with her horses, and that I would return for them.

In a little while we were carried before Colonel ——, commanding a detachment of an Ohio regiment then guarding trestle-work, some four miles from Iuka. He received me very coldly and, in a gruff voice, wanted to know who I was and where I belonged. I told him I was stationed at Iuka. At this moment I chanced to look around, and there stood the young man whom I had conscripted the day previous, with mouth wide open, grinning like an ape. Our eyes met, when, clapping his hands, he halloed out, "That's him; that's him;" and they all felt rejoiced to think that they had captured two secesh conscripting officers. I now requested to speak privately to the Colonel, who readily consented. I then told him he was very much mistaken respecting my character, and that if he would send me, under guard, to Iuka he would find me all right. I told him, further, that I would like to purchase the old lady's horses, and take along, as it would save me the trouble of returning again, and would be fulfilling the contract for which I was sent out. Thus the matter was satisfactorily arranged, and I paid the old lady eighty-five dollars, in greenbacks, for each horse.

I was taken direct to Iuka, and then to the Provost Marshal's office, who, on learning the facts, at once released me, telling the guard that they could return, and, if they ever saw me again around their camp, to treat me to the best they had. The boys left, looking as if badly sold. I now turned the horses over to Mr. Cotton buyer, who, in a few days, sold them to the government for one hundred and twenty-five dollars, each—a pretty neat, little speculation.

It was just after the above occurred that the General ordered me to take two of my scouts and go to Bay Springs, or below, and learn the whereabouts of Price, and his intentions. We proceeded afoot, keeping the woods and by-paths, avoiding the main roads, as much as possible, and traveling day and night. On arriving at Bay Springs we learned, from friends, that Price's whole force was then north of us, and shaping his course rather for Corinth or Iuka, and we turned right about, taking the most direct route through the woods for Iuka, striking the main road within twenty miles of the latter place, and crossing it between his cavalry and infantry. We traveled all night, reaching Iuka next morning, just in time to see the main column of our army leaving for Corinth.

The General was under the impression that Price was moving on that place. A small force was left at Iuka, under command of Colonel Murphy. We at once proceeded to Corinth and reported to General Rosecrans. Myself and scouts then had a chance to rest a few days, when the news came that Price had possession of Iuka. I was then ordered to distribute my men among the following commands, which were ordered to concentrate on the Tuscumbia road, east of Jacinto, Mississippi: Generals Hamilton, Stanley and Rosecrans, while General Grant would concentrate at Boonsville. On the morning of the day that the battle took place, a dispatch was received, at four o'clock, by General Rosecrans, from General Grant, ordering him to move immediately, and attack the enemy on the south side, precisely at four in the afternoon. This dispatch was carried by L. Bennet, one of my scouts. A letter also accompanied the dispatch requesting General Rosecrans to have the following read at the head of his command: "A great victory won in the East, by General McClellan"—which was complied with. According to order, the General was on the ground at the appointed time, having marched that day eighteen miles—myself acting as guide for the General!

It is useless to comment on this batttle, further than this that, for the number of men engaged, it was one of the most stubborn and hard fought battles of the war. The General displayed unquestionable generalship and bravery, and I shall never forget the noble charge made by Colonel Mower, and his brigade, while not a shot could be heard from General Grant, eight miles distant. Dark coming on ended the bloody strife, each army holding their ground. After the firing ceased, the General ordered me to assemble my scouts, and see who was the most competent to go to Iuka. On looking around I could not find a single man. I then proposed to go myself, and left immediately. I parted from our pickets on the ridge, near two tall pines, and, after proceeding a few rods, found myself among the rebels. A number of dead and wounded were scattered around. The first one I saw was leaning against a tree, apparently suffering much pain. I asked him what command, regiment and company he belonged to, and also his name. My intention was to assume his, if occasion required, as I knew he would soon be out of the way. I had not proceeded one hundred yards further when I came upon the rebels laying down in line of battle. I passed to the rear, without being questioned—as a number of wounded and dead were being carried in that direction. I was now within one and a half miles of Iuka, on the main road which I found full of men traveling each way. I pushed on into the place, and learned that they were loading up everything, and preparing to retreat. I now turned my attention to getting back. I reached the tall pines without difficulty, and was about to pass by the picket when I was halted. They then asked me if I had any arms, and I told them they knew I never went without them. I was then ordered to give up my arms. I asked them by what authority they demanded my arms, and one replied by Confederate authority. This was a stunner. I had not until this moment discovered the mistake, for while absent in Iuka our pickets had been driven from this post. You may well imagine my surprise, but presence of mind did not forsake me, and I replied no, never, and drew my revolver. In an instant, and before I could fire, I was thrown to the ground and my weapon wrested from me. I was then marched back into Iuka, and brought before the Provost Marshal. It was now two o'clock in the morning. After being questioned I was taken before General Price, who addressed me very kindly, and asked me what number of men we had. At first I was undecided what answer to make. I knew he was retreating, and so I concluded that the bigger scare I could give him the better, and told him that no private could tell the strength of our army. He said for me to tell him what I knew. I replied, "forty thousand." "Why," said he, "You did not fight as if you had so many." I said, "General you have been fighting only the advance brigade—the main column will be up in the morning." He then asked me what force General Grant had, and I told him that I had not seen General Grant's army, but, from all I could learn, supposed he had more men than Rosecrans. He then asked me how many pieces of artillery we had, and I told him that I counted thirty-six, when we left Jacinto. He then asked me what I was doing with those clothes on, and I told him that I was the Colonel's hostler, and he allowed me to dress as I pleased. He then sent for the Lieutenant who captured me, to know under what circumstances I was captured. The Lieutenant told him that I came to the picket post and claimed to be one of them, and when they tried to disarm me I told them that I would report them to General Rosecrans—which, at the time, created some laugh at my expense. The General then said he guessed I was out plundering the dead. I replied, "No sir! You can search me." He sent me to the Provost Marshal, with orders for him to examine my person, which he did, but found nothing—for, fortunately I had thrown away my pocket book, containing papers which would have condemned me.

I was then sent to the guard house, and, at four o'clock in the morning, was started on the road toward Bay Springs Factory. The whole army was then on the retreat, as follows: Six regiments of infantry abreast, three of them on each side of the road, while the artillery and wagons kept the road. This manner of marching accounts for General Price's rapid movements—especially when on a retreat—and I firmly believe that he can beat any general, Federal or Confederate, at that game. He marched this day thirty miles and camped near Bay Springs Factory. Just before night I was recognized, by an old acquaintance, as one of General Rosecrans' guides, and the Captain in charge of prisoners—of whom there were about sixty—said that he would put me in irons.

Our guard consisted of two companies of the Sixth Missouri Infantry. I had now fully made up my mind to attempt my escape, the first opportunity. That night we were correlled on a side hill in the woods. The guards were placed around us every six paces. I laid down on the ground near by where the Captain was seated. The night was dark. As I lay there, a major, belonging on General Price's staff, rode up to the Captain and asked him what he thought the orders were, from General Van Dorn. The Captain replied he did not know, when the Major said that a despatch had been received from Van Dorn, that evening, for them to make a forced march to Baldwin, when the combined forces would attack Corinth, and capture it before the Yankees could return. The Captain then swore like a trooper, saying that they had performed their part of the programme; that while they attacked Iuka, Van Dorn should have attacked Corinth; that he had a mind to break his saber, and never draw another in the Confederate cause; that they had all the fighting and marching to do. I had had nothing to eat since leaving Jacinto, the morning before, and I asked the Captain if we were not to have anything to eat. He said he was sorry to inform me that he had none for himself—that they had had no time to issue rations. I remarked to him, in a jovial way, that if he did not furnish me with some rations or whiskey, I would not remain with him. He replied, "Nary a whiskey." I then moved, carelessly, but cautiously, to the lower side of the prisoners, with nothing on but my shirt and pants, (the nights were somewhat chilly as it was September,) and I knew that I could not sleep much. As the moon would rise about twelve o'clock, my best time was after that hour, as the rebels needed rest as well as myself. About twelve o'clock I awoke and, peeping cautiously around, discovered a sentinel, not more than twelve feet from me, and apparently very drowsy. I had previously surveyed the ground, and made up my mind how to proceed. The moment had now arrived for action. No one was astir. Gathering myself up, in a sitting position, I sprang forwaad, throwing my whole weight against the guard, clasping my arms around him and his gun, we both went staggering down the hill. I gave him no chance to recover his equilibrium. In the meantime, the other sentinels were aroused, but dare not fire, for fear of hitting their comrade—nor could they leave their posts, for the other prisoners needed watching. After staggering in this manner, for about twelve paces, the sentinel fell to the ground, and at the same time I made one bound into a clump of bushes, where I lay sprawling at full length. At this moment two shots were fired toward me, but without effect. I did not stop until I had crawled about eighty yards. I then listened a few minutes, but could hear no one in pursuit—only some loud talking and swearing. In my scramble through the bushes I, unfortunately, crawled through one of those sinks so common around camps. The danger was not yet over, by any means, as the pickets had to be passed. After moving cautiously one-half mile, I discovered the picket, who I succeeded in eluding, by crawling on my hands and knees.

I now felt quite free again, and sat down to reflect, and study my course. The moon had risen, shedding a dim light. The stars were my compass and guide. The distance to Iuka was about thirty miles, in a northeasterly course; to Corinth about the same, in a northwesterly course. I then struck out, keeping the woods, striking across the country, going due north, wading through streams, across ravines, over hills and open fields. Just as the streaks of daylight began to appear, I heard the roosters crowing. This was a welcome sound, for I was so hungry that I had resolved to procure food, the first opportunity, at any risk. I approached the house, which was a double log cabin, cautiously. A bright fire was burning in the fire place, which showed very plain through the crevices and unplastered walls. My only fear was that there were men around. "Liberty is sweet but hunger will make a man bold." The only weapon of defense in my possession was a short, stout stick, about two feet long. I entered the little gate, and was making for the house, when I was assailed by six or eight dogs, of all sizes and colors. They made a dive at me. I now had to act on the defense, and kept backing up to the fence, but dare not turn to spring over, the dogs were so savage. I then threw my stick with all my might; at the same time the door opened and a woman made her appearance, but the stick, bounding, struck the door, scaring the woman most to death. She screamed, slammed the door shut, and could not be persuaded to open it again.

I concluded best to leave. Still pursuing my course, passing through a cornfield I got some corn and watermelons, which somewhat appeased my appetite. At times I saw squads of rebel cavalry, from whom I kept hid—they were all going south. Toward evening I came to a large open field which I must cross. As I went, I increased my pace, until I was making about two-forty time. I reached the timber on the opposite side and, springing over the fence, jumped right on top of a man, who lay concealed in the grass and vines. This was quite unexpected. He did not say a word, but jumped up and put into the woods, and was gone in less time than it takes to tell it. I never learned who he was, or why he was hiding there, but concluded that he was trying to avoid the conscription.

About an hour before sunset, I perceived a lengthy column of troops, moving westward, and, approaching them very cautiously, soon discovered, to my joy, that it was General Rosecrans' army, moving to Jacinto, and by dusk, that evening, I was with the General, who expressed unbounded satisfaction at my safe return. After a good supper—food never tasted better—and some good brandy, I reported to the General what I had learned respecting the intentions of the enemy— their meditated attack upon Corinth.

The next morning the General ordered the branding of the horses belonging to the Seventh Illinois Cavalry, which caused considerable excitement in camp. The Seventh owned their horses and equipments, and this proceeding was in violation of the contract entered into by the government, at the time of their organization. This same day the General moved his headquarters to Corinth, and at once commenced to fortify the place, while I was ordered to send out my scouts on all the roads leading south, and to watch closely Price and Van Dorn's movements—which I did.

Now follows the attack on Corinth, October 3d, 1862. The enemy gained some little advantage the first day, but the second day was the hardest fighting, and in it I participated, doing efficient service on the General's staff, for which he mentioned his scout (without name) in his report, in the highest terms. I will here make some comment on the proceedings of this battle, which will not only interest the reader, but throw some light upon the high esteem in which I was held by the General.

While General Davy was being hard pressed on the Mississippi and Charleston railroad, the first day, I was ordered to go to General Stanley, commanding division to the south on Tuscumbia, and tell him to reinforce General Davy, with one brigade of infantry and one section of artillery, and for me to guide them, which was accomplished, and I entered into the engagement with them, and came near being killed by the explosion of a shell from the enemy. I then left this brigade, led by Colonel Mower, and, under a perfect shower of shot and shell, reported back to General Rosecrans that they were in position. On the second day, when the rebels made their grand assault—which was the most magnificent charge I ever witnessed, and seldom equalled—I was with the General and staff. Adjutant General Clark was shot through the right lung, when sitting on his horse, immediately in front of me. Captain William Wiles, Provost Marshal, and myself carried him a short distance to the rear and laid him down, as we thought to die. The Captain remained and I returned to where I had left the General, but he was not there, while I found myself almost completely surrounded by rebels in their desperate charge. I managed to fall back, and at the same time our fort on the south of east of the town opened, and I never, in all my life, heard such screeching and whistling through the air. It was terrifying to listen to and witness. Directly after I had left this position I perceived that the rebel line was checked, and, for a space of two minutes, they stood wavering, undecided, when the most precipitate retreat imaginable took place—every man for himself and the devil for the hindermost. I hurried as close in their rear as possible, without exposing myself to the deadly discharge of our own artillery, which was making sad havoc with their retreating and disordered ranks. On advancing some three hundred yards beyond where our lines were formed that morning I discovered several members of the Yates' sharpshooters, and among them a Captain and orderly sergeant, both mortally wounded also the brave Lieut.-Col. Morsle, who called to me and requested me to hurry to the rear and procure some ambulances to convey his wounded to the hospital. I dismounted, leaving my horse with him, and started afoot. On my way, I overtook a squad of rebels, and ordered them to surrender. At the same time, seeing a man trying to hide in a clump of bushes, I ordered him out, and recognized him as an old neighbor, then a captain in the Forty-First Mississippi Infantry. His name was Thomas Cookwood. I then returned with them into town.

Thus ended the battle of Corinth. My scouts had all acquitted themselves honorably. The cavalry was in hot pursuit of the enemy. The General's body guard consisted of two companies of the Thirty-Sixth Illinois Cavalry, commanded by Captain Jenks, acting Major.

During the last day of this battle a rather amusing incident occurred, which I cannot refrain from mentioning. A certain captain, who could be seen occasionally around headquarters, had, that morning, imbibed somewhat freely of the ardent what-do-you-call-it—commissary whiskey. Myself and an orderly locked him up in his room, thinking it the safest place for him, under the circumstances. This was before the fighting become general. After the battle ended I sought the room, with the intention of finding some "commissary." I had forgotten all about the Captain, when lo, there he lay, soundly sleeping—locked fast in the arms of morpheus. After considerable shaking, he awoke. Rising up, he commenced rubbing his eyes. Advancing to the door he looked out, and the first object that met his eyes was a dead rebel, who lay within a few steps of the door. The Captain looked, and rubbed his eyes again and again. Was it imagination or was it some evil spirit, that appeared in that shape to annoy him? Stepping out through the door, he turned to the rear of the building, when, behold! there lay another dead rebel. It was truly laughable to witness the astonishment pictured on his countenance. I shall never forget his look and the expression depicted on his countenance, after he became satisfied that it was no delusion of the brain. Looking at me, with eyes protruding to their utmost capacity, he exlclaimed, "Who in hell has been killing all these men?" I then related to him the proceedings of the day, up to this time. Upon examining his room, it was discovered that some dozen balls had entered, passing through the weatherboards. The Captain gave it up. He is no coward—which he afterwards proved by his bravery at the battle of Stone River, Tenn.

The next day cannonading was heard toward the west. I inquired of some prisoners what that meant. They replied, "They are getting h—l on the Hatchie." This became a by-word afterward among the command. I participated in the pursuit of the rebels as far as Ripley.

On our arrival at Ruckerville General Rosecrans received a dispatch from General Grant, stating that if he carried the pursuit further he would have to do it with his own command, and that he could send him no assistance. This left General Rosecrans at liberty to act according to his own judgment, and he decided to follow them to Vicksburg. On reaching Ripley another dispatch was received from General Grant, with positive orders for the pursuit to end, and for him to return to Corinth. While returning I succeeded, with eight of my scouts, in capturing eleven rebels near the Hatchie, whom we delivered over to the proper authorities.

Some time had elapsed after this when one John Logan, from Edgar County, Illinois, arrived, bringing with him a high recommendation, approved by several officials of his State, Governor Richard Yates' being one of the signatures. The General, after examining the document, sent John to me, to be enrolled as one of my scouts. I found John a truly patriotic man, with a great degree of self-conceit, confident that he could go anywhere in the Southern Confederacy that he took a notion to. I saw at once that John had but a very faint idea of the different characters he had to deal with. John was very eager and solicitous for a trip. It was not long before an opportunity presented itself. A scout was needed to send to Grenada, Miss., and John was entrusted with the trip. After making the necessary preparations, and receiving instructions, he started. Some four or five days after this, while standing and looking towards the depot, who should I discover advancing on foot but John. At first I was in doubt whether it was him or not, he had changed so much in appearance, and was really such a sorrowful looking object—minus horse, fire-arms, and his good clothes; and from the manner in which he limped along I concluded that some one had taken a fancy to his boots, leaving him a pair that were a size too small. On presenting himself before me I was no longer in doubt that it was John, and extending my hand said, "Halloo, John, back from Grenada already?" "Back from h—l?" replied John. "Well, let us hear how you succeeded, John?" "Wait till I get breath and something to eat, won't you?" I saw that John did not feel in the best of humor, and allowed him to depart. After his appetite was appeased, and he was somewhat rested, I took him into my tent, when he proceeded about as follows:

"After leaving Corinth I shaped my course toward Blackland, meeting some mounted rebels, who did not appear to take much notice of me, and I passed along, congratulating myself that I was all right. I had not proceeded much further when I was met by six more, who stopped me and commenced questioning me, after which they came to the conclusion that if I was not a spy I would make a good conscript, and ordered me to go with them. As we proceeded along they were very active in finding and chasing deserters and conscripts. Night coming on they entered the woods and camped. After building a fire and making preparations for rest the question arose, what was to be done with me? Two or three of the party declared they would not guard me, and another swore he would shoot me before he would guard me all night. Things began to look very dubious, and there was no chance of escape. I had been deprived of my arms, &c. At last they concluded to make me fast to a tree, and they proceeded to fasten my hands behind me with a grass rope, made me sit down with my back against a hickory sapling, and secured my arms to it. They then all laid down and went to sleep. After feeling satisfied that they slept soundly I commenced to work and twist, and in doing so wore the skin all off my wrists. At last I managed to raise my body up to a standing position, and while straining every nerve I twisted my head around so as to be able to gnaw the rope with my teeth, one of which became fast in it, and while in the effort to release it one of my feet slipped and I fell. I felt a sharp, quick pain for an instant, and discovered I was minus a tooth. The longer I knawed on the rope the larger it seemed to get; I succeeded, however, in freeing my arms from the tree, and crawled cautiously along on my body about one hundred yards. I listened, but all was quiet. I then succeeded in working my legs back, one at a time, thus bringing my arms before me, which was quite a relief. I soon had them untied. I then shaped my course, as I then supposed, toward Corinth. After traveling all night and the next day until evening I found myself back on the same identical spot where they had tied me. Of course the rebels were gone, but let me tell you I was badly scared. I then proceeded to a house, where a woman directed me the course to pursue, and here I am."

John thought he had traveled about seventy-five

miles, when in fact he had not been more than twenty or thirty at most. I asked him why he did not go back, after releasing himself, secure their arms, and kill the last one of them. "Well," replied John, "I'll do it if ever I have the chance again, d——n me if I dont." I thought if John was not a better man he was a wiser one than before, and must have come to the conclusion that he could not travel where he pleased. I have since learned that he has rendered very efficient service to the Government. When last I heard of him he had gone to Vicksburg.

About the time of the above occurrence General Bragg's army was in Tennessee, after General Buell, while General Price had fallen back twelve miles south of Holly Springs, and was very active in collecting forces and organizing. General Rosecrans sent for me and told me that it was necessary for him to know what Price and Bragg were doing, and asked me if I could ascertain. I told him I would try. So I resolved that myself and my best scout, L. Bennett, of Mississippi, would each make a trip, one to visit Price's and the other Bragg's army. I gave Bennett his choice, and he chose Bragg. We both started about the same time. I left my scouts in charge of Captain Cameron, Provost Marshal. I started on an old horse, with no arms, and taking pretty much the same route that John previously took, avoiding public roads as much as possible, made my way to Water Valley, north of Grenada, and south of Price's army. I there learned that Price was not able to act on the offensive, but was busy collecting conscripts, &c.

I now started back for Corinth, and found it very difficult to travel north. I procured a home-spun sack, in which I carried sufficient corn to feed my horse two days. On reaching the vicinity of Rocky Ford, on the Tallahatchie River, I was arrested by a squad of the Fourth Mississippi Cavalry, commanded by Colonel Gordon, in the following manner: upon riding up to them they stopped me, and asked me where I was going. I told them I was going to Corinth, and asked if there was not a place by that name somewhere about there. They said there was, and wanted to know what I was going there for. I replied that I was going to have some salt in that sack before I came back. They said they would put me in the army. I told them I did not care for that, but I must have some salt—that I wouldn't fight without it. They told me if I went to Corinth the Yankees would get me and kill me. I told them I didn't care, I must have some salt, that my family could not live without salt, and that some of my old neighbors had been and got salt, and I knew I could, and if they would wait until I returned with my salt I would then fight as well as any of them. It was quite amusing to hear the remarks made respecting me. Some of them allowed I was a d——d old fool, and they did not think it would pay to keep me, for I would leave the first chance I got and go after my salt —that I was of no account. They laughed at me considerable, and thought I was soft in the upper story. Finally they concluded to send me to Holly Springs, along with two other prisoners, guarded by four men.

We went about twelve miles and camped. I had bought my sack full of sweet potatoes, which was all we had to eat. It was now night, and I sat up roasting sweet potatoes and talking about my salt. At last one of them wanted to know why in h—l I did not stop talking about that salt. At last they all lay down and went to sleep. I then got up and saddled my old horse, emptied my sack of potatoes on the ground, tied it on the saddle, mounted and started. Upon missing me in the morning my friends no doubt allowed I had gone after that salt.

About noon of the second day after this I reached Corinth, safe and sound, and in four days afterwards I was rejoiced to see my old friend Bennett, who had been conscripted, just south of Nashville, by Colonel Biffle, and carried to Mifflin, Tenn. After remaining a prisoner four days he succeeded in making his escape, and reached our lines with the necessary information.

At that time Iuka was considered neutral ground, and all the wounded of the two battles were placed in the hospitals there. A lady arrived from Missouri at this time and requested a pass through our lines, that she might go to Holly Springs to see her husband, who was wounded, also three surgeons, who were then attending the wounded belonging to General Price's army, and one Captain Bond, medical director on Price's staff. I was sent by General Rosecrans to Iuka, with instructions to proceed from there to Price's headquarters with this party, under a flag of truce, accompanied by four members of the Fourth U. S.

Cavalry, (regulars.) Our conveyance consisted of one ambulance, the escort being mounted. Upon reaching Ripley we stopped to procure rest and food.

An incident occurred here which I cannot refrain from mentioning. On the west side of town resided a lady in a very fine house, at the time our forces occupied Ripley just after the Corinth fight. At that time she professed to be the strongest kind of a Union woman, so much so that General Rosecrans had ordered a guard to be placed around her house, to prevent anything being disturbed. And now comes the funny part. After alighting Captain Bond proposed to go over to Mrs. ——'s, saying she was an old friend of his. We started, and as we neared the house the lady spoken of was seen standing in the door, apparently eyeing us very closely. I had on a Federal uniform, and the Doctor, previous to leaving Corinth, had purchased a suit of dark blue. We now halted at the gate, the lady still standing at the door, eyeing us with a look of silent contempt. The Captain thought it was time to say something, and calling her by name asked how her health was. Until then she had not recognized the Captain, when with a few bounds she reached the gate, and clasping her arms around his neck exclaimed, "Why, Captain Bond, I did not know you with those clothes on; I thought you were one of those cussed Yankees." The Doctor laughed heartily, while I bit my lips and could hardly contain myself. However, such is the fact, and there are many similar cases which might be recorded, and that the private soldier can testify to.

From here we proceeded to Lumkin's Mills, General Price's headquarters, and after being detained one day we were furnished a pass by the General and returned to Corinth. I had been absent twelve days, and on my return found that General Rosecrans had left to take command of the Army of the Cumberland, and left word that I was to follow.

General Hamilton was left in command of the forces. When I informed him that I wanted to join General Rosecrans he protested he could not spare me, but requested me to remain with him and keep charge of the scouts; that a combined movement of Generals Grant, Sherman, McPherson and himself, with their respective commands, was about to be made down into Mississippi, after old Price, and that my services as a guide were indispensable. Reader, that movement would lead me near my home, which I was anxious to see, so I consented, the General promising me good pay. The army soon took up its line of march for Grand Junction, where we were encamped for a few weeks, making preparations, during which time I took two or three trips south. On one of these trips I learned that Colonel Faulkner would rendezvous at Ripley on a certain day. On reporting the same to the General he ordered me to report to Colonel Lee, commanding cavalry division, left wing of the Sixteenth Army Corps, the day before Faulkner would be at Ripley. According to orders I reported, and the cavalry moved out at eleven o'clock, A.M. That night we camped at the residence of the notorious Samuel

Street, whom I expected to capture, but on reaching the house he was not to be found. At midnight we moved toward Ripley, fifteen miles distant, arriving there just at the dawn of day, entering the town from every direction at the same time. Previous to entering the town I had learned that Colonel Faulkner had changed his programme, and instead of meeting his command at Ripley they were to meet at Hickory Flat. About an hour after sunrise we struck out for the Flat, and on reaching there we found a portion of them collected. They fired upon our advance, and then scattered in all directions. We captured several prisoners and their baggage, and returned to Ripley that night. Next day we returned to Grand Junction with over sixty prisoners, without the loss of a man. I then formed a very high opinion of Colonel Lee's military talent as a cavalry officer, and he has honestly won his star.

Not long after this the army moved down the Central Railroad. I was then ordered to report to General Lee, to act as his guide, keeping with him and taking part in all the skirmishing from Holly Springs to Coffeeville, where I received a slight wound. Previous to this, and while at Waterford, I was sent with a dispatch through to General Grant, then at Tullahoma, where I found the General, whom I had not seen since the capture of Corinth. The General manifested a warm feeling toward me, and I loved him as a father. The next day I reached Oxford and reported to General Hamilton, who had reached there with the infantry.

While resting here a few days I employed an old gentleman to make a trip down into Chickasaw County and visit my family. I provided him with a horse and equipments, two hundred dollars in Confederate money and fifty dollars in greenbacks. After being absent six days he returned with the information that my family had left, and no one could tell him where they had gone—that my property had all been confiscated. This was the first news I had received from home since my visit there while on my trip to Columbus, Miss. He also stated that they took him into a room and made him strip naked, and searched him, expecting to find some letter or papers from me to my family, but they found nothing. I received a dispatch from General Dodge, at Corinth, saying my wife and family were there, which was joyful news, although I could not tell what was their condition. I got permission from General Hamilton to go to Corinth, where I found my family in a good house, provided them by General Dodge. He had also loaned them fifty dollars and furnished them with rations, for which I shall ever feel grateful. After remaining in Corinth a week I moved my family to Memphis, where General Hamilton had established his headquarters.

The next day Bennett and myself thought we would take a ride out in the suburbs of the city and see what we could discover. We directed our course toward the south part of the city, and soon found ourselves on the Horn Lake road, and passed out into the country, without seeing any guard or picket, which I thought very strange. We met a lad riding a horse and asked him how far it was to the pickets, and how the crossing was at the Nonconnah. He asked me what pickets I meant, and I told him any that might be on the road. He again asked me where I wanted to go, and I told him we wanted to go down into the Confederacy, that this emancipation proclamation and free negro fighting had played out. He then called our attention to several houses near by and told us that at certain ones, which he designated, we could procure anything we might want, but that the people living in certain other houses, which he pointed out, would betray us. He also informed us that if we wished to cross the stream we would find a raft, just above where the bridge had been burned, upon which he had himself crossed the day previous, with the mail, and that we would find some of our pickets there who would guide us further. We then proceeded down the road, and after riding about a mile discovered some fresh wagon tracks, which led me to suppose that some smuggling was going on. We now increased our speed, thinking that we might overtake the wagons before they could reach the creek. As we came in sight of the creek, which was about three hundred yards in our advance, we discovered two men walking toward us, and on meeting them I asked if they had met any wagons. They answered they had just assisted them across the creek and up the opposite bank. They then asked where we were going. I told them I did not wish to say where we were going, but they insisted upon knowing, and I told them we were going into the Southern Confederacy, in quest of friends, that the emancipation proclamation did not agree with our politics. As I concluded this speech I perceived that their countenances brightened up, and one of them remarked that it would not be safe for my friend to go down to the creek with blue pants on, but that I might go, and after stating my business to the pickets I could then return for my friend. I asked them where they were going, and one of them replied that he was going to Memphis to take the oath of allegiance, so that he might buy himself a revolver, after which he was coming back home to shoot a d——d Yankee for stealing his father's horse. I then dismounted, and leaving my horse with my partner I proceeded on foot towards the creek. I carried a revolver, which I kept concealed from view. As I came up to the crossing I saw two men standing upon the raft, one an old and the other quite a young man. To all appearance neither of them carried fire-arms. I inquired if they could take two men and two horses across the river, and they replied that they could. I then told the old man that I wanted to find some Confederate soldier who would convey me into their lines without running any risk of being shot by our Confederate or any other forces. The old man, after a hearty laugh, introduced me to his companion as a sergeant belonging to Major Blye's battalion, and who, extending his hand, greeted me warmly. I asked him to walk with me upon the bank, to which request he consented. After proceeding a short distance I drew my revolver, and presenting it at him ordered him to proceed at once to Memphis. A moment after my ear was startled by the sharp crack of a rifle, and at the same instant a ball whistled past my head, clipping my hair. I then ordered him to quicken his pace, and in a few moments we had come up to my comrade, and mounting my horse I persuaded my prisoner to quicken his speed. Before reaching the city we overtook the two men whom we had previously met, and I at once arrested them both, which somewhat surprised them. One of them allowed that he was all right, anyhow.

Upon arriving in South Memphis, I dismounted and, turning my horse over to my partner, told him to take care of him. We were decidedly a rough-looking set of men. My comrade's revolver, and my own, were fully exposed to view, which fact was noticed by a citizen, who stood, a short distance off, a silent spectator. As it afterwards appeared, he came to the conclusion that we were a portion of some guerrilla band, and away he started, as I afterwards learned, to General Veitch's headquarters—who was then commanding the post—and reported his suspicions. The General at once ordered a squad of cavalry to proceed and arrest the last one of us, requesting the citizen to act as guide, and conduct the cavalry to where we might be found. In the meantime, I had started my prisoners toward General Hamilton's headquarters, to report to him. On arriving at the General's headquarters, he had given me a note, directed to General Veitch, to whom I was to report. I at once started, with my prisoners, for General Veitch's headquarters. Arriving in due time, I reported to the General, handing him the note from General Hamilton. After reading it, he turned toward me and laughed very heartily, at the same time ordering me to bring in one prisoner at a time, in order that he might examine them separately. One of them stated to the General that he belonged to the Union army, telling the number of his regiment. At that moment a colonel announced himself, who at once recognized the prisoner as a member of his regiment, and, looking the man sternly in the face, asked him what in h—l he was doing with those clothes on. The Colonel then told the General that the man had deserted his regiment some fifteen days previous. This man was put in irons, after which he confessed his guilt. The other two were sent inside of the fort.

Reader, about this time there was great dissatisfaction in our army, owing to the emancipation proclamation, and hundreds were deserting our cause, and horse stealing, robbery and murder were common occurrences in the City of Memphis at that time.

After the prisoners were disposed of, the General told me that he had sent out a squad of cavalry, who had found and arrested my partner, and, after examining him, and finding certain papers upon his person, he had ordered his release, and had sent him to act as guide to a squad of cavalry which he had ordered to proceed to the Nonconnah and destroy the ferry. The General then gave me my orders, which were to hunt up and arrest every d—n deserter from the Union army

I could find, every horse thief and smuggler, and every citizen caught aiding deserters, or in any way violating the authority of the United States—and I assure you that Bennett and myself had our hands full for the following two months.

After arriving at home, that evening, I was glad to meet my friend, who had made a successful trip to the Nonconnah, destroying the ferry, &c. It had become necessary very frequently to go outside of the lines.

On one occasion, Bennett and myself were requested by the General to go down south of the Nonconnah, and, if possible, ascertain were Major Blye's command was camped. The next morning we started, on foot, and proceeded to the neighborhood where we supposed he was camped. About three oclock, in the afternoon, we found ourselves some fifteen miles from Memphis, seated on a log, in the timber, and near us was a small stream of running water. We had not been sitting more than ten minutes when we heard a rustling among the leaves. On looking to see whence it proceeded our sight was greeted by the presence of three Confederate soldiers, who were advancing toward us, each presenting a gun at us. Seeing that resistance was useless, they having the advantage of us, we delivered over our firearms, and were at once marched toward camp, which was about one mile and a half from where we then were. After proceeding about a mile, and being some ten paces in advance of my partner, and guarded by two of the men, the third keeping company with Bennett, I had just crossed over a fence and advanced some six or eight paces, when I was startled by the report of firearms. On looking around I heard another report, and, at the same moment, one of the men at my side fell. I caught hold of the gunbarrel of the other man, who was just in the act of firing at Bennet, and commanded him to surrender which he did. After disarming them I found that one was shot in the back of the head and the other in the shoulder. The third person was now our prisoner, and we at once made him wheel right about, and, on double quick time, retraced our steps, arriving in Memphis, about midnight, safe and sound. We had learned all that was required respecting the camp, and, under the circumstances, had been quite as near as was desirable.

I have omitted to tell an incident which occurred during the first two weeks after our arrival at Memphis, from Corinth, which was as follows: Bennett and myself started out one morning, with the intention of proceeding to Nonconnah Creek, for the purpose of discovering the crossing of contraband traders. After following the course of the creek for the distance of seven miles, we discovered a party of rebels busily engaged in building a flatboat. After reconnoitering, we withdrew, unobserved, and decided not to attack them—they being too numerous—and retraced our steps toward town. On arriving in the suburbs, on the south side, we saw two gentlemen approaching us, mounted on very fine horses. When within about sixty yards I observed one of them raise his hand to his mouth and, with his teeth, pull off his glove. This act at once aroused my suspicions, and I told my comrade to take the opposite side of the road, which would, on meeting, place the gentlemen between us. Just as they came up, I drew my revolver and, in a resolute voice, ordered them to halt, which they did instantly—my partner also ordering his man at the same time. One of them turned very pale, and hesitated, which led me to think that he would either make an effort to escape by flight, or draw his revolver, upon which his hand then rested, but, luckily for him, he did not make the attempt. I then demanded of them who they were, and they replied citizens. I then asked if those were government horses they were riding, and they answered no. I then inquired their name, which they, hesitatingly, told me, also stating that they lived two miles from town. I knew better than that, and did not hesitate to tell them that it was a falsehood, for there were no such men living in that place. I then asked them if they had any arms, and one of them said no, while the other, with some hesitation said yes, he had a small repeater. In the meantime my comrade stepped out into the center of the road before them, at the same time keeping his revolver pointed toward them. I continued to ask questiens, inquiring if they had any papers, and intimated that I thought they would make good soldiers, and I should be compelled to take them down into Mississippi, upon which one of them replied that he belonged to a command down in Mississippi, and was now at home on furlough. One of them produced a memorandum book, which I took, and the first thing that met my eyes was a discharge from the United States army. I then looked the man sternly in the face, asking him his name. He told me his name, and at the same time, I turned over another page of the book and saw it written in full, Captain S———, Chief of Detectives. Without further questions I returned to him his book and told him to keep his revolver—that I thought he was all right. We then allowed them to proceed, which they were not slow to do, and, putting spurs to their steeds they were soon out of sight, thinking, undoubtedly, that they had made a narrow escape. However, I felt satisfied in my own mind that they were all right. The name and position occupied, as written in the book, convinced me. The name I did not pretend to see, betraying every sign of ignorance in regard to reading.

We now proceeded to our homes, tired and hungry, resolved to make a report the next morning of our trip. Next morning Bennett and myself left home and directed our steps toward the Provost Marshal's office, where I found Lieutenant Bryan, Acting Assistant Provost Marshal, with whom I was well acquainted. While reporting to him about the boat, &c., some person had approached me, from behind, and the first intimation he gave me was a light tap on the shoulder, at the same time announcing that I was the same d—n scoundrel who had arrested him the evening previous. The Lieutenant then burst into a loud laugh, after which he told the gentleman that if I was the man who arrested him he did not wonder at it, for I would arrest the very devil himself if I should meet him. The Lieutenant then informed the gentleman that I was General Hamilton's Chief of Scouts. After this Captain S. treated me very kindly, invited me to his office, introduced me to several of his detectives, and told them that I was the cause of all the excitement, confusion and alarm in the last twenty-four hours. Until then I had not become acquainted with the particulars, which were really amusing. It appears that after the Captain and companion departed from us, they, with all speed, took a circular route into town, and at once deployed all the police force through the town, and several squads of cavalry were sent out, to hunt up and bring to his headquarters the persons of two desperadoes. I assure you I enjoyed the joke as well as the good brandy that was being freely offered and drank.

General Veitch had informed me that in all cases of emergency, where it required immediate action, and I needed assistance, in the shape of cavalry or provost guards, that the commanders of those detachments were instructed to furnish me the required force. The day after the above occurrance I was ordered to take a detachment of cavalry and proceed to the Nonconnah Creek and destroy the boat, which was successfully accomplished.

At this time it was impossible for a person to keep a horse or a mule, there were so many thieves in the place. My comrade, Bennett, had become intimate with a gang of them. On a certain night they were to make the attempt to steal the horses of Company A,

Thirty-Sixth Illinois Cavalry. Bennett informed me of this fact, and I went and informed Captain Willis, commanding the company, who at once made disposition to arrest them. At ten o'clock that night his guard succeeded in arresting three of them, but not until they had unhitched six or eight horses. This horse thieving was only a specimen of what occurred nearly every day.

I will now relate an incident that occurred during the first week in March, 1863. The reader will understand that for two months Bennett and myself had been operating in the city and vicinity, running many narrow escapes from persons who knew us and against whose interests we were working. On one occasion I chanced to meet some Confederate soldiers, numbering fourteen, two of whom were lieutenants. I had been drinking quite freely with them, and professed to be as good a rebel as any of them. My intention was to arrest the whole of them, but, unfortunately, one of the party recognized me and it was soon whispered among them who and what I was. Soon one of the party approached me behind and, unperceived, struck me on the back of the head, which felled me to the floor, where I lay, insensible, for nearly two hours. Upon recovering my senses I found myself alone, every person having disappeared, and, strange to relate, until this day I have not seen one of them to recognize them.

My friend Bennett, when reporting these occurrences to General Veitch, had been fired at, by some unknown enemy, and narrowly escaped with his life, and the

General very kindly advised me to leave the city, for a time, as my life was threatened, and I might be assassinated. Acting upon the General's advice, I was furnished transportation for myself and family to St. Louis, and, in the latter part of March, left for a more northerly clime, where I hoped to find friends. My wife was in very feeble health, produced by exposure to all kinds of weather, while stealing her way through the Confederacy into our lines. While on our trip to St. Louis, I had six hundred dollars stolen from me, leaving in my possession only forty dollars with which to locate my family, and that among strangers. The loss of nearly all my money was a sad stroke upon my wife's feelings. Her health had grown worse, since our departure from Memphis, and, four days after our arrival at Girard, Illinois, my dearly beloved wife died, leaving six motherless children. Pen cannot describe a father's feelings at this sudden and unreplaceable loss. I felt as though my last earthly hope was gone. I was a stranger in a strange land, reduced to poverty. But who should care for my children? This thought inspired me with a new feeling, and I resolved to try and care for them, and, with the help of God, assist my country too. After remaining in the State of Illinois a short time, I left my children in charge of a widowed sister.

I will now refer to my old chum and friend Bennett, who left Memphis, shortly after I started for Illinois, for the purpose of bringing in his family, who were then residing in the interior of the State of Mississippi. On my return from Helena I found him, he had just returned and was unsuccessful in getting his family through. It was not long after my return from up the river when I received a telegraph despatch from General Dodge, then at Corinth, commanding left wing Sixteenth Army Corps, requesting me to come at once if not engaged. At first I was undecided, being at this time in the employment of General Veitch. I had also, some time previously to this, received the following letter which is a true copy—

>HEADQUARTERS FOURTEENTH ARMY CORPS,
>DEPARTMENT OF THE CUMBERLAND,
>MUFREESBORO, TENN., Feb. 15, 1863.

MR. ——.

SIR:—I am requested by Captain William M. Willis, Provost Marshal General to Maj.-Gen. W. S. Rosecrans to write to you, that he would like to have you come to this army on special service, if not particularly engaged. If you can come do so without further delay or writing. He remembers your scouting at and around Corinth.

Yours very truly,

JOHN FITCH,
Provost Judge.

I soon decided to report myself at Corinth. Arriving at the latter place the next day and immediately reported myself to General Dodge, who requested me to take charge of his scouts. On seeing them I at first declined, they were not the kind of men for the business. I told the General if he had anything that myself or my friend Bennett could perform, that all he had to do was to command and we would undertake the job ourselves without the assistance of others. The General then told me that he wanted me to go down into the State of Mississippi and make arrangements so that he could receive from me papers every week—the Mobile Register, Augusta Chronicle, and Memphis-Grenada-Jackson-Atlanta-Appeal. Myself and Bennett started afoot, shaping our course south until we arrived into the interior of the State of Mississippi. I sent one man to Atlanta and one to Mobile, with instructions to take cognizance of the enemies' works, force and so forth, and procure the papers weekly. Myself and Bennett were visiting the latter's family; the most of the time being spent in the woods, to avoid being seen, where we had our meals brought to us. While remaining in this vicinity, General Rhoddy's command was moving down from the Tuscombia valley to join Chalmer, Ferguson and Lee at Okolono, Miss., then to move on toward Memphis and strike the Memphis and Charleston railroad, between Corinth and La Grange. I immediately sent a courier through to General Dodge who gave him notice of this contemplated move, which resulted in a Union force meeting the enemy at the Tallahatchie, near Rocky Ford, and severely repulsing the enemy; the road was not injured. This was in June, 1863. While yet remaining in that section of country an incident occurred of rather an amusing nature. I had learned that not more than eight miles from there was a gun shop which was repairing arms for Captain Warren, C. S. A., whose camp was about one mile from the shop. I at once decided to destroy it, and, accompanied by Bennett, started and succeeded in approaching to within one half mile of the shop. About one hour before sundown we had gained an elevated position so that we could perceive any movement made around the place. We discovered three cavalrymen, who remained until dark. After which time we concluded to advance and see if the cavalry had left; if there should be only three we felt confident we could overpower them if surprised.

After reconnoitering the premises closely, we could not see any signs of the cavalry. They had either left with their horses, or else had sent them away and were themselves in the house. I proceeded to the back door, which was wide open; my friend remaining in front, with a revolver in one hand and a shot gun in the other. I mounted the steps and saw a large mastiff standing in the open door, looking in at the darkies eating, who were gathered around a large table. I had not attracted the notice of the dog, and my mind was at once made up what to do. With one bound I landed behind the dog, at the same time allowing my foot to come in contact with his extremities, which had the desired effect of landing him under the table, where he commenced to growl, bark and bite. My unexpected appearance so frightened the niggers that they scrambled in every direction, screaming murder, murder, upset the table, breaking the dishes, and adding to the noise and confusion still more. I did not stop to see what mischief I had done, but, opening a door on my right, found myself in the presence of an old gentleman, his lady and son, a young man belonging to the Confederate army, and, by order of Captain Warren was detailed at this place to repair arms. I immediately ordered them to surrender, which they did, without any hesitation, but with wonder and astonishment depicted on their faces. They could not imagine what this intrusion meant. I told them to remain quiet and I would not harm them. They allowed that they had done nothing that they were afraid of, and thought it strange that one of their own men should visit them in such a manner. I then ordered them outside the door, where my partner took charge of them, ordering them to take the position of soldiers. I told them that Major Ham (Confederate army) was very much dissatisfied with them for trading and selling cotton to the Yankees, and that he had ordered me to come here and obtain the proceeds that they had received for it. Also to arrest them and seize upon all arms and ammunition they had about the premises. Also that Captain Warren was under arrest, and his command superceded by Major Ham. The old lady replied that the cotton she had taken to the Federal lines belonged to Captain Warren, and that she had paid the proceeds to him. I then permitted the old lady to enter the house, when she handed me three revolvers and one shot gun. We next proceeded to the shop, where we found ninteen muskets and shot guns, which I ordered the old gentleman and son to load themselves with, myself and Bennett taking the remainder.

We all, except the old lady, proceeded toward Captain Warner's camp, but, after traveling one-half mile, I concluded I had gone far enough in that direction, and the old gentleman and son desiring to return home for some blankets, I permitted them to do so, after they had pledged their word to report to Major Ham's camp, at seven o'clock next morning. We were now alone, and at once left the road, crossing a cornfield, until we reached a low bottom land, where we buried the guns in the mud—and there they undoubtenly remain until this day. From this place we made all haste back to our old section, and, the next day, sent an old man down into the vicinity of the gunsmith's, to ascertain what effect our visit had produced.

The old gentleman returned, in due time, and stated that the father and son had reported at camp, according to promise, but found Captain Warren still in command, and that he knew nothing about my Major Ham, and told the grieved party that they had been badly fooled by two d—n home made Yankees.

In the meantime, my newspapers, for which I had subscribed and paid for six months, had arrived at the post office, and my friends had arrived from Mobile and Atlanta, and all intermediate points, bringing all the necessary information. I now established a line of couriers, to ply between the post office and to within fifteen miles of Corinth. I also had plenty of Confederate money, having captured the Sheriff and County Treasurer of Franklin County, Alabama, who had in their possession fourteen thousand dollars. I expended this money freely among my scouts and couriers. The reader can perceive by this that there must have been good Union men residing in the South, without whose assistance many of my plans would have proved failures. While laying out in the woods, waiting for my scouts to report, my meals were brought to me by a young lady, and I promised that, if she would come to Corinth, her services would be rewarded.

I now had everything arranged to my satisfaction, and left for Corinth, which was sixty miles north, traveling all the way through the woods afoot, arriving on the second day of July, making the trip in forty hours, and reported to the General who was much pleased. He again requested me to take charge of his scouts, numbering fifteen, and to increase them to twenty-five, which I did. About one half of them were citizens, who were residing in the County, and the other half soldiers detailed from the ranks. My next plan was to establish three more lines of couriers, in different directions, whose business was outside the lines, not to come unless ordered to do so. I have every reason to believe that General Dodge, at this time, had better facilities for being posted than any other general in the Union army.

In the meantime, the young lady I have previously spoken of, made her appearance in Corinth. I knew of no better way to remunerate her than to offer her my heart and hand, which she, at once accepted—God bless her—and has, so far, proved a good, faithful wife and step-mother. An amusing incident occurred on the day of my marriage. Some of the boys came to the little frame house I was then living in, and, without waiting to see me, called out that Colonel Mercer, then commanding the post, in the absence of General Dodge, required me to saddle my horse immediately. I learned the boys were trying to play off a joke on me. About ten o'clock, that same night, an orderly came with the same message, but I paid no attention to it. Not long after this another came, knocking at the door. This annoyance began to bore me considerably, and I jumped out of bed and opened the door, expecting to see the fellow, but he did not wait, and I could not see who it was. I called after him, "Tell the Colonel to go to h—l." I had hardly got in bed before another rap, rap, rap, came, on the door, and a voice calling me said that the Colonel wanted me to come right away— and if I did not I had better. I at once opened the door and, shure enough, there stood the Colonel's orderly.

This was no joke. I was soon dressed, and reported myself to Colonel Mercer, who I found not in the best of humor, and, in broken English, he wanted to know, "Vat for, py God, you no report yourself to me, when I sends vor you? Ah, py God, and you keep me waiting all de hole night, py God. I sens my orderly some two, three times, and you no comes, py tam. I no like dis, and I vants to know de vy you tells mine orderly to say to me go to h—l, eh? Vat for you say dis? Ah, py God"—and thus he continued for some time. At last he told me he wanted a guide to send out with a scouting party, which order I filled in a few minutes. The next day I called on the Colonel, and explained to him why it was that I did not obey his orderly—that the boys had been plagueing me because I had only that day got married. This was a proceeding the Colonel had known nothing about, and when I finished he said, "So you gets married, eh? Vell, dat ish goot. I forgives you dis time, and hopes you have lots of little poys. Now we takes a drink of brandy. So good day"—and I left the Colonel in the best of spirits.

My position was of such a nature, at this time, that I had but little chance to participate in many of the scouts or raids, made into the enemy's country. Having twenty-five men under my immediate command and control, subject to no orders, except what came from myself; (I was at liberty to discharge and employ my men;) keeping my own books, without the help of a clerk or orderly; attending to the wants of my company for commissary and quartermaster stores, ordnance, camp and garrison equipage; making out of pay rolls, and receiving funds for paying my men—no one of whom got less than one hundred dollars a month; kept me constantly employed. I would have as many as eight scouts out at a time, operating in various directions, and be receiving reports daily, which had to be handed in at headquarters by myself. When I did absent myself I appointed a suitable man to conduct the business. I felt proud of my position, and my commanding officer, Brig.-Gen., since Maj.-Gen. Dodge, one of the bravest of the brave, was one who could appreciate valuable services, when rendered.

Twice a week I had to send scouts to communicate with the gunboats at Pittsburg Landing, twenty-one miles north. On the other hand, I had to have scouts out whose business it was to communicate with my outside cousins, fifteen miles from Corinth, bringing in the Southern papers, which kept about one-half of my men out all the time. In this way was business conducted most successfully, from July 1st, 1863 until November of the same year. Not unfrequently during this time have I taken ten or a dozen men, when learning of some rebel rendezvous, and surprised the enemy in their camp, and almost invariably with success. I must omit giving attention to a hundred or more incidents which occurred while scouting—they are too numerous to mention, and would occupy too much space. I will relate a few of the most startling and interesting ones.

About the last of July, having learned that a party of guerrillas and bushwhackers were making their headquarters at a certain house on Brown's Creek, some thirty miles south of Corinth, near Bay Springs, I resolved to capture them, although I could only take six of my men, the most of them being absent on duty. One morning, just as daylight began to appear, we started, riding all day, and arriving at the vicinity of our destination about four o'clock. After reconnoitering and satisfying ourselves as to their position, we charged their camp. It was a complete surprise, we, however, captured but two prisoners, and five horses—the rest being absent on a scout. We destroyed their camp and garrison equipage. It was now near sundown, and we learned, from reliable sources, that not more than two miles distant, there were camped some twenty-five Confederate Cavalry, who had only come into that section of country the day previous.

After talking the matter over, we came to the conclusion that we would retrace our steps toward home, taking the two prisoners along, and also a few extra horses, our own being tired and hungry. We must also procure corn for them before dark. After reaching the Tuscumbia and Fulton road, we crossed a bridge and turned into the woods, proceeded about four hundred yards and, dismounting, unsaddled and fed our horses, intending to remain at that place until midnight. Our arms, on this occasion, consisted of three double-barreled shot-guns and three fine shooting rifles, and two navy revolvers, each. Feeling confident that we would be pursued, I determined to fight them in their own style that night. After waiting about one hour we prepared for action. Leaving one man to guard the two prisoners and all the horses, with instructions if either of the prisoners tried to escape or made a noise to shoot him on the spot, we started for the main road. On reaching it, we selected a favorable position and laid down. We had not been waiting long when we heard the enemy approaching, as they crossed the bridge. Judging from the noise they made in crossing it, we supposed there were about fifteen of them. As they advanced to within about forty yards I halted them. They obeyed instantly. I then asked them to what command they belonged, and they answered to Major Ham's, at the same time inquiring to what one we belonged. I answered Rhoddy's, and, in the same breath, gave the word to my men to fire, which they did, pouring in a volley that somewhat disturbed the stillness of the night, and created a complete stampede of men and horses—some turning into the timber and others recrossing the bridge. All soon became quiet again, with the exception of a loose horse, stumbling over the fallen timber, and the groans of the wounded. Without changing our position, we reloaded our guns, and had been waiting about half an hour when several were seen to approach again, from the same direction. Halting at a more respectful distance they commenced to call loudly, and the following dialogue ensued:

"Halloo, there."

"Halloo."

"What in h—l do you mean?"

"You don't come that on me. You are the d—n Feds that went down the road this morning."

"No, by God, we are Rebels, and belong to Major Ham's command. You must be d—n fools."

"If you are Confederates, three of you advance."

(Three of them advanced to where they had been fired into and halted.)

"Dismount, and advance afoot."

"No, that is not right."

"I believe you are the d—n Yankees who went down the road this morning."

"No sir, we are pursuing them. They captured two of our men, this evening, five miles from here."

"Advance."

"No, one of you advance."

At this, I ordered the boys to let them have it, and we all blazed away—which caused another stampede. Very soon all became quiet again. The night was intensely dark. We again reloaded our guns, and all was ready. My attention was now attracted by a noise in the bush, on our left, which impressed me with the idea that a flank movement was going on. At the same time a voice was heard, coming from the direction of the bridge, to which I paid no attention. One of our men remarked that he would go and see what that groaning meant in our front. He had no sooner said it than a volley was poured into us from our left, which made things rattle around us. We instantly returned the fire, and a general fight ensued. Emptying our guns and revolvers, we silenced the enemy, and then began to fall back slowly, for about sixty yards, when we again took a position and loaded our guns and revolvers. Remaining quiet, we could now hear them coming out of the bush into the road, near the same spot we had left. One of them remarked that he reckoned they had given us h—l; to look sharp for he believed they must have killed some of us. At this I told the boys to let them have it, and away went another volley—and away went the rebels. We could not hear or see any more of them that night, and, returning to our horses, found our prisoners all right.

It being now midnight, we saddled up, mounted and started, arriving in Corinth the next morning. A few days after this occurrence, we captured two of Major

Ham's men. Upon questioning them about General Rhoddy's men, they replied, d—n Rhoddy's men; that they had had a fight with them the other night, and that two of their men had been killed and three wounded and five horses killed; that they were a set of d—n fools. This news pleased me very much and I did not dispute it.

About this time, there was a band of guerrillas, commanded by one Dr. Smith, who operated between Corinth and the Tennessee River. They became a terror to the Union inhabitants of that vicinity. The leader was a brave and desperate man. My instructions from the General were to break up the band, if possible. They had captured two of my scouts, while they were bearing dispatches to the Tennessee River, one of whom escaped, but the other I have never heard frome since. I now selected seven of my men, and, all being well armed, we started out, mounted, for their rendezvous, determined to give them battle, at all hazards, if found. After proceeding about fourteen miles, on the Hamburg road, we halted, dismounted, and, after concealing our horses, took up a position at a cross-road, where we remained all night, expecting them to pass that way. As they did their traveling in the night, and morning came without the guerrillas making their appearance, we mounted our horses and rode about a mile to a plantation, where we procured breakfast. We had just concluded our meal, and the order had been given to prepare to mount, when we discovered Dr. Smith, and seventeen of his men, advancing, following our trail. My men fell into line as quickly as possible, while shots were being rapidly exchanged from both sides, at not more than than two hundred yards. Dr. Smith, leading his men, ordered them to charge. I now had my men in line, and ordered them to charge, both parties firing and yelling like Indians. This movement was rather unexpected by them, and was made with so much determination, that they broke and fled in all directions, leaving on the field two men wounded—one of them mortally, and we also captured five guns. I had one man wounded, but not seriously. After caring for the wounded, we started for Corinth, but not by the direct road, which, had we taken, would have proved fatal to us—as I afterward learned that Dr. Smith rallied ten of his men and took a position on the direct road to Corinth, expecting us to pass that way. Neither party was satisfied with the result of this fight, and Smith was still at large.

It was now my intention to start out with a larger force and pursue Smith to the death; but before I was ready to start the Seventh Illinois mounted infantry, Colonel Rowett, commanding, while on a scout had come unexpectedly upon Smith's band and completely broken it up, Smith narrowly escaping. He left the country for other parts.

Myself and six of my men started out mounted, all dressed in Confederate uniform and armed to the teeth, directing our course toward Fulton, Miss. After riding three days, and finding nothing of any importance, we concluded to return home. When within about twenty miles of Corinth we stopped at the plantation of a very wealthy secessionist, where we procured supper, the inmates extending every courtesy, under the impression that we were good Southern men. While at supper a lady made her appearance, having just arrived from a neighboring house, to inquire to what command we belonged. I asked her why she wished to know, and she replied that there were twelve of Major Ham's command up at her house, getting supper, who wished to know. I told her we belonged to Captain Davenport's command (rebel.) Just as we were about ready to start an old gentleman made his appearance, coming from the same house, and inquired which way we were traveling, and what we were doing in that section. I told him to tell Major Ham's men that we would be up there in a few minutes to see them. We were soon ready and mounted, and as we approached the next house, which was by the road-side, we discovered a company of men mounted and drawn up in line, with their guns ready for instant use. The moon was shining brightly, and as we rode up to within a few yards of them the Captain commanding inquired which way we were going. I replied that we were skylarking around, to see what we could find, and that we expected to go up into the valley. I then asked them what they were doing there. He replied that they were sent out to watch the roads, and learn what they could about the Yankees, but as yet he had learned nothing. One of my men now proposed to swap horses, but could not agree, so we proceeded on our way, thinking it would not pay to attack them under the circumstances. They were in doubt as to our character. We arrived safely at Corinth, without meeting with any further incident.

Another incident occurred which is quite amusing to think of, though anything but profitable to us at the time. We had learned that at a wealthy old rebel's plantation, about forty miles south of Corinth, there were some very fine horses, and as our stock needed replenishing I concluded to take a few of my men and capture them. I selected B. and H., and we started, arriving in due time at the plantation. We concealed ourselves in the woods until night, when we proceeded toward the house. B. went to reconnoitre, and shortly returned, stating that a very fine stallion and two blooded mares were in the stable lot. We concluded to wait until the inmates of the house should retire before attempting to catch the stock. After waiting as we thought a sufficient length of time we started for the lot. The night was dark, and we did not discover, until close by, that the lot was full of horses, and at the same time we heard men talking and laughing. B. and H. started into the stable, while I kept concealed in a shed. Just then a number of men entered the lot and commenced catching their horses, saddling up, and preparing to start. This was unexpected company, and we were in doubt as to their number. I told the boys to hide, if possible, but if discovered to let into them, and we would get out the best we could. The new comers began to show themselves in every quarter, but I had a very indistinct view of them as they passed close by me, trying to catch their horses. I was then lying flat on my back, close in the pannels of the fence, and B. and H. were cooped up in the stable, under the mangers. It was not long before the horses were all secured and saddled, and nine men were seen to mount and ride off, followed by a negro, riding one and leading two, the same that we had come so far to procure. We now retraced our steps toward home, arriving there without meeting with any accident. While passing through a swamp two armed rebels rode up to us, and in a very rough manner demanded what we were doing there, and where we were going; they were under the impression that we were deserters from the rebel army. After parleying a few minutes I drew my navy revolver —which I carried concealed beneath my coat—and told them they were prisoners, and must accompany us. We brought them into Corinth, not meeting with any further trouble, but feeling very cheap over our disappointment in not getting the horses.

About this time General Rhoddy had his command scattered along Bear Creek, guarding all points where it was possible for any force to cross. Several attempts had been made to send scouts up into the valley. General Dodge told me it was highly necessary that he should obtain some reliable information from that quarter. I at once concluded to make the effort, and taking six of my men we started. After dark we arrived at the plantation of a doctor, with whom I had formerly been acquainted, and thought to be a good Union man, he having taken the oath of allegiance at the time our forces occupied Iuka. When within half a mile of his house we turned into the timber, where I left all my men except one, who accompanied me to the house, leaving our horses behind. On arriving at the house we found that the inmates had all retired to rest, but we at once aroused them, and they got up and went to work preparing us a supper. The old doctor did not recognize me in my Confederate uniform. They seemed to feel glad of our presence, and inquired where we were going. I informed them that we were rebel soldiers, belonging to the infantry, but we were going up into the valley to join General Rhoddy, for he was a fighting man. After finishing our supper we offered him pay for it, but he would not receive a cent, and expressed himself glad to think that we were going to join Rhoddy. I then inquired if he knew where we would find the pickets stationed, and he informed me that the first picket was stationed on this side of the creek, not more than four hundred yards from his house, and that two of them had taken tea with him that evening. I then asked him if the pickets had instructions to fire on any one approaching after dark without first halting them. He replied that they had not, and that when halted to halloo out "all right," and advance boldly. We then started down the hill, toward the creek, laughing and talking, with the understanding that when the proper time arrived, and I should give a certain signal, to draw our revolvers and demand their surrender. Upon reaching the foot of the hill we were halted and challenged. After answering in the usual manner, and adding that it was "all right," we were told to advance, which we did, and when sufficiently near I discovered there were but two of them. They inquired who we were, and I told them the same tale I had told the doctor, and gave them to understand that I knew they were here—that I had been informed so by the doctor, up at the house; in fact I made myself very familiar with them, and taking a seat upon a rock seemed to feel quite at home. They inquired if we had any arms, and we told them we had not. If they had searched us they would have found two navy revolvers concealed about the person of us both.

After obtaining all the information required about the disposition of Rhoddy's forces, and their contemplated movements, we also learned that their reserve picket was on the opposite side of the creek, which they crossed in a small boat, and that they would be relieved in about an hour, when they would ferry us over. After remaining as long as I thought it prudent I gave the signal, when we each drew a revolver and demanded their surrender, and, on peril of their lives, not to speak above a whisper. After securing their arms we marched them before us up the hill, and halted at the doctor's house. All this proceeding had taken considerable time, and the men I had left behind becoming alarmed at our lengthy stay had come up to the house, arousing the inmates a second time, and inquired if any Confederate soldiers had been there that evening. The old doctor told them that he had not seen one for more than a week. On reaching the house with the prisoners I found my men there. The old doctor looked at me and my party with the utmost astonishment. I now informed the old gentleman that we would have to draw on him for two horses for the prisoners to ride, knowing that we would be pursued before morning. At this request he produced his oath of allegiance and protection papers, signed by General Rosecrans. I told him to come down to Corinth and we would settle it. Without any further interruption or delay we proceeded to the latter place, and reported to headquarters. A few days after this the old doctor sent one of his neighbors in to see General Dodge, and have his horses returned to him. I had stated to the General all I knew respecting the doctor's loyalty, and the General sent the agent back as he came, without them. Not long after this latter trip one of my outside scouts sent me word that Captain Shackleford, of the Twenty-Sixth Mississippi Infantry, who lived twenty-eight miles south of Corinth, had returned home on leave of absence. I immediately started out, taking with me five of my men, arriving next morning, and surrounding his house before daylight. We found the Captain and two soldiers, all of whom surrendered to us without any resistance. After securing their horses, arms, &c., we mounted them, and brought them all safe into camp.

During all this time my scouts and couriers were operating in their different departments, with entire success, in obtaining the Southern papers, and also valuable information. Occasionally I would lose a man, either by capture or by being killed. Their services were invaluable to the generals, and were appreciated; they expressed themselves fully satisfied.

About the first of October General Dodge requested me to ascertain at what point the Tennessee River could be forded above Eastport. This was the first intimation that I had of the intended movement of our army towards Chattanooga, Middle Tennessee. Three days after I reported to the General that the river could be forded at Green's Bluff, one mile above the mouth of Town Creek, and one mile below the mouth of the Big Nancy, on the opposite side.

I now found it necessary to make some disposition of my wife. My friend Bennett was about to start for Illinois with his family, and I concluded to send my wife under his care.

The grand move of our army had now commenced. General Sherman and his command were already on the march. General Dodge was ordered to follow, my scouts, under my charge, constituting the advance guard for his command, taking the road leading to Pulaski, Tennessee. General Sherman had moved by the way of Florence.

I had received orders to scout the country in every direction, and secure all servicable horses and mules. We had been out several days when I learned that a number of Confederate scouts were in our advance. I started out with my men, determined to overtake and capture them, if possible. Four of my men and myself were dressed in the Confederate uniform, and occupied the advance. On reaching a cross-road we came upon them. At a considerable distance off they saw us, and demanded to know to what command we belonged. I answered, "Confederate." This announcement did not seem to satisfy them, for without any hesitation they pulled away at us. My company had received orders to keep within supporting distance of us, which they were at that time. I at once ordered them to charge, which they did, the enemy scattering in all directions, and my men also separating and pursuing them in the same manner. I soon found myself alone, and in hot pursuit of a single rebel. I was well mounted, and after a chase of about a mile my man dismounted and ran into a house. I followed him closely; at the same time I saw three or four of my men coming up the road at full speed. As I ran up to the door I was met by a nice looking young lady, who asked me if the Yankees were after me. I told her they were, and asked her if she could tell me where to hide. She told me she did not know. I then inquired where the other man was, and she replied that he was up stairs. She then opened a door leading to a room, and I ran into it, she following. Just then my men arrived, and were at the door demanding where in h—l them d——d rebels had gone that came in the house. The young lady had told me to stoop down in the corner, and standing before me screened me from their view by spreading out her crinoline. She told them they had gone out the back door, and as she finished speaking away they went, pell-mell through the hall, out at the back door, and had soon disappeared in the rear of the house. I now relieved the young lady, and could scarcely contain myself, I was so full of laughter. In a few minutes my men returned, when I told them that the man was up stairs, whom they soon found.

Nothing more occurred after this, except skirmishing and the capture of a few prisoners each day, until we arrived at Pulaski, where General Dodge received orders to repair the Nashville and Huntsville railroad, establishing his headquarters at Pulaski. General Sherman had by this time taken Lookout Mountain.

It was now about the tenth of November. Our forces were scattered along the line of railroad from Columbia to Huntsville, Ala. At this time there were but a very few rebels in that vicinity. My time was principally employed with my men, scouring the country in quest of horses, mules, etc., occasionally an incident occuring of a startling and amusing nature. I had learned that the rebel General Rhoddy was with his command in the Tuscumbia valley, with his headquarters established at Tuscumbia. He also had possession of some points along the river in the vicinity of Florence. Captain Phillips, with the Ninth Illinois mounted infantry, had almost daily skirmishing with them along the river. I had sent out some of my scouts in various directions; one of them returned, stating that two wagon loads of salt were at Lamb's Ferry. I took five of my men and started with the intention of destroying it, which we did near the river, within forty miles of Pulaski. On our return, and during the night time (which was very cool), we stopped, putting up at a wealthy planter's, who professed to be a good Union man. After stabling and feeding our horses and partaking of a good supper we retired to rest, feeling perfectly secure, being only twenty-seven miles from our army. At the same time, I took the neccessary precaution to keep one man on picket. About twelve o'clock (midnight) we were aroused by our guard, who told us the yard was full of rebel cavalry. I ordered the boys to get up, and without making any noise to dress and prepare their guns for instant use. I could then hear considerable noise in the parlor, which was the adjoining room. After all was ready, I ordered two of the men to step out on the porch and slip around to the back window, and, if necessary, to fire in through it, but not until they saw me enter from the inside through the door. Taking the other four men, each one with his revolver in hand, I approached the door and gently opening it I discovered six rebel officers seated around a fire. I at once demanded a surrender, to which they complied without any resistance, but very much astonished at our unexpected appearance. They ranked from a second lieutenant up to a major, which somewhat surprised me in turn. I afterwards learned they were a portion of Morgan's command, who were trying to make their escape, which was just after his defeat. We secured their arms and horses, keeping close guard over them until morning, when we started for camp, where we arrived safely with our prisoners and captured property, which pleased General Dodge very much.

A few days after the above occurrence, I sent out two of my scouts, dressed in Confederate uniform. While on their return to camp they met a young man dressed in rebel uniform, whom they conscripted for the rebel army. The young man was very indignant at first, and told them they were doing wrong, that he was on special business from General Bragg, all of which was of no avail, my scouts persisted in taking him before their Captain, who could act at his pleasure. They then demanded his arms which he hesitated for some time before delivering up, and said he did not believe they were Confederate soldiers, he would never give them up, that the whole Federal army could not take them from him alive. They had now approached to within about two miles of our camp, when this young man discovered that he was a prisoner in the hand of Federal scouts. He attempted to escape by putting spurs to his horse, but the scouts were on the watch, and the moment he made the effort one of the men caught his horse by the bridle rein. He was taken to headquarters, and upon examining his person was found a water-proof haversack filled with letters and papers for General Bragg. Among them was a despatch from General Bragg's chief of scouts in Middle Tennessee, giving the exact number of men in General Dodge's command, together with all his late orders and a late paper from Nashville. Other papers were found proving this young man to be a spy. The General then turned him over to me, with orders to deliver him to the Provost Marshal and to have him put into a cell, also, to tell him, that he had only a few days to live; except on one condition would his life be spared, that was, to tell who the person was that furnished him with those papers. He replied, that he would not confess anything. That when he entered the army he did not expect to live through this war, and if Tennessee could not be restored to the Southern Confederacy he would rather die than live. I could not but admire his brave manly spirit. At no time, while in my presence, did he seem to feel depressed. The next day a commission was called to give him a trial. The prisoner was called out, who confessed to the charge preferred against him. He was sentenced to be hung on the following Friday. When he was taken to the scaffold I was permitted to talk to him. I addressed him thus; "Davis, you are not the man that should be hung, and if you would yet tell me who General Bragg's chief of scouts was, so I might capture him, your life would yet be spared." He looked me steadily in the eye, and said—"do you suppose were I your friend that I would betray you?" I told him I did not know, but life was sweet to all men. His reply to this, was, "Sir, if you think I am that kind of a man you have missed your mark. You may hang me a thousand times and I would not betray my friends." I then left him, only to witness in less than two minutes afterwards his fall from the scaffold, a dead man. Thus ended the life of Samuel Davis, one of General Bragg's scouts, a noble, brave young man, who possessed principle. I have often regretted the fate of this young man, who could brave such a death when his life rested in his own hands. His mind was one of principle, though engaged in a wrong cause.

Guerrillas were becoming more numerous, and receiving information from two of my scouts that a force of rebels, moving north, had crossed the river at Lamb's ferry; I reported the same to the General, and he ordered me to take my scouts and see if it was so. I started with eleven men, and, after proceeding about twelve miles, in the direction spoken of, we saw six mounted rebels emerge into the road in our front, and form a line across the road. We immediately ordered a charge, when they fired a volley, turned about and retreated in hot haste. We were mounted on good fleet horses, and very soon began to overtake them, picking them up, one at a time. After chasing them about half a mile, my men succeeded in picking up all but two of them. I still continued the chase followed by six of my men, the remainder having halted some distance in the rear with the prisoners. On reaching the top of a hill, under full headway, I unexpectedly found the road full of rebels, forming in line of battle, and not more than twenty yards in our front. There was but one course to pursue, and that was to charge through. In fact, it was impossible so check our horses, and away we went, firing our revolvers right and left. The rebels were thrown into confusion by this unexpected appearance in their midst, and thought the whole Federal army was charging them. It was now each man for himself, and through them we went. The next question was to get away from them, and the only chance was to wheel about and return as we came. No sooner said than away we went, charging about three hundred and fifty men, formerly Rhoddy's old regiment, commanded, at this time, by Lieut.-Col. Johnson. A portion of them had formed a line and, as we passed them, they fired a volley into us, wounding three. One rebel stood beside the road and, as I came up, leveled his revolver within two inches of my head and fired, the ball just grazing my neck, and powder burning my face and singing my hair. We had now returned back, still keeping under full headway, while the rebels continued to fire after us, but not daring to pursue. We soon came up with the rest of my men, who had remained with the prisoners, and, without any delay, we retraced our way to camp, all arriving safely, and feeling rejoiced that we had escaped so well. My wound was not of a serious nature. My two companions, however, were less fortunate, one having his arm broken, and the other his thigh fractured. As soon as we arrived in camp I reported to the General, who ordered out a detachment of the Seventh and Ninth Illinois Mounted Infantry, who were to find and attack this rebel force, if possible, but they returned without finding them, for the rebels had retreated and re-crossed the Tennessee River.

My wound now began to trouble me, and I applied to the General for leave of absence, to visit my family up North. I now felt that I had had my fill of satisfaction. The following is a correct copy of the Special Order relieving me from duty for a certain time:

HEADQUARTERS LEFT-WING SIXTEENTH ARMY CORPS,
PULASKI, TENNESSEE, Dec. 15th, 1863.

SPECIAL ORDER,
  No. 39.

VI. L. H. N——, in employ of United States Government, is hereby ordered to Illinois, on business for this command. The Q. M Department will furnish transportation. He will turn over his quartermaster and ordinance stores to James Hansel, taking proper receipts therefor. During N——'s absence James Hansel will act as Chief of Scouts.

By order of
BRIG.-GEN. G. M. DODGE.
J. W. BARNER,
Lieut. and A. A. A. G.

After making preparations, I started for Nashville, remaining there about one week. My health was not good and I experienced considerable pain in my wound. I had been in Nashville but a few days when I found one of my old scouts, who had been absent from me a long time. While stationed at Pulaski, during the month of November, I sent out three of my best scouts, with instructions to reconnoiter up and down the Tennessee River. After being absent about three weeks, one of them, Biffell, a Tennessean by birth, returned. He was wounded through the shoulder, and reported as follows: After scouting along the river four or five days, finding that they were going to be arrested or pursued, they began to retrace their steps. Being very weary they stopped at a plantation, about midnight, to feed and rest. They were at some distance from the house, at the lower end of the plantation. After feeding their horses, they crept into a corn-crib, and, laying down, were soon asleep. The first intimation they had of danger they were aroused and found themselves surrounded by nine men, who had their guns leveled upon them. They surrendered, without any resistance, and were marched back to the Tennessee River, where it was decided they should be hung. They declared that they were Rhoddy's scouts, when it was decided to send them to Rhoddy.

After crossing the Tennessee River, their guards were reduced to five men. They halted at a plantation to feed and rest. The prisoners now fully determined to escape—knowing that if they were carried before General Rhoddy they would be recognized by some of his men, and certain death would await them. One of the party had kept concealed, in his boot, a small revolver. While three of the guard were in the house, eating dinner, the other two remained on guard. Two of the prisoners then seized the guns belonging to the guard while the other drew his revolver from his boot leg, but it would not fire—the caps being damp. He then struck one of the guards over the head with his pistol, knocking him down, while the other was knocked down with a musket. By this time the three men in the house were alarmed, by the noise, and made their appearance, only to see their two bleeding comrades lying on the ground, and the prisoners making the best possible use of their legs in crossing a corn field. The three guards commenced firing on them, and wounded Biffles, who then became separated from his companions—whom he saw no more.

This ended Biffle's narrative, and, until my arrival at Nashville, I had not heard anything of the other two—Joe, from Mississippi, and Haines, of the Second Iowa Infantry. One morning, while in the quartermaster's depot, at Nashville, I was asked by a gentleman to what command I belonged. I told him, General Dodge's scouts, and he then said that one of the d—d'st looking cases he had ever seen was then up at the Soldier's Home; that he had arrived that morning, from the vicinity of Chattanooga, and professed to belong to General Dodge's scouts. It occurred to me at once, after hearing the description of this strange looking being, that it must be either Joe or Haines. Without any delay, I proceeded to the Soldiers' Home, and about the first man I saw was Haines, and, true enough, he was a hard looking case, reduced almost to a skeleton, covered with dirt and rags. Pen cannot describe the meeting that there took place. He was overjoyed at seeing me, and clasped his arms around me and caressed me like a child. I immediately took him to the barbershop and had him shaved and shampooed. I also procured an order for a suit of clothes, after which I presented him to Generals Sherman and Dodge, who were then in the city, stopping at the St. Cloud Hotel. They received him kindly and heard his report. He furnished me the following narrative. I will commence at the time they had knocked the guard down and effected their escape, by running across the cornfield—when they became separated from Biffles:

After making their escape, they concluded to make their way toward Corinth—Joe being familiar with the country—though they were, at this time, in the midst of Rhoddy's scattered forces. Rhoddy, having learned the circumstances, had sent out detachments of men, in various directions, to watch for them, and, after traveling two days and nights, without provisions, they were discovered by his cavalry. After running some distance, they came to a narrow defile. Haines, having now become so exhausted that he could proceed no further, told Joe to go ahead and try to make his escape, and that he would get behind a stump—having yet in his possession one of the guns taken from the guard, but no percussion caps. Joe continued running, while Haines, took up a position behind a stump and, as the pursuers came up within fifty yards he leveled his gun at them, and they retreated. Thus it continued until they succeeded in flanking him, when he arose to a standing position and, breaking his gun over a stump, surrendered. Joe, in the meantime, had effected his escape from this party, and has not been heard of by me up to this time.

Haines, now a prisoner, was conveyed to Tuscumbia, where he was recognized as one of the men who killed the guard, and was ordered to be put in heavy irons. After keeping him closely confined for several days, orders were received to remove all the prisoners to Rome, Georgia. As the Federals were advancing into the valley at that time, Haines was taken along handcuffed. As they were taking their departure, the

Provost Marshal told the Captain of the guard that he would hold him strictly responsible for that man, as he was a desperado, and if he made his escape he would have to take his place.

After marching several days across the sand mountains, they came to the Coosa River, near Rome, at which time he said he was nearly in a state of starvation. While seated on the river bank, waiting for the boat which was to convey them to Cahawba, a young lady made her appearance, carrying a basket of eatables, consisting of pies and cakes, and, addressing him kindly, asked him to eat some of her pies. He told her that he had no money, but she replied that he must eat some anyhow, saying that she did not want any pay from him. (She had been informed that he was a Federal spy, and was to be shot.) He then asked her name and where she lived. She told him her name and said that she lived with her brother-in-law, some distance out west, also telling his name. After eating abundantly of her pies and cakes, he felt very much refreshed. This young lady appeared to him like an angel sent to soothe and relieve his troubled mind. She was the first person who had shown any sympathy toward him since his capture.

The boat now making its appearance he was ordered aboard, and was chained, by the Captain of the guard, to one of the uprights of the boat. A lieutenant who was on the boat, at the time of her landing at this point, on passing Haines saw that he was chained, and, without consulting any person, released him, saying that it was a shame and not right to chain a man on water. Immediately after this, the Captain of the guard, in passing, saw that Haines was released, and immediately rechained him, cursing and swearing at the Lieutenant, and threatening to report him. After dark, the Lieutenant, watching for an opportunity, told Haines that, if he would jump overboard, he would relieve him of his chains and break his handcuffs—that he would let the d—n Captain see if he could treat a man in that manner. Haines, of course, consented, and the Lieutenant managed to release him, without being observed, which was no sooner done than Haines made one jump, and plunged headlong into the Coosa River, on the west side of the boat, and swam ashore, nearly chilled to death by the cold.

After scrambling up the bank, he proceeded north, finding himself in a wild, barren and mountainous country. After traveling all that night and the next day, until late in the evening, without any food, except roots and wild herbs, he unexpectedly, upon gaining the top of a high ridge, and looking down into the valley below, saw with inexpressible joy, the smoke curling up through the tree tops, and upon closer observation, he could see a few log houses and people moving about. Being hungry and nearly naked, he resolved to venture, at all hazards, so moving cautiously, he approached the house from the rear, and had got within one hundred yards when he perceived a female emerge from it and approach the spot where he lay concealed. Upon seeing her face what was his inexpressible joy and astonishment at beholding the kindhearted lady who had furnished him with pies and cakes, on the banks of the Coosa River.

He at once attracted her attention, and she, in turn, was surprised at seeing him there. She told him that she would bring him some food and clothing, but that as the country was full of rebel cavalry, he must lay concealed through the day. After dark she went to him, accompanied by her brother-in-law, who told him to keep secluded all the next day, and the next night he would convey him fifteen miles and turn him over to other friends. This promise he faithfully kept, and the second party conveyed him to within a few miles of the Tennessee River, and gave him instructions necessary to enable him to avoid danger, and the course to pursue to reach Nashville. The reader is already acquainted with his arrival and condition.

Shortly after meeting my old friend Haines, I took my departure for the North, arriving in Illinois the first day of January, 1864, where I found my wife and family all well, and happy at seeing me alive once more. I remained at home until the first day of October, when I started for Tennessee. In the meantime, I had learned that General Dodge had been wounded and was absent from his command, which was the reason for my visiting Memphis. It had also been reported to me that he was coming to the latter place, to assume command of that Department, and I was anxious to again tender him my services. In this I was disappointed. I found General Washburne in command,

and also learned that General Dodge was assigned to the command of Missouri, with headquarters at St. Louis.

I at once tendered my services to General Washburne, and they were accepted, for a short time. The General, however, told me that he would not remain long in Memphis, and recommended me to the notice of Brig.-Gen. Grierson, to whom I at once reported. I was greatly surprised at meeting my old friend, S. L. Woodward, formerly General Sherman's Chief Clerk, now Captain and Acting Adjutant General on General Grierson's staff, who was pleased to see me. My services were at once accepted by the General, who was making preparations to send a cavalry force into Mississippi, to tap the Mobile and Ohio railroad south of Corinth.

This expedition was entrusted to the command of General Grierson, who questioned me respecting the roads, streams, &c. I told the General that I could guide him and his command through the proposed route without having to swim a horse over any steam of water. On the morning of the twenty-first of December, 1864, the expedition left Memphis, Tennessee. It was comprised of three brigades. The first was commanded by Colonel Karge, and was composed of the Second New Jersey, Fourth Missouri, Seventh Indiana and First Mississippi Mounted Rifles. The second brigade, commanded by Colonel Winslow, included the Third and Fourth Iowa and Tenth Missouri. The third brigade, commanded by Colonel Osborne, consisted of the Fourth and Eleventh Illinois, Second Wisconsin, Third U. S. Colored and fifty men of the Pioneer Corps, colored, commanded by Lieutenant Lewis, of the Seventh Indiana Cavalry, numbering in all about thirty-three hundred men. The whole commanded by Brig.-Gen. B. H. Grierson. His staff consisted of the following members: Major M. H. Williams, Tenth Missouri Cavalry, Acting Assistant Inspector General, and Captain S. L. Woodward, Assistant Adjutant General, U. S. A., accompanied by a telegraph operator, whose quick hand is lightning.

Previous to the departure of this expedition, reliable information had been received, from scouts, that the enemy were accumulating a large quantity of supplies on the line of the Mobile and Ohio railroad and Mississippi Central railroad, for transportation to Hood's army. On the morning of the nineteenth, a brigade was sent forward, to make a demonstration toward Bolivar, and thence to swing south-east and join the main column near Ripley, Mississippi, but owing to heavy rains on that and several previous days, it was impossible to cross Wolf River, and, therefore, the intended junction could not be effected, and the command returned to Memphis.

On the morning of the twenty-first, the expedition started from Memphis, accompanied by a considerable force of infantry, moving along the line of the Memphis and Charleston railroad, as far as Moscow, making a demonstration toward Corinth. The cavalry, under General Grierson, cut loose from the infantry near

Germantown, and pursued the most direct route for Ripley, passing through Lamar and Salem.

From Early Grove, a detachment of one hundred men, commanded by Captain Neet, of the Tenth Missouri, was ordered to proceed to the neighborhood of Grand Junction, and cut the railroad and telegraph lines there. He regained the command between Salem and Ripley, having successfully accomplished the work assigned him.

The transportation for the expedition consisted of pack mules, carrying ten days' rations, and one hundred rounds per man of extra ammunition. No artillery, ambulances or wagons accompanied the expedition. Such encumbrances, which have proved fatal to so many well contemplated raids, were dispensed with, that the command might be able to move with great rapidity. General Grierson's orders from General Dana were to cut the Mobile and Ohio railroad effectually, if possible. Further than this the General was at liberty to use his own discretion—and the sequel will show with what masterly skill it was exercised. The march to Ripley was unopposed, very few of the enemy being seen.

Arriving at the latter place in time for dinner, on the twenty-fourth, two detachments of the Second New Jersey, under the command of Major Van Rensalaer, were immediately sent out with orders to proceed to Booneville, on the Mobile and Ohio Railroad, to destroy it and the government property there, and rejoin the command at Ellistown, twenty miles south of Ripley. I was ordered to accompany this expedition as guide.

The other detachment of two hundred men, under the command of Captain Search, of the Fourth Illinois, was to strike the same road at Gunntown, and rejoin the command at Ellistown. This the detachments successfully accomplished, the former capturing and destroying a large quantity of quartermaster stores, five cars, cutting the telegraph, burning railroad bridges and trestle-work, and paroling about twenty prisoners. At the same time the attention of the enemy at Corinth was diverted from the proceedings. They were led to anticipate an attack on that place. The track and the telegraph line were destroyed at Gunntown. While this was being done the main column, after a few hours' rest, left Ripley and moved rapidly toward Tupelo, arriving there on the afternoon of the twenty-fifth without meeting with any opposition. From this place the Eleventh Illinois, Lieut.-Col. Funk, commanding, was sent to destroy a bridge and some trestle-work over the Old Town Creek. In the meantime Colonel Karge was ordered to move rapidly upon Verona Station, seven miles south, with his entire brigade, information having been obtained that a force of seven hundred dismounted cavalry, belonging to Forrest's command, were stationed at that place, guarding an immense amount of quartermaster stores. About ten o'clock that evening a gallant charge was made into the place, led by the Seventh Indiana Cavalry, Captain Skelton, commanding. The surprise was so complete that little resistance was offered, most of the garrison, aided by the darkness, escaping into the timber. This affair resulted in the easy capture of eight buildings filled with fixed ammunition, variously estimated at from 250 to 300 tons, 5000 stand of new carbines, 8000 sacks of shelled corn, a large quantity of wheat, an immense amount of quartermaster stores, clothing, camp and garrison equipage, a train of sixteen cars, and two hundred army wagons, the same that were captured by Forrest from General Sturgis, at his disastrous defeat near Gunntown the June previous. After effectually destroying all this property, tearing up the track, burning the bridges and cutting the telegraph wire, the brigade started to rejoin the command, leaving a fire in their rear for miles. The explosion of ammunition, which continued at intervals all night, added much to this magnificent scene, which must have produced a peculiar effect upon the minds of the citizens, who were not aware of our presence.

On the morning of the twenty-sixth the command moved out from Tupelo. The third brigade was ordered to proceed down the railroad and destroy the bridges, trestle-work, water-tanks, etc. On arriving at Shannon they surprised and captured a large train of cars, containing one hundred new army wagons on the way for Forrest's forces, besides a quantity of quartermaster and commissary stores, and also several government buildings, all of which were destroyed. After the main column arrived at this place the third brigade was relieved by the second, which received orders to proceed down the railroad, destroying it as they went. The remainder of the command kept the public road leading toward Okolona, and camped that night on Chawappa Creek.

On the morning of the twenty-seventh the command moved out at an early hour, the second brigade in advance. After proceeding a few miles the enemy was encountered. They numbered about one hundred men, who kept falling back and exchanging shots with our advance guard, just as we came in sight of Okolona. Here a rebel courier was captured, bearing a dispatch for the captain commanding the post. The dispatch stated that thirteen hundred infantry would reinforce him, arriving by railroad from Mobile.

While making preparations for the fight I sent one of my comrades into Okolona, who returned with a favorable report. The same scout was sent from this place with a dispatch to Memphis, for General Dana. He succeeded in arriving safely with it, but had some narrow escapes. He was arrested once, carried back and closely searched, but no papers were found and he was permitted to proceed, telling them that he was a good rebel. Being acquainted with many of the citizens of that county his story was believed. He was nick-named "Perseverance."

A fight was now anticipated, and the order was given to form squadrons. The command "forward" was sounded. It was a grand sight to witness the cavalry moving along in perfect order over the prairie, with banners gaily fluttering in the breeze, each company bearing its guidon. Peaceable possession was taken of the town, a large quantity of commissary stores and several thousand pounds of finished leather captured and destroyed, and sufficient tobacco obtained to supply the whole command. The telegraph wire was tapped at this point, and dispatches were intercepted from General Dick Taylor, Maj.-Gen. Gardiner and others, ordering the commanding officer at Egypt to hold that place at all hazards, and intimating that reinforcements would be sent from Mobile and other points. The promised reinforcements soon made their appearance. A long train of cars was seen approaching from the south. When within two miles of town they could see the burning buildings, and they concluded to retreat to Egypt Station, ten miles south. After effectually destroying all the government property the command moved to within five miles of Egypt and camped for the night. During the night several deserters came into our lines, bringing with them their guns. They said they belonged to our army, had been prisoners a long time, and had joined the Confederate army in order to avoid a lingering and horrible death in the prison pen at Andersonville, Ga. As soon as this fact became known among the men they at once conferred upon them the title of "Galvanized Confeds." These men stated that the rebels offered inducements to all those of foreign birth who would join them, promising that they should be required to do only garrison duty. They further stated that about two hundred of their own stamp were in the stockade at Egypt, and would be compelled to fight us in the morning if attacked. The morning came, and at an early hour the command started for Egypt. The General did not anticipate a fight there, but was under the impression that the rebels would evacuate. However, the opposite fact was soon ascertained, and the whole command, except the Fourth Iowa, was ordered to move by the wagon-road; the latter regiment moved down the railroad. The second brigade was ordered to follow as a reserve. They had not proceeded far before a squad of mounted rebels was seen; they kept retreating, and occasionally exchanged a shot with our advance. The command soon emerged from the timber into the open prairie, where were plainly visible to the eye, about a mile distant, the few houses, depot, and stockade, which comprise the town or station of Egypt. On nearer approach it was discovered by the third brigade that Colonel Karge, commanding first brigade, had come well up to the enemy's works, and heavy skirmishing was going on. General Grierson and staff accompanied the first brigade. A train of cars stood on the track, and a four-gun battery was mounted on one of them; all were within supporting distance of the garrison. The enemy's skirmishers were driven into their works, where they were well protected, while our forces were exposed on the open prairie. While forming the troops for a charge a movement was discovered which led the General to suppose that the train was about to leave. He at once ordered Colonel Karge to charge the works. Drawing his sabre he ordered a detachment of the Fourth Missouri and Seventh Indiana to follow him, and away he dashed for the train, which was by this time moving off. So closely did the General, his staff and escort press them, that the engineer detached fourteen cars, leaving them in our possession—thus escaping with the battery, which was attached next the tender.

An exciting chase was now kept up for nearly a mile, the cavalry firing rapidly their carbines and revolvers, while the gunners threw grape, canister and shell. It was soon discovered that two other trains were approaching from the south. They were loaded with troops. Captain Woodward, General Grierson's assistant adjutant-general, a young, brave and dashing cavalry officer, was ordered to take the detachment that had been chasing the train and proceed down the road rapidly and tear up the track. This he successfully accomplished, preventing the trains from approaching nearer than within two miles of the station, and keeping in check General Gardiner, with reinforcements to the number of about two thousand infantry. The Captain was ably assisted by Captain Hencke, of the Fourth Missouri, and Captains Elliott and Skelton, of the Seventh Indiana. The former fell wounded while charging the enemy, who had disembarked, thrown out a line of skirmishers, and begun to advance. The Captain, with only one hundred men, fell back from the railroad, the infantry pursuing. When about six hundred yards from the train Captain Woodward ordered a left about, and with a will and a spirit stirring yell he charged them, driving them back in confusion. His loss was two men killed and five or six wounded, and thirty horses killed. While this brave little band was so gallantly fighting the first brigade charged the enemy. The charge was made by the Second New Jersey, Lieut.-Col. Yorke, their brave commander, leading the attack. Mounted on their horses they charged right up to the stockade, so that they could fire directly into the garrison. They were armed with that splendid carbine, the Spencer seven shooter, and poured, in quick succession, volley after volley into their ranks. The rebels could not withstand the fire. They were flanked on both sides, while the third brigade lay back in the rear not more than sixty yards, dismounted and ready to participate in making a charge. The charge was not necessary; the rebels saw that there was no chance for retreat, and that their reinforcements could not reach them; they therefore surrendered the whole garrison to Lieut.-Col. Yorke. The prisoners numbered about eight hundred, infantry and cavalry. Their loss in killed and wounded was not less than sixty or seventy. Among the killed were Brig.-Gen. Gohlston, commanding post, and a colonel. Our loss was fifteen killed and seventy wounded, thirty of whom had to be left behind. Over one hundred horses were killed at Egypt, and one thousand stand of arms captured and burned with the cars. After burying the dead and caring for the wounded the command moved west and southwest toward Houston. The prisoners were taken along.

This fight was a very spirited one, and reflects great credit upon the officers and men engaged. It has been seldom, if ever before during this rebellion, that a charge has been made and successfully carried out by a mounted force against an equal force protected by a stockade. General Grierson participated in the victory with his brave followers, and complimented them very highly. Just as the garrison surrendered the rebel General Gardiner and his force left on their trains, retreating towards West Point. Beside the fourteen cars mentioned that were abandoned, ten more were captured at the station. They were loaded with two large pontoon bridges, shelled corn and quartermaster stores, all on the way for Hood's army.

I do not think it had been the intention of General Grierson to attack this place, and I believe he did so principally with a view to the recapture of our own men, who appeared to feel very much rejoiced at their deliverance. He hinted that the capture of so many prisoners had saved the command several days hard riding, as he would now be compelled to take them to Vicksburg. The General governs his actions according to circumstances, being quick both to plan and to act. On the night of the 28th the command camped within three miles of Houston, on the plantation of Norton & Co. They remarked that we were the first Yankees they had ever seen, and that "weuns" looked like their folks. General Grierson somewhat surprised the ladies by displaying his musical talent on the piano, after which one of the ladies favored the General and staff with one of Longfellow's beautiful songs, "Hiawatha." At its conclusion one of the officers complimented her by saying that he thought the song very beautiful, and that her singing was excellent. She replied that she did not suppose he would like it, as it was seldom appreciated except by persons of literary tastes. This was said as a compliment to the Captain, she being under the impression that the Northerners were an ignorant race, and was surprised to meet any one possessing a cultivated taste in the Yankee army.

The next morning the General missed his saddle blanket, when, in the way of a joke, I suppose, he remarked to the inmates that he thought it was not treating him well to steal his blanket, when he had taken so much pains to guard their property. So I thought, also, especially in view of the fact that there was not a chicken or turkey left alive on the plantation.

On the morning of the twenty-ninth, the whole command moved out, passing through Houston, from which place two detachments were sent—one south-east, toward West Point, and the other north, toward Pontotac—for the purpose of misleading the enemy. On returning, they destroyed the bridge across the Houlka River. Orders were soon issued to the command to sequestrate, for the use of the prisoners—who were in a pitiable condition—all the blankets, shoes and such clothing as was required, that might be met with. Nothing worthy of note transpired this day, and the command camped at Hohenlinden.

Morning of the thirtieth, left camp at an early hour and proceeded to Bellefontaine, capturing a few prisoners, among whom was the notorious Captain Tom Ford, whose business it had been, for the past two years, to conscript and hunt down—with bloodhounds—good Union men, and who confessed to having assisted in hanging several of them. He was placed in custody of a special guard, but, by some means, succeeded in making his escape. From Bellefontaine a detachment was sent toward Starkville, again threatening the Mobile and Ohio railroad, while one hundred and fifty men, under Captain Beckwith, of the Fourth Iowa, were sent to Bankston, where they arrived at midnight.

They found the place quiet—the inhabitants having had no intimation of the Yankees being in their vicinity. At this place a large manufacturing estalishment, which was turning out one thousand yards of cloth and two thousand pair of shoes per day, was completely burned down. It was working five hundred hands. A large supply of cloth, shoes, cotton, wool and commissary and quartermaster's stores were also destroyed. A large flouring mill underwent the same fate. The following incident will show how completely the enemy was surprised. Just as the fire got well started, the superintendent of the factory made his appearance, in his night clothes, swearing, threatening to arrest the guard and night watchers, and wanting to know what in h—l they were about that they did not extinguish the fire. It was amusing to hear him, and still more so to witness his astonishment when he discovered who and what we were. The Captain perceiving his mistake, told him that the night was so very cold that he had concluded to have a fire. "H—l and d—nation," said the man, "would you burn up the manufactory to make a fire to warm by?"

On the morning of the thirty-first, left camp at six o'clock, the first brigade in advance. At about nine o'clock, the command was joined by Captain Beckwith, who returned from Bankston, reporting his complete success. The column proceeded along the Bellefontaine and Middletown road, passing through a hilly country, and arriving at Lodi about eleven o'clock in the morning. At that place we captured seven hundred and ninety fat hogs, which were enroute for Hood's army, and also two thousand bushels of wheat, which was at once destroyed. After a good deal of speculation, and about one thousand and one ideas being advanced, as to what disposition should be made of the grunting stock, it was finally concluded to drive it before us. This was done amid a good deal of fun. Just imagine about eight hundred hogs before you, in the road, and about two hundred jolly fellows driving them, and then picture to yourself the various remarks and expressions they used. The General and staff participated in the fun, and directed the movements. After putting the hogs through for five miles, they being found to be too troublesome, it was decided, by a council of officers, to put them all to death. They were too fat to be driven further, averaging, as they did, two hundred and fifty pounds each. The men constructed a large pen, and into it they were driven. The idea was then advanced after killing to burn them. This being decided about a whole brigade dismounted and, with drawn sabres, charged in among the squealing herd, splitting each of them open in the back. They then piled rails upon them, which were fired. This soon made a glorious barbecue. H. V., a clerk declared that, a few years hence, new discoveries would be made in that section of the country, in the shape of lard oil wells—the genuine oil. According to Mobile prices, pork was worth, at that time, five dollars a pound.

While the destruction of hogs was going on, Colonel Karge commanding the first brigade, was moving toward Middletown. He struck the Mississippi Central railroad within one mile north of Winona, cutting the railroad and telegraph. Before cutting the wires Colonel Karge intercepted a dispatch, which contained an inquiry respecting the operation of Wirt Adams, at Canton— whether he had sent any reinforcements up the road? A reply could not be obtained. Nine locomotives were destroyed at Winona, and also the depot and a large quantity of quartermaster stores. From this place the command proceeded to Middletown and camped for the night, with the exception of the Third Iowa, commanded by Colonel Noble. After feeding, and resting a few hours, this regiment was ordered to proceed up the road to Grenada, and to destroy the bridges on the route and all government property in that place, after doing which he was to rejoin the command at Benton, sixty-five miles south of Middletown. The distance from the latter place to Grenada is twenty-five miles.

On the morning of January 1st, 1865, the command left camp, the main column moving south, toward

Benton, while the third brigade was sent down the Mississippi Central railroad, with orders to destroy it, and to rejoin the command at Benton. Nothing transpired on the march that day, worthy of notice, the main column camping that night within four miles of Lexington, Holmes County, Mississippi.

On the morning of the second we left camp, passing through Lexington. Some little skirmishing occurred in the advance, on the direct road to Ebenezer. We arrived there about noon, and passed through the town without halting. Shortly after leaving the place a rebel lieutenant belonging to the Fifth Texas Cavalry was captured. He stated that a force of rebel cavalry, numbering eleven thousand men, with artillery, was then at Benton, awaiting our approach. This story was not credited, at least it made no impression further than to increase our speed toward that point. About four o'clock, P.M., a dispatch was received from the second brigade, stating that they had moved down the railroad, which they destroyed as far as Gooman's, and then struck west through Franklin in the direction of Ebenezer. While at Franklin they were attacked by five or six hundred of Wirt Adam's cavalry, under the command of Colonel Woods. After a very spirited fight the latter was repulsed with the loss of twenty-five killed and left on the field. Among them was one major and one captain, also several wounded; twenty prisoners were taken. Our loss was five killed and fourteen wounded. Too much praise cannot be awarded the whole brigade for their conduct in this fight, and particularly that of the Third U. S. Colored Cavalry, commanded by Major Mann. They alone repulsed several desperate charges, having their adjutant killed and several wounded. Colonel Osband, commanding the brigade, is all fight. About six o'clock, P.M., the main column arrived at Benton, without meeting any opposition, and camped for the night. About ten o'clock, P.M., the third brigade arrived, having met with no opposition after their fight.

While the main force was lying at Benton Colonel Noble joined it. He came with tidings of success, that added largely to our victories. After destroying twenty-five miles of the Mississippi Central Railroad he surprised and took Grenada, where he captured four serviceable engines and ten others in process of repair, a very extensive machine shop, which had but recently been completed—the machinery for which was brought from Georgia—several buildings, containing immense quantities of commissary and quartermaster stores, twenty cases of Enfield rifles—which had been lately received for the purpose of arming the State militia—together with a considerable amount of ammunition. Colonel Noble entered the office of the Grenada Picket, where he picked up a paper of the day previous, in which was an article stating that the Yankee raid on the Mobile and Ohio Railroad had played out, that Grierson's vandals had been repulsed and were making for Memphis with all speed. After reading this the Colonel remarked to a citizen that it was not the intention of General Grierson to slight them so much as to fail in paying them a New Year's visit. He ordered the destruction of the Picket press, saying that if he could have done so consistently he would have left it untouched, so that the editors might proclaim what a warm call they had had from their Northern brethren.

The General now felt comparatively satisfied, as the main object of the expedition was to reach Benton without disaster. On the morning of the third the whole command left camp, proceeding southwest in the direction of Vicksburg, passing through Mechanicsburg. They arrived at the latter place before dark, camping there for the night. From this place, four scouts, members of the Fourth Iowa, were sent to Vicksburg, forty miles distant, with dispatches for General Washburne; also with a request that rations might be sent to Clear Creek.

On January fourth, we left camp at an early hour, and marched all day through canebrakes. Considerable bushwhacking was done this day, in which we lost one man killed—a member of the Third Iowa. The roads were good, but were not unlike the Mississippi River in one respect—they were very crooked, and were in a really God-forsaken country. We arrived at Clear Creek about five o'clock in the afternoon, having marched twenty-five miles. At this place we were met by the provision and forage train, which had been sent for the day previous. Just as old Sol was disappearing behind the western horizon, our ears were greeted by the report of the sundown gun at Vicksburg, which had the effect of eliciting hearty cheers from our weary command. Captain Whiting, of General Washburne's staff, brought in the late Northern papers, containing news of the glorious successes of Sherman and Thomas. This night we camped within fifteen miles of Vicksburg, feeling perfectly secure and safe, after a sixteen day's ride through the enemy's country, and having traveled over five hundered miles. Our loss was twenty-five killed and eighty wounded—many of the latter slightly. We brought in six hundred prisoners, six hundred extra horses and mules, and about a thousand negroes. The amount of property destroyed cannot be estimated. It would take all the figures in the calendar, and the Philadelphia lawyers to sum it up. Seventy miles of railroad were effectually destroyed, with bridges, etc. Some private property was destroyed, not intentionally, but owing to its close proximity to burning rebel government property.

Too much praise cannot be awarded the four scouts who operated during this raid. Their services were duly appreciated by the Generals. I have refrained somewhat from entering into details respecting myself, while on this raid, although I might make mention of many startling and amusing incidents that occurred. I occupied the advance all the time, of either detachments or the main column. At one time I had an exciting chase after three rebels, and fired three shots at them, but they, being mounted on fresh horses, succeeded in making their escape. I afterward learned that one of them was my own brother. I am only sorry that I did not succeed in taking him a prisoner.

At one time I was within three miles of my home, and met with several of my old neighbors, many of whom expressed a strong desire that I should return and reside among them again—which I would willingly do could I be guaranteed a peaceable life, without changing my opinions respecting this rebellion.

The question of arming negroes was freely discussed by our men with many of the citizens, who assert that they must resort to every means to obtain their independence, though they do not like the idea of making soldiers of negroes. Prisoners brought in stated that thirty days' furlough was given to every rebel soldier who shot a Yankee prisoner, who might be caught in the act of trying to escape.

On several occasions when government property was destroyed, General Grierson allowed the many poor families around to help themselves to salt, flour, sugar, bacon and molasses. With the exception of the first three days and the last, the weather was delightful. On the morning of the fifth of January, 1865, the command started from Clear Creek, for Vicksburg, in a pelting rain—it was cold and dreary—arriving at the latter place about two o'clock, amid the cheers of thousands, who flocked to the roadside to welcome us. The meeting between Maj.-Gen. Washburne and Brig.-Gen. Grierson was very cordial. In a few days we arrived at Memphis, by the river, from which place I intended to leave for Illinois, to visit my family.

I will now close my lengthy but true narrative by extending my sincere thanks to Brig.-Gen. Grierson,

Captain S. L. Woodward, Assistant Adjutant General, for their marked attention and generous appreciation of my services. Also to H. B. Paris, of the Seventh Illinois Cavalry, who is General Grierson's Chief Clerk, for his many acts of kindness, and to his Assistant Clerk, Edward Jones, of the Second Iowa Cavalry, who is a most agreeable comrade.

CONCLUSION.

I will take the liberty of expressing a few opinions respecting the winding up of this rebellion. My long acquaintance with the Southern people, and my knowledge of their dispositions, traits of character, etc., give me some ideas I would like to see carried out.

In the first place, a war is existing between the people of the Northern or Free States and the people of the Southern or Slave States, which has yet to be settled. As there are various opinions as to how this settlement is to be effected, I will confront the public with mine. Two ideas seem to be prevailing among the public—one to subjugate the South, and the other to use mild measures, or, rather, to buy them back. The first two years the war was conducted on the latter plan, and the South, laughing at the very idea, asked, "Have you any more to give us now than when we seceeded?" The last two years the war has been conducted on the former principle, and the South, with thousands of others, say that you only aggravate them and will make them fight the more desperately. I am of the opinion that, to finally settle this question, and to have a permanent peace, we must have a majority of loyal people in the Southern States. Now, the question arises how is this to be effected—for the administrations of the Northern and Southern States have been conducted in such ways that the loyalty which was in the Southern States is now nearly extinct. The Confederates would not tolerate a loyal man in their midst, while the Federal authorities would tolerate disloyalty any where within their jurisdiction, and, therefore, most of the loyal men who were in the Southern States have gone to the North. Now, when the Southern people lay down their arms, let all the lands in the rebellious States be confiscated, and one hundred and sixty acres of it be given to the head of every white family in the Southern States. This course, I claim, would largely increase the number of friends of the government, for there are thousands of men in the South who never owned an acre of land. Such a course would not only make friends of them, but would prevent large numbers from becoming paupers and outlaws. The remainder of the lands of the South should be given to actual white occupants who have served three years in the United States army. In this way there would be placed in the Southern States a majority of loyal men, who would represent tnemselves in Congress, and enforce the laws at home, and in this way the Southerners would become an enterprising, flourishing, law loving and abiding people. On the other hand, were the Southern people to lay down their arms to-day, and take the amnesty oath *en masse,* and establish civil law, their first

Representative would be as vile a rebel as Davis or Wigfall, and they would exterminate within their bounds every loyal man who had given aid or comfort to the Federal government. And who would be the judge to try the secessionist assassin? Who would say to the secession murderer you served him right? On the other hand, to enforce civil law by force of arms would require a standing army of at least two hundred thousand men, and we would have neither a peaceable nor a republican government.

CHICKASAW.

FAREWELL ORDER OF BREVET BRIG.-GEN. COON.

HEADQUARTERS 2D BRIGADE, 5TH DIV. C. C. M. D. M.,
DECATUR, ALA., July 9th, 1865.
GENERAL ORDERS,
NO. 11.

VETERAN COMPANIONS! This day the identity of the old Second Brigade is lost, and its unflinching battle line, that covered our retreating forces at West Point and Prairie Station—that saved a disorganized command at Okolona—that raised the well earned battle-cry of "victory!" at Hurricane Creek and Tupelo—that presented its unbroken front to Hood's advancing hosts at Shoal Creek, Mt. Carmel, Campbelville, Linnville, Louisburg Pike and Franklin—and that taught the world a new lesson in cavalry warfare when it waved its victorious battle-flags over the captured redoubts at Nashville—that unwavering, battle-scarred line has at last, by order of your department commander, been broken. And in parting I feel proud in giving expression to the heart-felt "God-speeds," and sincere ' well-wishes," mutually exchanged by the officers and men of the brigade.

You have endured storm, hunger, fatigue, and disaster; and enjoyed sunshine, plenty, and many a victorious march together. Under each other's faithful watch you have slept without fear in many a dangerous bivouac. Shoulder to shoulder you have stemmed the battle tide on many a sanguinary field, and the greatest good I could wish for you is that your future happiness and prosperity may be as great and unremitting as your past patriotism, fidelity and courage—while better cause for honest pride I shall never possess than this : I once commanded the Second Brigade. Officers, soldiers, comrades, farewell !

By order of

DATUS E. COON,
Brevet Brigadier-General.

JOHN H. AVERY,
Capt. and A. A. A. G.

To commanding officer Seventh Illinois Cavalry.